GREAT
CIVILIZATIONS
OF THE
EAST

GREAT CIVILIZATIONS OF THE EAST

Discover the remarkable history of Asia and the Far East

MESOPOTAMIA ◆ ANCIENT INDIA
THE CHINESE EMPIRE ◆ ANCIENT JAPAN

DAUD ALI • FIONA MACDONALD • LORNA OAKES • PHILIP STEELE

southwater

CONTENTS

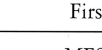

First Civilizations......6

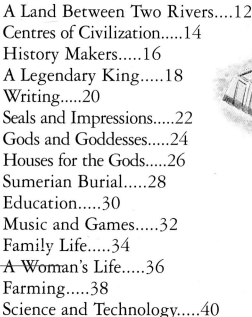

MESOPOTAMIA......10

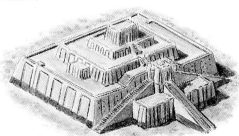

ANCIENT INDIA......70

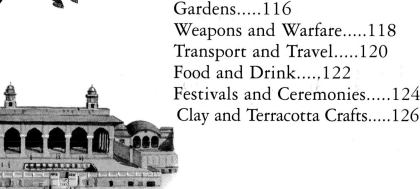

THE CHINESE EMPIRE.....128

ANCIENT JAPAN.....186

First Civilizations

The early civilizations of the East influenced the way our world is today. The ancient peoples of Mesopotamia, India, China and Japan were among the first peoples to write down their history. A great deal is known, not only about what they wore and where they lived, but also what they thought about. They transformed wilderness country into a network of villages and small towns. Gradually they formed civilized societies and settled communities that were governed by a leader and run according to commonly accepted rules.

SAFE AS HOUSES
Japanese nobles and courtiers lived in splendid *shinden* houses like this. Each *shinden* was designed as a number of separate buildings linked by covered walkways. The Japanese built single-storey houses made of straw, paper and wood. These materials would bend and sway in an earthquake but usually would not collapse.

Trying to Survive

The earliest human beings lived in small groups. They moved from place to place, collecting wild plant foods and hunting wild animals. As the years passed, people began to settle down in one place where they grew crops of wheat, rice and fruit. They learnt how to domesticate animals and bring them up, although they still went hunting to add meat to their diet and provide furs and bones for clothes and furnishing their homes. Every part of an animal was used.

Many villages were on the flood plains of great river systems because the land there was fertile and had a good supply of water. Such settlements grew up around the Yellow River in China and the Indus in Pakistan. Other people lived in more difficult places with very dry weather or poor infertile land. In the 4,000

PLOUGHING THE LAND
A Chinese farmer uses a pair of strong oxen to plough his land. Oxen saved farmers a lot of time and effort. The Chinese first used oxen for farming in about 1100BC.

islands of Japan, the first settlers coped with a harsh environment battered by sea and storms.

Gradually, at different times in different places, larger towns, cities and civilizations began to develop. More than 5,000 years ago, cities began to develop in Sumer, the region at the head of the Gulf. The River Tigris bordered this area to the east and the River Euphrates was to the west, so the region became known as 'The Land Between the Rivers'.

MEDICAL MEN
Hundreds of modern medicines were first developed in ancient times. Here a group of Assyrians extract essential oils from herbs using a distillation process.

Growing Crops

People in farming communities in Sumer worked together to dig canals to carry water from the River Euphrates to the crop fields. Eventually the farmers grew more food than they could eat themselves, creating a surplus which they could sell to people in the new towns. It was no longer necessary for everyone to work in the fields, and some people took up specialist jobs as craftworkers, weavers and metalworkers. Others became leaders and organizers in their communities. Villagers moved into larger communities, which gradually became cities some time before 3000BC.

The First City-states

Civilizations did not always develop in the same way. Mesopotamia was a collection of many small, independent city-states. Each state had its own king and god but shared a common culture known as the Sumerian civilization. The neighbouring country of Egypt developed a very different civilization at around the same time. It became a united country with a single ruler who was called the pharaoh.

The people of Mesopotamia made important discoveries in science

USEFUL AND BEAUTIFUL
Paper-making and calligraphy (beautiful writing) were two important art forms in Japan. This woodcut shows a group of people with everything they need to decorate scrolls and fans – paper, ink, palette, calligraphy brushes and pots of paint.

and technology – learning how to farm the land, how to use the wheel, how to make pottery and work with metal. They developed trading links with the cities of the Indus Valley in northern India.

SIGNED AND SEALED
The Sumerians were one of the first peoples in the world to develop writing. They used cylinder seals to identify property.

Reading, Writing and Arithmetic

The south of Mesopotamia became the home of the Sumerian civilization, which was one of the first cultures to use writing. Later, the Babylonian kings carefully preserved the old Sumerian culture and carried on its traditions of learning and the arts, while adding their own contributions in the fields of medicine and mathematics. Later the Chinese were to make their own investigations into medicine, particularly herbalism and acupuncture.

After 1000BC the kings of Assyria in northern Mesopotamia became important and often ruled the whole country from the capital cities of Nimrud and Nineveh. They preserved the learning and history of the country in clay tablets at the great library of King Ashurbanipal at Nineveh.

In India, religion inspired the great Hindu epics, the Ramayana and the Mahabharata, while the Muslims made beautiful copies of their holy book, the Quran.

Ruled by the Gods

Each of these civilizations developed their own beliefs about gods. The people of Mesopotamia thought about the problem of why there is suffering in the world. These thoughts are expressed in the various flood stories from Mesopotamia, which are similar to Noah's Ark in the Bible. In ancient India, poverty, disease and suffering may have been the major reason why religion played such an important part in the development of their culture. India is the home of Hinduism and Buddhism, and Islam also became widely accepted there.

From the time of the Zhou dynasty, which began in China in about 1100BC and lasted nearly a thousand years, the Chinese believed in the Mandate of Heaven. This means that, like the people of Mesopotamia, they thought their rulers had been chosen by the gods and were responsible to them for the well-being of their people.

A POEM IN STONE
Many ancient buildings are still a source of wonder today. The Taj Mahal in India was built entirely of gleaming white marble as a tomb for the Emperor Shah Jahan's wife. It is one of the most magnificent buildings in the world and is the high point of Mughal art.

Japanese sailors are tossed around by wind and waves in a rough sea. Bad weather made it very hard for early peoples to fish the seas and farm the lands.

The Birth of Art

Religion often inspires great works of art and architecture. Beautiful temples and palaces were built in all these great civilizations. One of the most famous buildings in the world, the Taj Mahal in India, was a memorial to the beautiful wife of the Emperor Shah Jahan. Eastern buildings were decorated with wonderful carvings in wood and stone.

The Chinese developed great engineering skills. The Great Wall of China stretches for hundreds of kilometres. Like the Grand Canal and the thousands of bridges all over China, it is a testimony to the work of these ancient engineers and builders. The Japanese knew how to construct buildings that would survive earthquakes. Their houses had fine strong paper in their windows rather than glass, which would shatter. Their ancient wooden buildings are beautifully designed and carved.

Such civilized societies as those of China and Japan had a highly developed culture producing great works of art, including fine china and paintings. The Japanese learned many valuable skills from the Chinese and Koreans, including writing and woodblock printing. Going to the theatre and listening to music were especially popular pastimes in ancient Japan and India. Music, poetry and drama flourished at the courts of the kings of India.

The First Industrial Revolutions

The Chinese are famous for their scientific and technical advances. They invented paper, a fine china called porcelain, and lacquer work, and they were very skilful metal workers and sculptors. They invented the wheelbarrow, gunpowder, the magnetic compass, locks and keys, and umbrellas hundreds of years before these things were known in the West. Silk production in China is said to go back to 2640BC. Silk was exported to the West along a trade route known as the Silk Road. Exotic silks and muslins produced in India and China were much sought after in the Western world in the 1800s.

Human civilization began with the remarkable cultures of Asia. Art, science and technology evolved in quite distinct ways in different societies – although some developments, such as the use of money, and the invention of the wheel and the plough, happened at the same time in different nations.

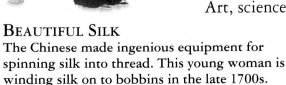

BEAUTIFUL SILK
The Chinese made ingenious equipment for spinning silk into thread. This young woman is winding silk on to bobbins in the late 1700s.

MESOPOTAMIA

Thousands of years before the Parthenon was built in Athens or the Roman Empire ruled Europe and North Africa, the people of Mesopotamia established one of the very earliest civilizations. The Sumerians, Assyrians and Babylonians were among the first people to develop writing, mathematics and the science of astronomy. They traded with Egypt and the Indus Valley in India and fought battles all over the ancient world.

LORNA OAKES

CONSULTANT: DR JOHN HAYWOOD

A Land Between Two Rivers

MESOPOTAMIA is the name of an ancient region where some of the world's first cities and empires grew up. Today, most of it lies in modern Iraq. Mesopotamia means 'the land between the rivers' – for the country lay between the Tigris and the Euphrates, two mighty rivers that flowed from the highlands of Turkey in the north down to the Gulf.

The first farmers settled in the low, rolling hills of the north about 9,000 years ago. Here, there was enough rainfall to grow crops and provide pasture for animals. The first cities developed about 3,500 years later, mostly in the flat, fertile flood plains of the south. Rivers and marshes provided water to irrigate crops, plenty of fish, and reeds to build houses and boats. Date palms grew in abundance. At first the south was called Sumer. Later it was known as Babylonia. The land in north Mesopotamia became known as Assyria.

SUMERIAN WORSHIPPERS

Statues of a man and woman from Sumer are shown in an act of worship. The Sumerians were some of the earliest people to live in the south of Mesopotamia. They lived in small, independent cities. At the centre of each city was a temple built as the home for the local god. These two Sumerians had statues made of themselves and put in a temple, so that the god could bless them.

THE WORK OF GIANTS

Most of what we know about the ancient civilizations of Mesopotamia has come from excavations by archaeologists over the last 150 years. In 1845, the British archaeologist Henry Layard unearthed the remains of a once-magnificent palace in the ancient Assyrian city of Nimrud. He found walls decorated with scenes of battles and hunting, and a statue of a human-headed, winged lion so huge that local people were astonished and thought it had been made by giants.

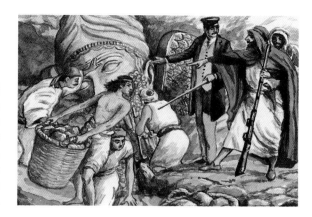

TIMELINE 7000–2100BC

Humans have lived in northern Iraq since the Old Stone Age, when hunter-gatherers lived in caves and rock shelters and made stone tools. Mesopotamian civilization began when people began to settle in villages. They learned how to grow crops and keep animals. Later, city-states grew up, and people developed writing. They became good at building, working metal and making fine jewellery.

painted pottery

7000BC The first villages are established. Edible plants and animals are domesticated, and farming develops. Pottery is made and mud-bricks used for building.

6000BC Use of copper. First mural paintings, temples and seals. Irrigation is used in agriculture to bring water to the fields. Decorated pottery, clay and alabaster figurines. Wide use of brick.

clay figurine

4000BC Larger houses and temples are built. Terracotta sickles and pestles are developed.

3500BC Growth of towns. Development of the potter's wheel, the plough, the first cylinder seals and writing. Bronze, silver and gold worked. Sculptures are made. Trading systems develop.

writing tablet

3000BC Sumerian civilization begins. City-states and writing develop.

7000BC   4000BC   2700BC

TEMPLES OF THE GODS

The ziggurat of Nanna, the Moon god, rises above the dusty plains of modern Iraq. It was once part of the massive temple complex in the city of Ur. Ziggurats showed how clever the Mesopotamians were at building. They were designed as a link between heaven and earth.

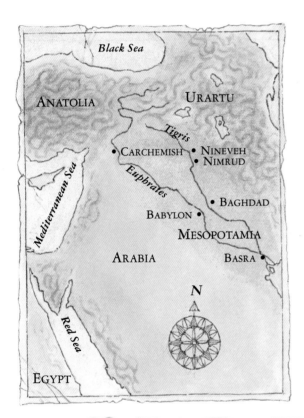

WRITING TABLET

A clay tablet shows an example of some of the earliest writing in the world. The symbols were pressed into a damp clay tablet using a reed pen. The Sumerians originally used writing to keep accounts of goods bought and sold including grain and cattle. Later on, kings used clay tablets as a record of their victories and building activities. Scribes wrote letters, poems and stories about heroes.

POWERFUL NEIGHBOURS

The kingdom of Egypt lay to the south-west of Mesopotamia. In about 2000BC the Assyrians traded with Anatolia in the north-west. They later conquered Phoenician cities in the west and fought Urartu in the north.

Sumerian chariot

2700BC Early Dynastic period. Kings and city administrations rule.

2600BC Royal Standard of Ur made, probably as the sounding box of a lyre.

2500BC Royal Graves of Ur made. Queen Pu-abi and other wealthy individuals buried in tombs with soldiers, musicians and court ladies.

2440BC Inter-state warfare. Kings of Lagash go to war with Umma.

2334BC Sargon of Agade becomes king. He creates the world's first empire, which is maintained by his grandson Naram-sin.

Pu-abi

2200BC The Agade Empire comes to an end. The Gutians, a mountain people, move into Mesopotamia and take some cities.

Ziggurat of Ur-nammu

2141BC Gudea takes the throne of Lagash. Ambitious temple-building programme at Girsu.

2112BC Ur-nammu of Ur tries to re-create the Agade Empire. He builds the famous ziggurat of Ur.

2500BC   2200BC   2100BC

Centres of Civilization

BEFORE THE RISE of the great empires in Mesopotamia, there were many small city-states, each with its own ruler and god. Each state consisted of a city and the surrounding countryside and was the centre of a brilliant civilization. Uruk, in the south, was the first to become important.

Around 2300BC, Sargon, a usurper, conquered all the cities of Mesopotamia and several beyond, creating the world's first empire. After his dynasty died out in about 2150BC, the kings of Ur, a city near the Gulf, tried to re-create Sargon's empire, but with limited success. About 100 years later, Ur fell to the Elamites, invaders from ancient Iran. A nomadic people called the Amorites gradually moved into Mesopotamia and took over the old Sumerian cities, including Babylon, and several of their chiefs became king. The sixth king of Babylon was Hammurabi, famous for his collection of laws.

In the 1500s BC, the Kassites took over Babylonia and ruled well for 400 years. Meanwhile, in the north, the Assyrian Empire had grown from its beginnings in the city-state of Ashur in the third millennium BC. It developed slowly over 2,000 years and reached a glorious peak around 645BC. The empire crumbled when the Babylonians conquered their key cities in 612BC. Babylonia became the most powerful empire in the known world until conquered by the Persian king, Cyrus, in 539BC.

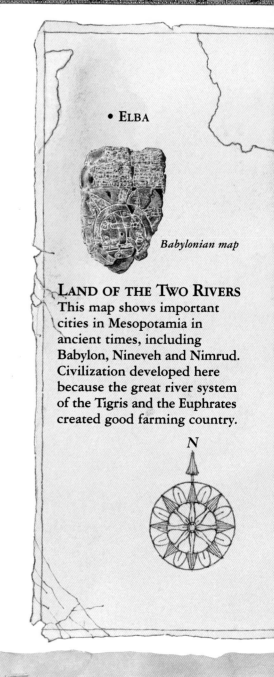

• ELBA

Babylonian map

LAND OF THE TWO RIVERS
This map shows important cities in Mesopotamia in ancient times, including Babylon, Nineveh and Nimrud. Civilization developed here because the great river system of the Tigris and the Euphrates created good farming country.

N

TIMELINE 2050–1000BC

2004BC Ibbi-Sin, last king of Ur, is captured by Elamites and taken to Susa.

2000BC Fall of the Sumerian Empire. Amorites interrupt trade routes. Ur attacked by Elamites and falls. Assyria becomes independent and establishes trading network in Anatolia.

1900BC Amorite chiefs take over some cities as rulers.

1792BC Hammurabi, an Amorite ruler, becomes King of Babylon.

Hammurabi

1787BC King Hammurabi conquers the major southern city of Isin.

1763BC Hammurabi conquers the city of Larsa.

1761BC Hammurabi conquers Mari and Eshnunna and may have conquered the city of Ashur.

1740BC Expansion of the Hittite kingdom in Anatolia, based on the city of Hattusas.

Scorpion man

1595BC The Hittite king, Mursulis, conquers North Syria. Marching further south, he destroys Babylon but does not take over the city.

1570BC The Kassites, a foreign dynasty, begin a 400-year rule of peace and prosperity. King Kurigalzu builds a new capital city, naming it after himself. Babylon becomes a world power on an equal level with the kingdom of Egypt.

2050BC   1790BC   1600BC   1500BC

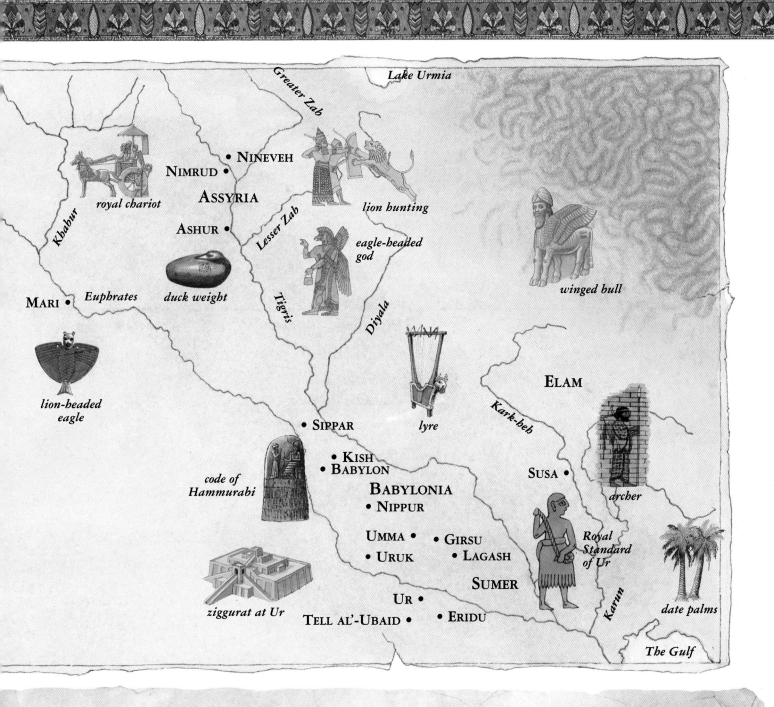

Lake Urmia

Greater Zab

NINEVEH •

NIMRUD •

royal chariot

ASSYRIA

lion hunting

Khabur

ASHUR •

Lesser Zab

duck weight

eagle-headed
god

Tigris

winged bull

MARI • Euphrates

Diyala

lion-headed
eagle

lyre

ELAM

Kark-beh

• **SIPPAR**

code of
Hammurabi

• **KISH**
• **BABYLON**

BABYLONIA

• **NIPPUR**

Susa •

archer

UMMA •

• **GIRSU**

Royal
Standard
of Ur

• **URUK**

• **LAGASH**

SUMER

Karun

date palms

ziggurat at Ur

UR •

TELL AL'-UBAID •

• **ERIDU**

The Gulf

1500BC Mitanni, a new state, develops
to the north of Mesopotamia. The people
speak Hurrian and fight in
two-wheeled horse-drawn chariots.
They conquer land from the
Mediterranean to the Zagros Mountains,
including Assyria.

1365BC Ashur-uballit becomes King
of Assyria and gains Assyria's
independence from Mitanni.

1150BC The Elamites conquer Babylon,
ending Kassite rule.

copper peg

1124BC Nebuchadnezzar I, a later
king of Babylon, successfully
attacks Elam, bringing back
large amounts of booty,
including the statue of Marduk, the
Babylonian god the Elamites had
captured some years earlier.

1115BC Tiglath-pileser I becomes
king. He expands Assyrian territory
and captures Babylon and other
southern cities. First written
account of the royal hunt in
Mesopotamia. Egyptian king sends
him a crocodile as a present.

1076BC Death of Tiglath-pileser I.

1050BC Ashurnasirpal I becomes king.

1000BC Assyria is attacked by
many enemies, including the
nomadic Aramaeans,who
move into Mesopotamia
and take over large
areas. Their language,
Aramaic, and its
alphabetic script gradually
replace Akkadian and
cuneiform.

Humbaba the giant

1130BC

1100BC

1000BC

History Makers

THE NAMES OF Mesopotamian kings are known because their victories and other achievements were recorded on clay tablets and palace wall decorations. The kings wanted to be sure that the gods knew that they had ruled well, and that their names would be remembered for ever. The names of ordinary soldiers and temple builders, the craftsmen who created the beautiful painted wall reliefs and the authors of the sagas and histories were not written down. Some astrologers, army commanders and state officials are known by name because they wrote letters to the king.

SARGON OF AGADE (2334-2279BC)

The man who created the world's first empire, by conquering all the cities of Sumer, Mari and Ebla. He founded the city of Agade, no trace of which has yet been found. A legend tells that when Sargon was a baby, his mother put him in a reed basket and set him afloat on a river. The man who found him trained him to be a gardener. When Sargon grew up, it was believed that he had been favoured by the goddess Ishtar, and he became cup-bearer to the king of Kish (a city north of Babylon).

EANNATUM OF LAGASH (C. 2440BC)

A king of Lagash, a city in southern Sumer, who was a great warrior and temple-builder. His victory over the nearby state of Umma was recorded on the Vulture Stela, a limestone carving that showed vultures pecking at the bodies of dead soldiers.

ENHEDUANNA(C. 2250BC)

The daughter of King Sargon of Agade is one of the few women in Mesopotamian history whose name is known. She held the important post of high priestess to the Moon-god at Ur. Her hymn to the god made her the first known woman author.

TIMELINE 950BC-500BC

911BC Adad-nirari becomes king. Assyria recovers some of her lost possessions and defeats the Aramaeans and Babylon.

879BC Ashurnasirpal II holds a banquet to celebrate the opening of his new palace at Nimrud.

858BC Shalmaneser III, son of Ashurnasirpal II, spends most of his 34-year reign at war, campaigning in Syria, Phoenicia, Urartu and the Zagros Mountains.

Stela of Ashurnasirpal II

c. 845BC Palace of Balawat built.

744BC Tiglath-pileser III brings more territory under direct Assyrian control. Deportation of conquered peoples begins.

721BC Sargon II decorates his palace at Khorsabad with carved reliefs showing his battle victories.

Black obelisk of Shalmaneser III

705BC Sennacherib becomes king of Assyria.

701BC Sennacherib attacks Hezekiah in Jerusalem.

694BC Ashur-nadin-shumi rules Babylon on behalf of his father Sennacherib. He is captured by the Elamites and taken to Susa. In revenge, Sennacherib burns Babylon to the ground.

Balawat Gates

950BC   850BC   710BC   690BC

ASHURBANIPAL OF ASSYRIA (669-631BC)

A great warrior king, who reigned at the peak of the Assyrian Empire. Ashurbanipal fought successfully against the Elamites, Babylonians and Arabs, and even made Egypt part of his empire for a time. But his greatest gift to civilization was the vast library in his palaces at Nineveh. Here, over 25,000 clay tablets were collected, including letters, legends and astronomical, mathematical and medical works.

NEBUCHADNEZZAR II (604-562BC)

As crown prince, Nebuchadnezzar fought at the side of his father, the king of Babylon, and brought the Assyrian Empire to an end. Under his own rule, the Babylonians conquered neighbouring countries, such as Palestine, and became one of the world powers of the time. Nebuchadnezzar built great fortifying walls around the city of Babylon and a magnificent ziggurat. He features in the Bible, as the king who captured Jerusalem and sent the people of Judah into captivity.

HAMMURABI (1792-1750BC)

The king of Babylon who collected 282 laws concerning family, town and business life and had them recorded on a black stela, a large stone. Other rulers had made laws, but his is the largest collection to survive. The picture shows Shamash, god of justice, giving Hammurabi the symbols of kingship. Towards the end of his reign, he went to war and created an empire, but it did not last long after his death.

681BC Sennacherib killed by his eldest son. His youngest son Esarhaddon becomes king.

671BC Esarhaddon invades Egypt and captures the Egyptian capital of Memphis.

668BC Ashurbanipal becomes king of Assyria. His brother Shamash-shum-ukin becomes king of Babylon.

Tiglath-pileser III

664BC Ashurbanipal invades Egypt and destroys the southern city of Thebes.

663 or 653BC Ashurbanipal begins a series of wars with Elam.

652BC Rebellion of Shamash-shum-ukin. Ashurbanipal invades Babylonia.

648BC Ashurbanipal lays siege to Babylon, which suffers starvation.

631BC Death of Ashurbanipal. Assyrian Empire begins to collapse.

Nimrud

612BC Babylonians attack and burn the Assyrian cities of Nimrud and Nineveh.

605BC Assyrians defeated by the Babylonians at the battle of Carchemish.

Ashurbanipal on horseback

604BC Nebuchadnezzar II becomes King of Babylon, and Babylon becomes a world power.

562BC Nebuchadnezzar II dies.

539BC Cyrus of Persia takes Babylon.

663BC

620BC

500BC

A Legendary King

THE ADVENTURES of one king of ancient Sumer were so exciting that they became the subject of some of the oldest stories in the world. Gilgamesh was king of Uruk, one of the most important cities of ancient Sumer, probably around 2700BC. He was said to be two-thirds god and one-third human and seems to have become a legend in his own lifetime. His deeds were first written down about 4,000 years ago and recounted in stories and poems over many generations, passing from the Sumerians to the Babylonians and Assyrians. Finally, in the 7th century BC, the Assyrians wove the individual tales together into an exciting adventure story called an epic and wrote it down on clay tablets. The *Epic of Gilgamesh* was stored in the great libraries of King Ashurbanipal of Assyria, where it was discovered by archaeologists over 100 years ago.

Gilgamesh was not a good king at first, so the gods created Enkidu, a wild, hairy man, to fight him. The king realized he had met his match, and the two then became good friends and went everywhere together.

GIANT ATTACK
The giant Humbaba guarded the Cedar Forest, far away, in Lebanon. His voice was like thunder, his breath was fire, and he could hear the faintest noise from far away. To test their courage, Gilgamesh and Enkidu decided to kill this monster. They were terrified by the giant's dreadful face and taunting words, but finally cut off his head with one stroke.

THE BULL OF HEAVEN
Ishtar, the goddess of love and war (on the left), tries to stop Enkidu and Gilgamesh from killing the Bull of Heaven. Ishtar had fallen in love with the hero-king, and she wanted to marry him. Gilgamesh knew that the goddess was fickle, and turned her down. Ishtar was furious and asked her father, Anu the sky god, to give her the Bull of Heaven so she could take revenge on Gilgamesh. The Bull was a deadly beast who had the power to bring death and long-term misery to the city of Uruk. The two friends fought and killed the bull. Enkidu (on the right) hung on to its tail, as Gilgamesh delivered the death blow with his sword.

THE CITY OF URUK

There is very little of Uruk left today, but it was a very important city when Gilgamesh was king. The city had splendid temples dedicated to Anu, the sky god, and his daughter Ishtar who fell in love with Gilgamesh. The king also built a great wall round the city. When his friend Enkidu died, Gilgamesh was heartbroken, and also frightened because he realized he would die one day, too. He wanted to live for ever. In the end, he decided that creating a beautiful city was his best chance of immortality. He would be remembered for ever for creating the fine temples and massive walls of Uruk.

THE PLANT OF ETERNAL LIFE

A massive stone carving of a heroic figure found in the palace of King Sargon II may be of Gilgamesh. The hero set out to find Utnapishtim, the ruler of another Sumerian city who was said to have found the secret of eternal life. The way was long and dangerous, and led into the mountains where lions prowled. The moon god protected Gilgamesh and led him to a great mountain, with a gate guarded by scorpion men. After a terrifying walk in total darkness, Gilgamesh emerged on the other side of the mountain into the garden of the gods. Beyond the garden were the Waters of Death, but our hero found a ferryman to take him safely across. At last he met Utnapishtim, who told him he would never die if he found a plant that grew on the sea bed. Gilgamesh tied stones on his feet, dived into the sea and picked the plant. However, on the way home, he stooped down to drink at a pool. A water snake appeared and snatched the plant. With it went Gilgamesh's hope of immortality.

LASTING FAME

The figures on this stone vase from Uruk probably show Gilgamesh. The king found the lasting fame he wanted because his name lived on in stories and legends, and in statues and carvings such as this.

The Development of Writing

MESOPOTAMIA WAS ONE OF the first places in the world to develop writing. The earliest examples are about 5,000 years old and come from the Sumerian city-state of Uruk. At first, writing was in the form of pictures and numbers, as a useful way to make lists of produce such as barley, wine and cheese, or numbers of cattle and donkeys. Gradually, this picture-writing was replaced by groups of wedge-shaped strokes, arranged in different ways. This type of writing is called cuneiform, which means 'wedge-shaped', because of the shape the reed pen made as it was pressed into the clay. To begin with, cuneiform writing was only used to write Sumerian, but later it was adapted to write several other languages, including Assyrian and Babylonian.

CLAY TABLET

Writing was done on clay tablets with a stylus (pen) made from a reed. The writer pressed the stylus into a slab of damp clay. This was left to dry and harden. The clay tablet in the picture, from around 3000BC, has symbols on it. One symbol looks like a hand, and others resemble trees or plants. It is not clear which language they represent, although it is likely to be Sumerian.

TWO SCRIBES

The scribe on the right is writing on a clay tablet with a stylus. He is making a list of all the booty and prisoners that his king has captured in battle. He is writing in Akkadian, one of the languages used by the Assyrians. The other scribe is writing on a leather roll, possibly in Aramaic, another language the Assyrians used. Aramaic was an easier language to write because it used an alphabet, unlike Akkadian, which used about 600 different signs.

SHAPES AND SIZES

Differently shaped clay tablets, including prisms and cylinders, were used for writing. Many tablets were flat but some were three-dimensional and hollow like vases. One like this, that narrows at each end, is called a prism. It is about 30cm long and records the military campaigns of King Sargon of Assyria.

A CLAY TABLET

You will need: pen, stiff card, ruler, scissors, modelling clay, cutting board, rolling pin, blunt knife, paper, paint and paintbrush, cloth.

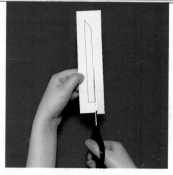

1 Draw a pointed stylus 20cm by 1.5cm on to the stiff card with the pen. Use the shape in the picture as a guide. Cut the shape out with the scissors.

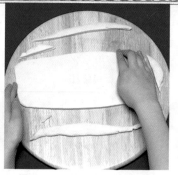

2 Roll out the clay on the cutting board with the rolling pin until it measures about 30cm by 15cm. Use the knife to cut out the clay as shown.

3 Take your card stylus and start writing cuneiform script on your clay tablet. Use the wedge shape of your stylus to make the strokes.

WRITING DEVELOPMENT

Cuneiform signs gradually came to be used for ideas as well as objects. At first, a drawing of a head meant simply 'head', but later it came to mean 'front' and 'first'. The symbols also came to represent spoken sounds and could be used to make new words. For example, in English, you could make the word 'belief' by drawing the symbols for a bee and a leaf. The chart shows how cuneiform writing developed. On the top row are simple drawings. In the middle row the pictures have been replaced by groups of wedges, and in the bottom row are the even more simplified versions of the signs.

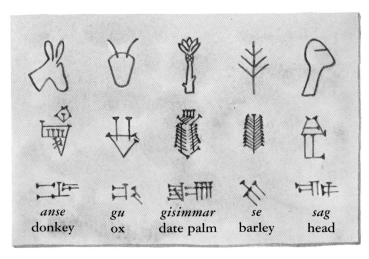

| *anse* | *gu* | *gisimmar* | *se* | *sag* |
| donkey | ox | date palm | barley | head |

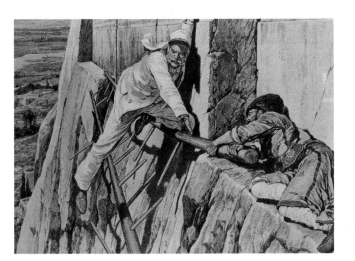

The tablet you have made is about half the size of the original. Flat tablets were used for everything from scholarly works on medicine and mathematics to dictionaries and stories. The Epic of Gilgamesh *took up 12 large tablets. Letters were written on tiny tablets.*

WRITING ON THE ROCK FACE

Henry Rawlinson, a British army officer who helped decipher cuneiform in the mid-1800s, risks his life climbing a cliff face at Behistun to copy the writing there. The inscription was in three languages, Old Persian, Elamite and Babylonian (Akkadian). He guessed that the cuneiform signs in Old Persian represented letters of the alphabet and found the name of Darius, the King of Persia. This helped scholars work out all three languages.

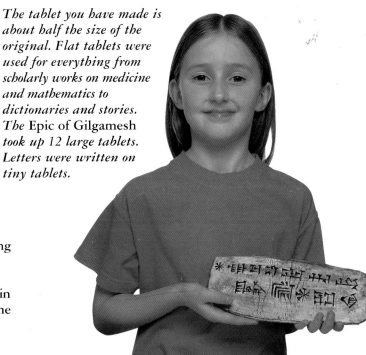

4 Copy the wedge shapes of the cuneiform script shown here. See how each group of strokes combines to make a particular letter or word.

5 Move your tablet on to a piece of clean paper. Take the paintbrush and paint and cover the clay, working the paint well into the cuneiform script.

6 When the painting is finished, wipe across the clay with the cloth. Most of the paint should come off, leaving the lettering a darker colour.

7 Leave the clay and the paint to dry. The lettering on your finished tablet reads: Nebuchadnezzar King of Babylon

Seals and Impressions

A SEAL IS A small piece of a hard material, usually stone, with a raised or sunken design on it. When this design is rolled across soft clay, it leaves an impression in the clay. In Mesopotamia, seals were impressed on to lumps of clay that sealed jars of wine or oil. Sometimes the clay was attached to ropes which tied up boxes or baskets. Seals were also rolled across clay writing tablets and their clay envelopes. Impressions in the clay identified who owned the object and made it harder to pass on stolen goods. Seals were often worn as jewellery, as part of a necklace or worn like a brooch. People thought seals also had magical powers that would protect them from illness and other dangers. They sometimes included pictures of the gods for added protection.

PERSONAL STAMP
This is the base of a long cylinder-shaped seal. It also has a design which the owner could use to stamp his or her mark on to objects. The base of a cylinder might only be 1cm in diameter, which made cylinders very hard to carve. Perhaps this seal once belonged to a priest since it shows a priest performing a ritual.

ROLLING DESIGN
Most seals were cylindrical in shape so that designs could be rolled over a clay tablet and repeated several times. This design shows the storm god, Adad, brandishing his special symbol, forked lightning. The seal was made in Babylon around 600BC. It is made of lapis lazuli, and is 12cm long about four times as long as most cylinder seals.

MIRROR IMAGE
A design showing a king or official being led by a goddess into the presence of a great god was a common design on cylinder seals. The design was cut into the seal the opposite way round to the way it would look when it was rolled out.

A CYLINDER SEAL
You will need: cutting board, rolling pin, self-hardening clay, ruler, paintbrush, glue, cardboard roll, scissors, cocktail stick, clay or plasticine.

1 Take the cutting board, rolling pin and self-hardening clay. Carefully roll out the clay until it measures roughly 15cm by 15cm. Trim one edge.

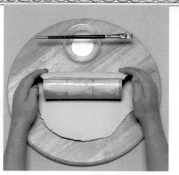

2 Paint glue on to the outside of the cardboard roll. Place the glued roll on to the clay and carefully cover the roll with the clay.

3 Make sure the roll is completely covered with clay. Trim away the excess clay at the edges. Smooth over the join of the clay with your fingers.

ROLL IT OUT

Seals were rolled over clay, so that the design was repeated. Cylinder seals are known from about 3000BC at Uruk, and at Susa in ancient Iran. Various kinds of stone, or glass, bone, shell, ivory or metal were shaped into cylinders. The length of the cylinder was then carved with intricate designs, either hand cut with flint or copper tools, or drilled with bow drills.

SHEEP SEAL

One of the earliest seals ever made comes from the city of Uruk. Its cylindrical base is carved out of a piece of limestone. The sheep-shaped knob on the top is made of copper. Nobody knows who invented the first cylinder seals but some people think they may have been made from the knuckle bones of sheep. Later designs copied the knuckle shape, complete with knobs.

The cylinder seal you have made is very much larger than those used in Mesopotamia. Cylinder seals were usually only 2 or 3cm tall and 1 to 1.5cm in diameter.

4 Use the cocktail stick to mark out a pattern in the clay. When you are happy with your pattern, you will use these marks as guides.

5 Following the marks made with the cocktail stick, use the end of a thin paintbrush to engrave your pattern deeply in the clay. Leave to harden.

6 Take the cutting board and rolling pin again. Roll out the second piece of clay, or plasticine, until it measures roughly 20cm by 14cm.

7 Make sure the clay on your cylinder seal is hard. Roll the seal across the clay or plasticine, pressing down firmly. Watch the pattern appear!

Gods and Goddesses

THE PEOPLE OF MESOPOTAMIA had many gods and goddesses. Every city had a temple to its own chief deity (god), and there were often temples dedicated to other members of the god's family too. The Sumerians and Akkadian-speaking peoples who lived in Mesopotamia worshipped the same gods and goddesses, but had different names for them. The Assyrians and Babylonians also worshipped these gods. The Sumerians called the moon god Nanna, but in Akkadian his name was Sin. The chief Sumerian god was called Enlil, who was often also referred to as King, Supreme Lord, Father, or Creator. According to one Sumerian poem, no one was allowed to look at Enlil, not even the other gods. The Mesopotamian kings believed they had been chosen by Enlil.

The god's chief sanctuary was at the city of Nippur. Legends tell that when the Nippur temple was raided by the army of the King of Agade, Enlil was so angry that he caused the Agade dynasty to come to an end. Enlil owned the Tablets of Destiny, which were thought to control the fates of people and the other gods.

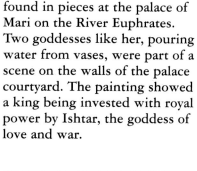

GODDESS
This statue of a goddess was found in pieces at the palace of Mari on the River Euphrates. Two goddesses like her, pouring water from vases, were part of a scene on the walls of the palace courtyard. The painting showed a king being invested with royal power by Ishtar, the goddess of love and war.

BEFORE THE GOD
A scene on a 4,000-year-old seal shows an official called Lamabazi being led into the presence of a great god by a lesser god. The great god is sitting on the throne, and before him is a brazier for burning incense. Lamabazi is holding his hand in front of his face as a sign of respect for the god.

IN THE BEGINNING
Marduk was the god of Babylon. He is shown here standing on his mushushshu (snake dragon). In the *Epic of Creation*, a Babylonian story about how Marduk created the world, he fought against a female monster, Tiamat, and her son, Kingu. After Marduk had killed them, the other gods made him their king. Marduk then brought the rest of creation into existence. He made models of human beings by mixing some clay with the blood of Kingu and then brought them to life.

CLUES TO IDENTITY

Most of our ideas about what the Mesopotamian gods and goddesses looked like come from their pictures on cylinder seals. This one shows Ishtar, the goddess of love and war, carrying her weapons. She is accompanied by a lion, which was her sacred animal. Shamash, the sun god, is recognizable by the flames coming from him, as he rises between two mountains. Ea, the water god, has streams of water gushing from his shoulders.

GOD OF ASSYRIA

Ashur was the chief god of the Assyrians. It was thought that he was the god who chose the Assyrian kings and went before them into battle. He is often symbolized by the same horned cap as Enlil, the chief Sumerian god. Sometimes he is shown standing on a winged bull or on a mushushshu (snake dragon) like Marduk, the god of Babylon. Both gods were honoured in New Year festivals when their priests slapped the reigning king's face, pulled his ears and made him bow low. The king then said he had served his people properly and was re-crowned for another year.

FERTILE MIND

Nisaba was originally a goddess of fertility and agriculture, although she later became the goddess of writing. Good harvests were very important to the people of Mesopotamia, and almost everyone ate barley bread and dates. This carving of Nisaba shows her covered with plants. She is wearing an elaborate headdress composed of a horned crown and ears of barley. Flowers sprout from her shoulders, and she is holding a bunch of dates.

Houses for the Gods

THERE WAS A TEMPLE at the centre of every Mesopotamian city, which was regarded as the house of the local god or goddess. A statue of the deity was put in a special room in the temple, and daily ceremonies were held in his or her honour. One of the main duties of kings was to build or repair temples. King Gudea of Lagash built 15 temples in his city-state. One was inspired by a dream in which the king saw a huge man with two lions and a woman with a writing tablet. Another man appeared with a temple plan, a basket and a brick mould. A dream interpreter told Gudea that the man was the god Ningirsu and the woman was Nisaba, the goddess of writing. This dream meant that Ningirsu wanted Gudea to build him a temple.

TEMPLE BUILDER
King Gudea was one of the great Mesopotamian temple builders. He described the process of building the temple to Ningirsu, near Lagash, on two large clay cylinders. Before installing the god's statue, he purified the temple by surrounding it with fire and anointing the temple platform with aromatic balm. Next day the king washed himself and offered prayers and sacrifices. Finally, the statue was taken to its temple with great ceremony.

FORMER GLORY
All that is left today of the ziggurat (temple-tower) at Ur is the lowest level. In 2100BC it was a three-staged tower built of mud-brick. Three staircases met at the top of the first stage, and the worshippers went on up a single staircase to the temple at the top. Ziggurats may have developed their stepped structure because new temples were often built on top of old ones, and so a huge platform gradually built up. Ziggurats were first built by King Ur-nammu of Ur.

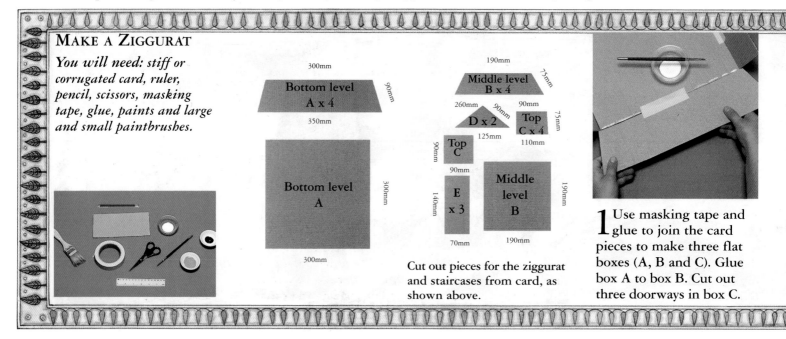

MAKE A ZIGGURAT

You will need: stiff or corrugated card, ruler, pencil, scissors, masking tape, glue, paints and large and small paintbrushes.

Bottom level
A x 4
300mm
350mm
90mm

Bottom level
A
300mm
300mm

190mm
Middle level
B x 4
75mm

260mm
D x 2
125mm
90mm

Top
C x 4
90mm
75mm
110mm

Top
C
90mm

Middle
level
B
190mm

E
x 3
90mm
140mm
70mm
190mm

Cut out pieces for the ziggurat and staircases from card, as shown above.

1 Use masking tape and glue to join the card pieces to make three flat boxes (A, B and C). Glue box A to box B. Cut out three doorways in box C.

FOOD FIT FOR THE GODS

The building on this clay impression may be the ziggurat at Babylon, where the seal was found. The figure of a man seems to be offering a sacrifice. The people of Mesopotamia believed they had been created to serve the gods so they gave them special food, including fish, meat, cream, honey, cakes and beer.

THE TOWER OF BABEL

The ziggurat of Marduk, the protector god of Babylon, was thought by modern Westerners to be the Tower of Babel mentioned in the Bible. This is an imaginary picture of the tower the Babylonians built to get closer to heaven. The story says God was angry with them for thinking the way to heaven was so simple. He made the builders speak different languages so they could not understand each other and finish the work.

LAYING THE FOUNDATIONS

A statuette and clay tablet of Ur-nammu of Ur show that the king took his temple-building duties seriously. To make sure the gods knew who had built temples for them, the kings put a clay or stone tablet beneath each of the four corners of the temple, with their names on. They often also put statues of themselves like this one, complete with bricks and carrying a brick basket. Ur-nammu built temples at Ur and several other cities.

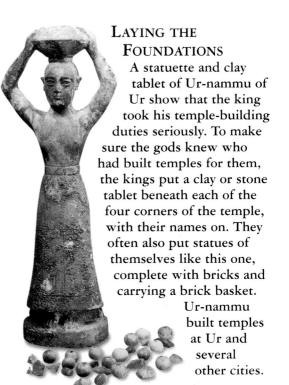

A real ziggurat was a solid stepped temple-tower of mud-brick. Worshippers climbed the stairways to the god's shrine on the top. It is sometimes seen as a ladder between heaven and earth.

2 Cut out four pieces of card 9 x 2cm, and cut out the edge as shown in the picture. Glue them on top of box C. Then glue box C on top of the ziggurat.

3 Glue triangles D to the first strip E for the main staircase. Cut out two triangles of card for the side stairs and glue them to the other two strips E.

4 Glue the staircases into position as shown. Add strips of card for more doorways and the sides of the main staircase. When dry, paint the ziggurat brown.

5 When completely dry, add details such as the stairs on the staircases and the markings on the sandstone, with black paint and a fine brush.

Sumerian Burial

W HEN the Sumerian city of Ur was excavated in the 1930s, archaeologists found hundreds of graves. The discovery gave an insight into how the inhabitants regarded death and burial. Little evidence about death rituals in other parts of Mesopotamia survives.

In Ur, most people seem to have been buried in family graves under the courtyards of their houses. Their children were put in jars and placed in chapels above the family graves. Other people were buried in the city cemetery. Most bodies had been wrapped in reed mats or placed in baskets (which no longer existed but the patterns of their weaving were pressed into the soil). Most people had a few belongings buried with them, but 17 of the graves contained many precious objects. They may have belonged to kings and queens, and so were called the Royal Graves.

FIT FOR THE QUEEN'S COURT
A headdress of gold and semi-precious stones, with finely worked golden leaves and ribbons, was found in the grave of Queen Pu-abi at Ur. It may have belonged to one of the ladies of her court. The body of the queen herself was bedecked in gold earrings, finger rings and necklaces. Tiny threads of wool suggested that she had been wrapped in a red woollen cloak.

CEREMONIAL HELMET
An exquisitely decorated helmet of electrum (a mixture of gold and silver) may have belonged to Meskalamdug, whose name was found on two golden bowls in the grave. The wig-like pattern is hammered from the inside. The holes around the edge were provided so that a lining could be sewn in to make it more comfortable.

RAM IN THE THICKET
No one knows why this ram was placed in a mass grave called the Great Death Pit. A pair of rams or goats in a thicket was a common image in Mesopotamian art. This ram was one of a pair. It was made of wood decorated with bright blue lapis lazuli to show the animal's hairy coat and a silver plate over its belly.

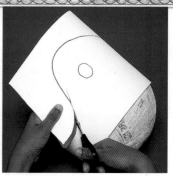

A GOLD HELMET

You will need: balloon, flour, water and newspaper to make papier mâché, scissors, card 60cm by 20cm, masking tape, pen, pieces of white cotton fabric, glue, string, gold and black paint and paintbrushes.

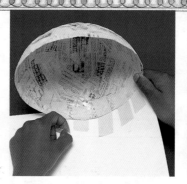

1 Blow up the balloon until it is as big as your head. Dip newspaper strips in flour-and-water paste, and cover the balloon with layers of papier mâché.

2 When the papier mâché is completely dry, pop the balloon. Trim the edge of the helmet. Attach the piece of card to the helmet with masking tape.

3 With the pen, draw the shape of the sides of the helmet as shown. Cut round the shape with the scissors. Draw and cut out holes for the ears.

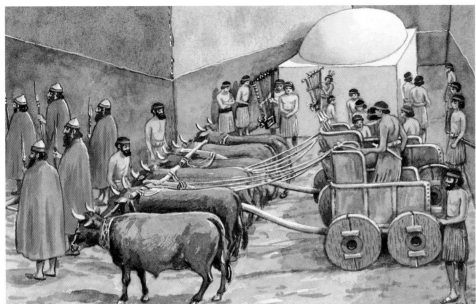

ROYAL FUNERAL

The bodies of six guards and 68 court ladies were found in a grave at Ur called the Great Death Pit. Woolley thought they were the servants of kings and queens who had been chosen to accompany them to the afterlife. They walked down into the grave in a great funeral procession. Then they drank a drugged drink and fell asleep never to wake again.

You have made a copy of Meskalamdug's ceremonial helmet. One meant for real use would have been made of a stronger metal such as copper.

GOLDEN TABLEWARE

So many beautiful golden objects, such as these fluted bowls and tumblers, were found in certain graves at Ur that Woolley called them the Royal Graves. In 1989, the tombs of some Assyrian queens were found under the palace floor at Nimrud. The queens were buried with their exquisite jewellery of gold, but unlike Queen Pu-abi of Ur they were not buried with their servants.

4 Take three strips of white fabric 100cm by 4cm. Tie them together with a knot at one end and plait the three strips loosely and knot the other end.

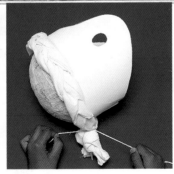

5 Glue the plait around the helmet, covering the join between the papier mâché and card as shown. Tie off the end with string to make a tail.

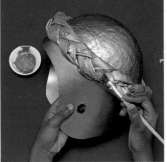

6 Paint the whole helmet, inside and out, with gold paint. Use a broad paintbrush. Paint over the cloth plait, too. Allow the paint to dry thoroughly.

7 Add detail of hair to the helmet using the black paint and a fine paintbrush. You can use Meskalamdug's helmet to give you some ideas!

Education

SCHOOL BUILDINGS in Mesopotamia looked very similar to ordinary houses. Archaeologists have been able to identify the schools because large numbers of clay tablets containing mistakes and corrections were found there. The tablets had been corrected by the teachers just as modern teachers mark books. A school was called edubba, which means tablet house.

The tablets show which subjects were taught and how schools were run. The headteacher was called ummia (expert), but was also known as the school father. The teachers' job was to write out tablets for students to copy, to correct their exercises and listen to them recite what they had learned by heart.

The school day was very long, lasting from sunrise to sunset. Discipline was very strict. One boy was caned several times in one day – for getting his clothes in a mess, making a mistake on his tablet and talking in class.

MUSIC LESSONS
Students learned music at school. In examinations they were asked questions about playing musical instruments, different types of songs and how to conduct a choir. This figure showing a man playing a lyre is on a highly decorated box called the Royal Standard of Ur because it was once thought it was a standard that was carried into battle.

LEARNING ABOUT HEROES
When students were good at reading and writing, they studied the Mesopotamian myths and legends, such as the stories of the heroic king of Uruk, Gilgamesh, and his friend Enkidu.

CIVIL SERVANT
Ebih-il was Superintendent of the Palace at Mari. The main aim of schools was to produce scribes and civil servants like Ebih-il. Some students became scholars who worked in the temple and royal libraries, or teachers. At school, boys learned the two main languages, Sumerian and Akkadian, by copying and learning by heart groups of related words. They also studied other subjects, such as botany and zoology, by copying out lists of plants, animals, insects and birds.

EXCLUSIVE EDUCATION
If these modern-day Iraqi boys had been born 5,000 years ago, they would probably not have gone to school. Only boys from well-off families went to school in ancient Mesopotamia. They were the sons of high-up officials, officers in the army, sea captains or scribes.

PLAYING WITH NUMBERS

Maths was very important in Mesopotamian schools. Clay tablets, such as this one, had mathematical problems written on them. Some of these related to practical matters, but most were just brain-teasers. The Mesopotamians obviously liked playing with numbers. Students also had tables for multiplying and dividing, and for working out squares and square roots. There were two number systems, one using 10 as a base and the other, 60. We use 10 as a base too, and 60 to measure time, for example.

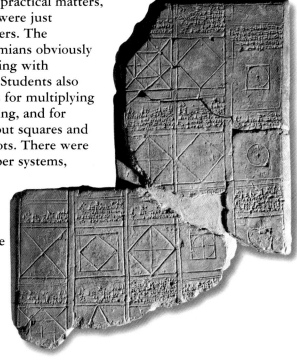

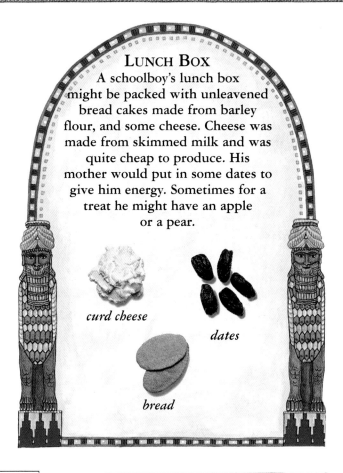

LUNCH BOX

A schoolboy's lunch box might be packed with unleavened bread cakes made from barley flour, and some cheese. Cheese was made from skimmed milk and was quite cheap to produce. His mother would put in some dates to give him energy. Sometimes for a treat he might have an apple or a pear.

curd cheese

dates

bread

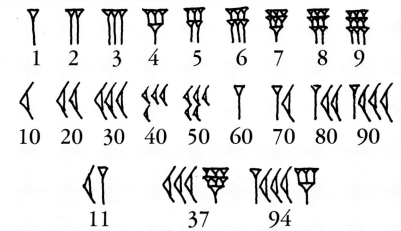

1	2	3	4	5	6	7	8	9
10	20	30	40	50	60	70	80	90
	11		37		94			

WRITING NUMBERS

This chart shows how numbers were written in Mesopotamia. Numbers were written on clay tablets using a system of wedge-shaped signs. For the numbers 1 to 9 the appropriate number of wedges was arranged in groups. 10 was one slanting wedge, 20 two slanting wedges, and so on up to 50. The figure 60 was written with an upright wedge. There was no sign for zero. The same symbol is used for the numbers 1 and 60. You can tell which number is which by looking at the order of the wedges. For example, if the slanting wedge comes first the number is 11 (10+1). If the slanting wedge comes afterwards the number is 70 (60+10).

PRINCE'S EDUCATION

Learning to drive a chariot and fight in battle were part of King Ashurbanipal's education when he was crown prince. Officials taught him the Sumerian and Akkadian languages, which he found difficult. He also studied multiplication and division, astronomy and ancient literature, and learned to ride a horse and hunt.

Music and Games

INSTRUMENTAL MUSIC and singing played an important part in Mesopotamian life. Musicians entertained at the court of the king and played in temple rituals. King Gudea of Lagash wrote a learned work about music. Most of the musical works that have come down to us are hymns to gods and kings. For example, we know that Sargon of Agade's daughter, Enheduanna, composed a hymn to the moon god at Ur. People may have amused themselves with music, singing and dancing in their homes and in the market place. One Sumerian poem about the goddess Inanna and her lover Dumuzi speaks about them going to see an entertainer singing and dancing in the public square. In the Middle East today, musicians and storytellers still entertain in the open squares of cities.

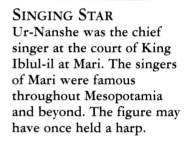

SEVEN-STRINGED HARP
Harps and lyres were two of the most popular musical instruments in Mesopotamia. They were sometimes played in funeral processions. The harp on this Babylonian terracotta relief has seven strings, which were probably made from animal gut.

ROYAL GAME OF UR
A beautiful board game was found in the Royal Graves of Ur. It is made from wood covered in bitumen (tar) and decorated with a mosaic of shell, bone, blue lapis lazuli, red glass and pink limestone. The game may have been a bit like Ludo, with two sets of counters and four-sided dice, but the rules have not been found!

SINGING STAR
Ur-Nanshe was the chief singer at the court of King Iblul-il at Mari. The singers of Mari were famous throughout Mesopotamia and beyond. The figure may have once held a harp.

MAKE A LYRE

You will need: pencil, card, scissors, 3 pieces of dowel 55cm long, masking tape, glue, flour, water and newspaper for papier mâché, sandpaper, paints and paintbrushes, pins, piece of balsa wood, string or elastic.

1 Draw a bull shape 40cm long by 25cm wide on to the card, following the shape shown above. You will need two of these card cutouts. Cut out two horns.

2 Cut four card strips 3cm by 55cm. Use masking tape and glue to attach a strip to each side of two of the pieces of dowel.

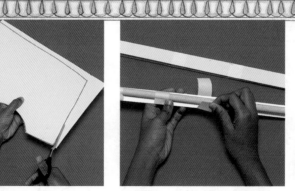

3 Fix the two dowel pieces to one of the bull shapes, one coming out of the head, the other out of the rump. Tape the other bull shape on top.

DRUMS AND CYMBALS

Musicians pictured on a palace wall are playing cymbals and a drum as well as stringed instruments. There were several kinds of drums in Babylonia. One was the balag, which was shaped like an hour-glass. It was used in temple rituals to soothe the gods. Another was the lilissu, which was set up in temple courtyards and beaten when there was an eclipse of the Moon. Flutes were also played. Just over a hundred years ago a Babylonian clay whistle was found. Unfortunately it has now been lost.

CEREMONY WITH MUSIC

Musicians play in victory celebrations. They are playing at a ceremony to celebrate King Ashurbanipal's victory over the King of Elam. Musicians took part in other rituals too, such as one after a lion hunt when Assyrian kings offered the dead animals to the gods.

Your lyre is like one found in the Royal Graves of Ur. It was made of wood and decorated with a mosaic in shells, blue lapis lazuli and limestone. The bull's head was made of gold and lapis lazuli with ivory horns. It had 11 strings.

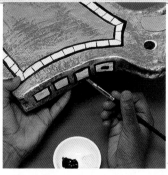

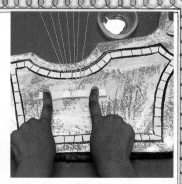

4 Use masking tape to attach the horns. Make a flour-and-water paste and use papier mâché to fill the gap between the two bull shapes and cover the bull.

5 Take the third piece of dowel and tape to the top of the other two pieces. Smooth with sandpaper and paint. Add cardboard pegs as shown and paint.

6 When the papier mâché is dry, decorate the body of the lyre with the paints. Use different coloured paints to create an inlaid mosaic effect.

7 Cut 7 strings from string or elastic. Tie them to the balsa wood and pin it on the bull's body. Tie the other end of the strings to the top piece of dowel.

Family Life

MOTHERHOOD
Having lots of healthy children, especially sons, was very important because families needed children to grow up and work for them. Most women stayed at home to look after their families. Women did not usually go out to work, but some had jobs as priestesses. Some priestesses were single but others were married women.

LIFE WAS HARD for ordinary families in Mesopotamia. Many babies and young children died from disease or because of poor maternity care. Boys from poorer families did not go to school but worked with their fathers, who taught them their trades. Girls stayed at home with their mothers and learned how to keep house and look after the younger children. Some of the details of family life are described in ancient clay tablets. In one tablet, a boy rudely tells his mother to hurry up and make his lunch. In another one, a boy is scared of what his father will say when he sees his bad school report.

In some ways, Mesopotamian society was quite modern. The law said that women could own property and get a divorce. However, if a woman was unable to have a baby, she had to agree to her husband taking a second wife. The second wife and her children had rights too. They remained part of the household even if the first wife had a child after all.

HOUSEHOLD GOODS
Pottery was used in Mesopotamian homes from the time of the first villages. At first it was hand-made, but later a potter's wheel was used. This pottery jug may have been modelled on a jug made of metal. Tools and utensils were made of stone or metal. There was not much furniture in a Mesopotamian house, just mud-brick benches for sitting or sleeping on. There may have been rugs and cushions to make the homes more homely and comfortable, but none have survived.

MODEL HOUSE
From models such as this one, we know that homes in Mesopotamia were similar to village houses in modern Iraq. They were built of mud-brick and were usually rectangular, with rooms around a central courtyard. Doors and windows were small to keep the house warm in the cold winters, and cool during the hot summers. Flat roofs, reached by stairs from the central court, could be used as an extra room in summer.

MESOPOTAMIAN FASHIONS

A statue of a worshipper found in a temple shows the dress of a Sumerian woman. Dresses were of sheepskin, sometimes with a sheepskin shawl as well, or of woollen cloth. One shoulder was left bare. Some women, who may have been priestesses, wore tall, elaborate hats like this one. Later fashions included long, fringed garments. Sumerian men wore sheepskin kilts, but men in the Assyrian and Babylonian Empires wore long, woollen tunics. Both sexes wore jewellery.

EARNING A LIVING

Most families in ancient Mesopotamia depended on agriculture for a living, just as many people in the Middle East do today. Farmers rented their land from bigger landowners, such as important officials, kings or temples, and had to pay part of what they produced in taxes. Many townspeople had jobs in local government or worked in the textile and metalwork industries.

BUILD IT UP

Mud-bricks are made from a mixture of clayey mud and straw mixed with water. The straw stops the bricks from cracking. The mixture is put in square or oblong moulds and left to dry in the sun for several weeks. The bricks are usually made in the summer after the harvest, when there is plenty of straw available and it is less likely to rain (which would damage the bricks).

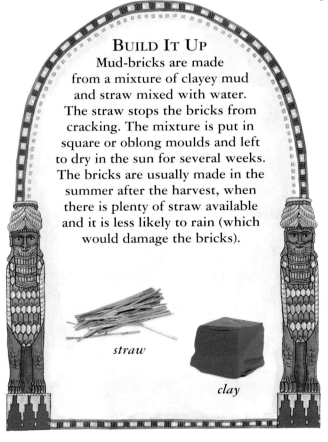

straw

clay

GONE FISHING

There were lots of fish in the rivers and fishponds of ancient Iraq, and fish seem to have been an important part of people's diet. Fishbones were found at Eridu, in the south of Sumer, in the oldest level of the temple. Perhaps fish were offered to the water god Enki as an offering. (He is the god with streams of water containing fish springing out of his shoulders.) Some of the carved reliefs from the Assyrian palaces give us rare glimpses into everyday life and include little scenes of men going fishing.

A Woman's Life

MOST MESOPOTAMIAN WOMEN married in their early teens. Sometimes, two families agreed on a marriage when the future man and wife were still children. After the agreement was made, the children lived with their parents until they were old enough to set up home together. Then the young man took a betrothal present to his bride's family, such as some clothing, some silver and a ring. When the marriage took place, the wife's father would give her a dowry of jewellery, clothes or furniture to take to her new home. She might be given a field or an orchard as her property.

Some women had a lot of responsibility. Queen Shibtu, wife of King Zimri-lim of Mari, ran the palace while her husband was away and kept him informed about everything that went on.

A queen seems to have become important only after producing a son. The mother of a king often had higher status than his wife.

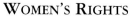

WOMEN'S RIGHTS
The laws of King Hammurabi of Babylon are carved on this stone pillar. They tell us about some of the legal rights held by women in Mesopotamia. They could own property and engage in business. A woman could get a divorce if her husband treated her badly. If she could prove her innocence, she could reclaim her dowry and return to her parents' home. But if she neglected her duties as a wife, the laws said she could be thrown into water.

OF ROYAL BLOOD
The fine clothes and jewellery on this statue show that it is a figure of a princess. She belonged to the family of King Gudea of Lagash. Her name was once written on her statue, but unfortunately it can no longer be read. The statue was found at Girsu, where King Gudea built his temples, so she may also have been a priestess.

MAKE A NECKLACE
You will need: self-hardening clay, cocktail stick, paper, pen, scissors, paintbrushes, glue, paints in bright colours, wire and pliers, strong thread.

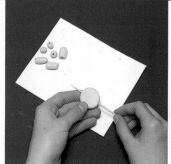

1 Make a variety of beads using the self-hardening clay, in long shapes and round shapes. Use the cocktail stick to make a hole through each bead.

2 Cut shapes out of the paper following the pattern shown above. The shapes should be about 3cm long. They will be used to make cylindrical beads.

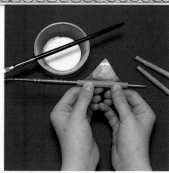

3 Roll the pieces of paper tightly around a fine paintbrush as shown. Glue the tail of the paper to secure it to itself and leave it to dry.

WOMEN'S WORK

A relief shows a woman spinning. A great deal is known about the women who worked at Mari, a city on the River Euphrates, because they are mentioned in letters that archaeologists found in the palace ruins. Many women worked in the textile industry. There were several female musicians. Other women worked in the royal kitchens, or were midwives who helped mothers in childbirth. The biggest surprise of all was to find that one woman was a doctor.

EDUCATING DUDU

Although usually only boys went to school, a few women were educated and became scribes, such as this woman, Dudu. There were nine women scribes at Mari. Their names appear on ration lists, showing that they were palace employees. We do not know how they trained.

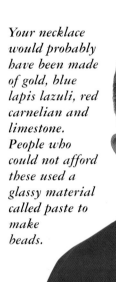

EXPENSIVE NECKLACE

Only a rich woman would have worn a necklace like this, as it would have been quite expensive. The blue lapis lazuli was imported. It was mined in the mountains of Afghanistan and made into beads in workshops in Iran. The necklace was made about 4,500 years ago.

Your necklace would probably have been made of gold, blue lapis lazuli, red carnelian and limestone. People who could not afford these used a glassy material called paste to make beads.

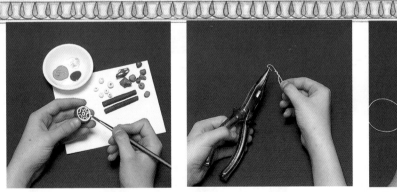

4 When the beads are dry, paint them. If you are using different colours, allow the paint to dry thoroughly between before adding the next coat.

5 Cut two small pieces of wire. Use the pliers to make two hooks. One side of each hook should be closed as shown, the other should be left open.

6 Tie a long piece of strong thread firmly to the closed side of one hook. Push the end of the thread through the painted beads to string the beads.

7 When you get to the end of the thread, or have used up all your beads, attach the end of the thread to the closed end of the second hook.

Farming

NORTHERN MESOPOTAMIA had enough rainfall to let farmers grow crops, but in the dry south farmers had to use the Tigris and the Euphrates rivers to irrigate the land. The main crop was barley. Wooden ploughs were used to break up the soil before the seed was sown with seed drills. A Sumerian almanac or diary told farmers what they should do at various times of the year. Vegetables and fruit were also grown, dates being particularly valued. They also kept cattle, sheep and goats on the grasslands between the cultivated areas. The landscape looked much the same as it does today, although rivers have changed course over the years. The weather has always been unpredictable and sometimes crops are spoiled by sudden storms.

SHEPHERD WITH LAMB
A Sumerian shepherd holds a lamb. Sheep not only provided meat and milk, but the sheepskin garments that were commonly worn. Wool was also woven into cloth to make long tunics, dresses and shawls. People had to pay a proportion of the goods they produced as taxes to the city-states.

FOOD SOURCE
Cows were an important part of the Mesopotamian economy. Many different kinds of cheese and other dairy products are mentioned in clay tablet records. One Sumerian temple frieze shows work in a dairy, with two men churning butter in large jars. Other men are straining a substance from one vessel to another to make cheese.

WATER LIFELINE
Summers in Mesopotamia were very hot and dry. From the earliest settlements in Sumer to present-day Iraq, farmers have dug channels to carry water from the Tigris and Euphrates rivers to their fields. Mesopotamian kings believed that organizing the building of canals was a religious duty.

MAKE A RAM-HEADED DRINKING CUP

You will need: paper cup, newspaper, masking tape, scissors, flour and water to make papier mâché, fork, fine sandpaper, paint and paintbrushes, varnish.

1 Scrunch up a piece of newspaper. Attach the ball of newspaper to the bottom end of the paper cup with pieces of masking tape.

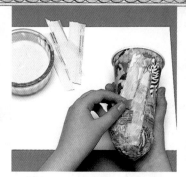

2 Make a paste with water and flour using the fork to mix the paste. Tear strips of newspaper and dip them into the paste, then cover the cup.

3 Twist two pieces of newspaper into coil shapes for the horns and fix them to the cup. Cover the cup inside and out with papier mâché. Leave to dry.

A HEALTHY DIET

By looking at ancient seeds, archaeologists have been able to find out what people ate in the past. The Mesopotamians ate fruit and vegetables such as apples, pomegranates, medlars and grapes, onions, leeks and turnips. The country's most important crop was barley, which was used for making bread and beer. Wheat was grown to a lesser extent. Barley was made into a porridge-like mixture flavoured with cumin, mustard, coriander and watercress.

apples

medlars

grapes

pomegranates

DATE ORCHARDS

Some of the biggest date orchards in the world are in the south of modern Iraq. The fruits were important in ancient times because they were an excellent source of energy. Dates could be dried and stored so that they were available all the year round, and were made into wine. Date syrup was used as a sweetener.

Animal-headed cups for drinking wine have been found at Nimrud. Your cup is copied from a pottery one. Wealthy people also used cups of bronze.

ANCIENT TOOLS

Agricultural tools were made of copper and bronze, and included axe-heads, knives and sickles for harvesting. Ancient farmers also had seed drills and wooden ploughs drawn by oxen, like the ones still used today, although many modern farmers also use tractors.

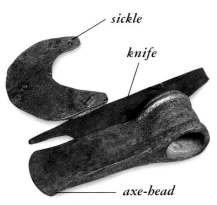

sickle

knife

axe-head

4 When the papier mâché is completely dry, smooth it down with sandpaper. Paint the whole cup in a creamy beige colour.

5 When the base coat is dry, use a fine paintbrush and brown paint to add details to your cup. Paint in the ram's horns and face.

6 Use red paint to add stripes to your drinking cup. Paint three red stripes around the neck, and two red stripes around the open end.

7 When the paint is completely dry, coat the drinking cup with a water-based varnish. Allow the first coat to dry before applying a second coat.

Science and Technology

THE PEOPLE OF MESOPOTAMIA developed many different aspects of technology including metalworking, pottery, glassmaking, the manufacture of textiles and leather-working. They were also experts at irrigation and flood control, building elaborate canals, water storage and drainage systems. They were among the first people in the world to use metal. An early copper sculpture, made in 2600BC, comes from the temple of Ubaid near Ur. It shows a lion-headed eagle clutching two stags in its talons. The armies used vast amounts of bronze for their weapons and armour. King Sennacherib used striding lions, cast in solid bronze and weighing hundreds of kilograms, to support the wooden pillars of his palace at Nineveh.

SUPPLYING THE CITY
Water wheels and aqueducts such as these are still used in the Middle East today. The Assyrians built aqueducts to take water to the cities to meet the needs of their growing populations. The Assyrian king Sennacherib (701-681BC) had 10km of canals cut from the mountains to the city of Nineveh. He built dams and weirs to control the flow of water, and he created an artificial marsh, where he bred wild animals and birds.

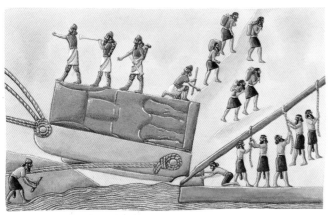

A WEIGHTY CHALLENGE
Workers in a quarry near the Assyrian city of Nineveh prepare to move an enormous block of stone roughly hewn in the shape of a lamassu (human-headed winged bull). The stone is on a sledge carried on wooden rollers. At the back of the sledge, some men have thrown ropes over a giant lever and pull hard. This raises the end of the sledge and other workers push a wedge underneath. More workers stand ready to haul on ropes at the front of the sledge. At a signal everyone pulls or pushes and the sledge moves forward.

MAKE A PAINTED PLATE
You will need: a plate, flour, water and newspaper to make papier mâché, scissors, pencil, fine sandpaper, ruler, paints and paintbrushes.

1 Tear strips of newspaper and dip them in the water. Cover the whole surface of the plate with the wet newspaper strips.

2 Mix up a paste of flour and water. Cover the newspaper strips with the paste. Allow to dry, then add two more layers, leaving it to dry each time.

3 When the papier mâché is dry, trim around the plate to make a neat edge. Remove the plate. Add more papier mâché to strengthen the plate.

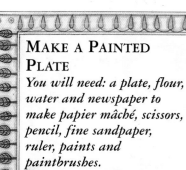

MAKING CLOTH

Spinning and weaving were usually done by women in the home or in state or temple factories. Large herds of sheep and goats were kept to produce wool, to make clothing. Flax was grown for its fibres, which were used to make linen as early as the 3000BC. Cotton was not introduced until the reign of Sennacherib in the 700s BC.

sheep's wool

wool

sheep's fleece

METALWORKERS

Ceremonial daggers demonstrate the Sumerians' skill at working with gold. Real weapons would have had bronze blades. The Sumerians cast metal by making a wax model of the object required which they covered with clay to make a mould. A small hole in the side let the wax escape when it was heated, so that molten metal could be poured into the mould. When the metal cooled, the mould was broken and the object removed.

You have copied a plate from Tell Halaf, a small town where some of the finest pots in the ancient world were made. They were decorated with orange and brown paints made from oxides found in clay.

HAND-MADE VASES

Vases found in Samarra in the north of Mesopotamia were produced about 6,000 years ago. They were shaped by hand and fired in a kiln, then painted with geometric designs. Later, a wheel like a turntable was used to shape the clay, which speeded up the process.

4 When the papier mâché is completely dry, smooth it down with fine sandpaper. Then paint the plate on both sides with a white base coat.

5 When the paint is dry, use a pencil and ruler to mark a dot in the centre of the plate. Draw four large petals around this point and add details as shown above.

6 When you are happy with your design, paint in the patterns using three colours for the basic pattern. Allow each colour to dry before adding the next.

7 Add more detail to your plate, using more colours, including wavy lines around the edge. When you have finished painting, leave it to dry.

Travel by Land and Water

THE TIGRIS AND EUPHRATES rivers and their tributaries provided a very good communications network around the country, so most people travelled by boat rather than on foot. In the south, boats were made of reeds, and were very convenient for getting about in the marshy areas at the head of the Gulf. Once the wheel had been introduced, some wealthy people travelled by horse and chariot along roads and local tracks. Chariots were mainly used by the Assyrian kings and their courtiers when hunting and in battle. At rivers, the chariots were dismantled and carried across on boats. The soldiers swam across using inflated animal skins as lifebelts. The horses had to get over as best they could.

TRANSPORTING LOGS
Phoenician ships tow logs of cedar wood along the Mediterranean coast. There was no wood in Assyria that was suitable for the palace roofs, so cedar was imported from Phoenicia. When they reached land, the logs were dragged overland on sledges. Once they reached the rivers, the timber could be floated again. Heavy goods were also often transported on rafts supported by inflated animal skins.

BEST FOOT FORWARD
People without transport had to walk, but everyone travelled by boat or cart whenever possible. Conquered people often travelled hundreds of kilometres from their original homes to new ones in Assyria and Babylonia. These people have been conquered by the Assyrians, and they are taking heavy bales of woollen cloth as a tribute to their new king. Armies marched vast distances too, wearing high leather boots. King Nebuchadnezzar I of Babylon led his armies on a gruelling march to Susa at the height of summer to recapture the statue of Marduk, the chief god of Babylon.

MAKE A BOAT
You will need: cutting board, modelling clay, piece of dowel about 20cm long, cocktail stick, paints and paintbrushes, glue, varnish and brush, string, scissors.

1 Make an oval dish shape out of the clay. It should measure 14cm long by 11cm wide by 4cm deep. Make a mast hole for the dowel and attach it to the base.

2 Trim round the top of the boat to neaten it. Use the cocktail stick to make four holes through the sides. Leave the boat to dry out completely.

3 Paint the boat all over with a light brown base colour. Then using a brush and your finger, flick contrast colours to create a mottled effect.

SEAFARING NATION

The Phoenicians of the eastern Mediterranean, whose cities were conquered by the Assyrian kings, were the great sailors and shipbuilders of the time. They traded fine ivory and metal work, and richly coloured woollen cloth, throughout the Mediterranean and beyond. The ships were large and many-oared, and the sailors worked out how to navigate by the stars. The Phoenicians may have been the first people to sail around Africa – via the Strait of Gibraltar, the southern tip of Africa, and along the east coast to the Red Sea.

OVERLAND EXCURSIONS

By about 900BC, spoked wheels had replaced the earlier wheels made from a single piece of solid wood. In Sumerian times, onegars (wild asses) hauled chariots, while oxen and mules were used for heavy goods. Traders carried their goods on long caravans (lines) of donkeys that were sturdy enough to travel long distances. From about 900BC the Assyrians used camels as well. Local roads were little more than tracks, but messengers and state officials sped on horseback along the well-maintained roads between the main centres of the Assyrian Empire.

Small boats are still used today on the River Euphrates. Your boat is based on a model clay boat from 4000BC. It has a mast for a light sail. It might have been steered using oars or a punt pole.

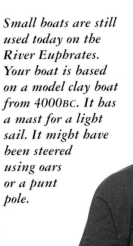

4 Put a blob of glue inside the mast hole. Put more glue around the end of the dowel and push it into the hole. This is your mast.

5 Wait until the glue has dried and the mast is firm. Then paint a layer of water-based varnish all over the boat. Leave to dry and repeat.

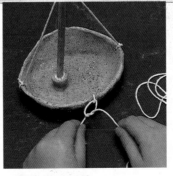

6 Take two lengths of string about 60cm long. Tie the end of one piece through one of the holes, around the top of the mast and into the opposite hole.

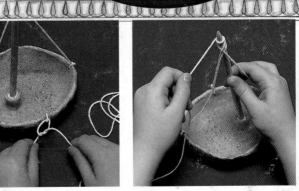

7 Complete the rigging of the boat by tying the other piece of string through the empty holes and around the top of the mast as before. Trim the strings.

Banking and Trade

THE PEOPLE OF MESOPOTAMIA were very enterprising and expert business people. They travelled long distances to obtain goods they needed, importing timber, metal and semi-precious stones.

Around 2000BC, the Assyrians had a widespread, long-distance trading network in Anatolia (modern Turkey). The headquarters were in the northern Mesopotamian city of Ashur and the trade was controlled by the city government and by large family firms.

The head of a firm usually stayed in Ashur but trusted members of the family were based in Anatolian cities such as Kanesh. From here they conducted business on the firm's behalf, going on business trips around Anatolia, and collecting any debts or interest on loans. Deals were made on a credit basis, for the Assyrian families acted as money-lenders and bankers as well. On delivery, goods and transportation (the donkeys) were exchanged for silver, which was then sent back to Ashur. In about 2000BC, one Kanesh businessman failed to send back the silver, and the firm threatened to send for the police.

TROPHIES AND TAX
Carved ivory furniture, like this panel, and bronze bowls were often carried off after successful battles. There is little evidence of trade in Mesopotamia from 900 to 600BC. The Assyrian kings took anything they wanted from the people they defeated. They collected as tax whatever was needed, such as straw and food for horses.

TRADE TO KANESH
Donkeys or mules are still used to transport goods from one village to another in modern Iraq. When trade with ancient Turkey was at its peak, donkey caravans (lines) took large amounts of tin and textiles through the mountain passes to Kanesh. A typical load for one donkey would usually consist of 130 minas (about 65kg) of tin (which was specially packed and sealed by the city authorities), and ten pieces of woollen cloth.

PRECIOUS THINGS

The marvellous jewellery in the Royal Graves of Ur not only demonstrates the skills of the jewellers who made it, but is also evidence that the Sumerians went in for long-distance trade. None of the materials used to make the jewellery was available in Sumer, so the precious stones had to be imported. The gold may have come from Oman, the lapis lazuli from Afghanistan and the carnelian from the Indus Valley.

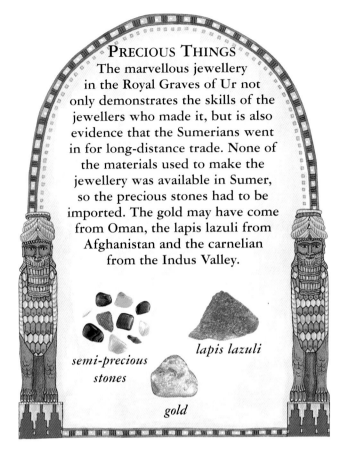

semi-precious stones

lapis lazuli

gold

STRIKING A DEAL

Two merchants make a contract. One is agreeing to supply goods for a certain amount of silver, and the other is promising to pay by a certain date. The details of a deal were written on a clay tablet and impressed with the cylinder seals of the two men. Often a copy was made and put in a clay envelope. If there was a dispute about the deal later, the envelope would be broken and the agreement checked.

LETTERS FROM KANESH

The site of the trading settlement of Kanesh, where the Assyrians did an enormous amount of business, has been excavated. A great many clay tablets were found, many of them business letters. From these letters, it is clear that the Anatolian princes had the first pick of the goods brought by Assyrian merchants. They charged the merchants taxes on their donkey caravans. In return, the princes protected the roads and provided insurance against robbers.

CASH AND CARRY

There was no money in Mesopotamia, so goods were usually paid for in silver. Silver was measured in shekels and each shekel weighed about 8g. It was carefully weighed to make sure that the person paying gave an amount equal to the value of the goods bought.

An Important City

The city of Ashur was where the country of Assyria began, in the third millennium BC. When the Assyrian Empire grew vast and mighty, the province of Ashur was called 'The Land', because it was the original land of Assyria.

By around 2000BC, Ashur was a flourishing business centre, the focus of the wealthy trade with Anatolia. The City Council, which included the heads of important local families, controlled trade and was very powerful. Although the king was the leading member of the Council, he had to take the Council's advice. In later times, kings had greater power, but the Council still retained some special privileges. As time went on, Ashur became the capital of a growing state, and several kings built temples and palaces there. During the Assyrian Empire, Nimrud or Nineveh became the capital cities, but Ashur remained both the chief religious centre, the home of the god Ashur, and the place where Assyrian kings were crowned and buried.

TOP GOD
Ashur was chief god of the Assyrians and protector of the city that bore his name. He was the god responsible for appointing the Assyrian kings. King Sargon II made a special trip to the city so that he could read a letter he had written to Ashur and the people of his city to tell them about the successful campaign he had fought on their behalf. Scholars argue about whether the city was named after the god or the other way round.

DEFENSIVE POSITION
Only traces of the many temples and palaces of Assyria's greatest city can be seen today. The city was built on this rocky spur, above the River Tigris. It was protected by the river on one side and a canal on the other, while steep cliffs enclosed the town to the north and east. The remains of what was once the most impressive building, the ziggurat of Ashur, the city's chief god, are on the skyline.

CITY SCENE

This painting shows what the city of Ashur might have been like at its peak. It is based on a painting done by Walter Andrae, the German archaeologist in charge of excavations there in the early 1900s. Although there was no longer much to see above ground, Andrae had uncovered the foundations of so many temples and palaces that he felt he had a very good idea of what the city had been like.

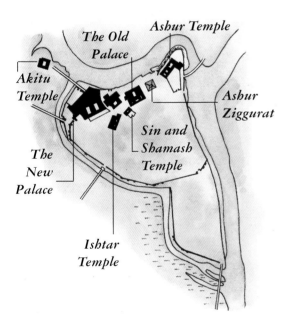

CITY PLAN

Ashur was built high on a rocky outcrop above the River Tigris. To the north and east, the city was protected from attack by steep cliffs. There were temples to the goddess Ishtar and to Sin, the moon god, and Shamash, the sun god. The main temple to the city's god, Ashur, was built in the north-east. The Akitu Temple where the New Year Festival was held lay outside the city walls.

HOME OF THE GODDESS

A statue of Ishtar, goddess of love and war, stands in a niche in her temple. Her temple is made of mud-brick and is the oldest in Ashur. It was begun in about 2500BC and rebuilt seven times. In one of the lowest levels, the archaeologist Walter Andrae found the remains of this cult room, where the goddess was worshipped. Priests and priestesses conducted rituals every day. Along the sides of the room, there were benches where Assyrian people placed statues of themselves, so that they could be seen in a constant act of worship and gain Ishtar's blessing. In the central area were offering tables where food could be left for the goddess. This area also contained copper braziers for burning incense and pottery altars in the shapes of houses.

Running the Empire

From the beginning of the 800s BC, the country of Assyria began to grow into a vast empire. The land was divided into provinces, each one named after its main city, such as Nineveh, Samaria, Damascus, or Arpad, each with its own governor. The governor had to make sure that taxes were collected, call up soldiers in times of war, and supply workers when a new palace or temple was to be built. He had to provide safe passage for merchants and was responsible for law and order. If the king and his army passed through the province, the governor supplied them with food and drink. A vast system of roads connected the king's palace with governors' residences and all the important cities of the Empire.

ENFORCED REMOVAL
Conquered people are banished from their homeland to go and live in Assyria. These people were from Lachish, near Jerusalem, and were moved to the Assyrian city of Nineveh. The men were used as forced labour in the limestone quarries.

THE KING'S MEN
A king was constantly surrounded by bodyguards, astrologers and other members of the court including provincial governors who helped him run the empire. His attendants included scribes to write down his orders, messengers to deliver them and an attendant to hold a parasol and shield him from the sun. King Ashurnasirpal is celebrating a successful bull hunt with priests and musicians.

MAKE A PARASOL

You will need: pencil, coloured card 60cm x 60cm, scissors, masking tape, paints in bright colours and paintbrushes, white card, string or twine, glue, dowel.

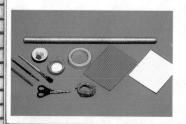

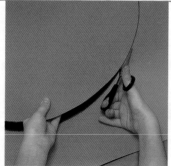

1 Draw a circle on the coloured card measuring roughly 60cm across. Cut out the circle with the scissors keeping the edge as neat as possible.

2 Cut a slit from the edge of the circle to the centre. Pull one edge of the slit over the other to make a conical shape. Secure with masking tape.

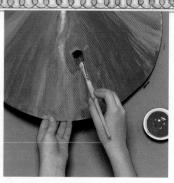

3 Paint your parasol with red paint. Leave to dry. Then paint stripes in lots of different shades of orange and red from the top to the bottom.

TOWARDS A NEW LIFE

Defeated people camp out en route to a new life in Assyria. The Assyrian Empire grew so big, that it could take months to travel back from a newly conquered territory. People were usually kept together in families and given homes in the countryside. Often they were set to work to cultivate more land.

KEEPING ACCOUNTS

Assyrian scribes at the governor's palace at Til Barsip on the River Euphrates make a note of taxes demanded by the king. Taxes were exacted not only from the local Assyrian people, but also from the conquered territories. They could be paid in produce, such as grain, horses or cattle, and wine.

Kings were accompanied by an attendant carrying a sunshade, which was probably made of fine woollen material and decorated with tassels.

USEFUL TRIBUTE

Horses are given as tributes to the Assyrian king from a conquered people. They will be used to swell the chariot and cavalry units in the Assyrian army. The best-bred and strongest horses came from the foothills of the Zagros Mountains to the east of Assyria. The king also demanded food for the horses.

4 Cut 20 oval shapes about 5cm by 4cm from the white card. Cover with a base colour of gold. Leave to dry, then paint with bright designs.

5 Use the scissors to make holes around the edge of the parasol and in the ovals. Attach the ovals to the parasol with twine, knotting it as shown.

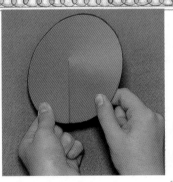

6 Cut a small circle out of coloured card measuring 10cm across. Make a slit to the centre, and pull one edge over the other as before. Paint the small cone gold.

7 Glue it to the top of the parasol. Paint the handle with gold paint and allow to dry. Attach it to the inside of the parasol using plenty of masking tape.

Fighting Forces

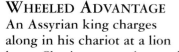

THE EARLIEST HISTORICAL RECORDS of Mesopotamia tell of city-states at war with one another. These were usually local disputes over pieces of land or the ownership of canals. Later, when powerful kings created empires, they went to war with foreign countries. King Sargon of Agade, for example, subdued all the cities of Sumer and then went on to conquer the great cities of Mari on the River Euphrates and Ebla in northern Syria. Assyria and Babylonia were often at war in the first millennium BC. The walls of Assyrian palaces are decorated with reliefs showing frightened groups of Babylonians hiding among the reeds of the marshes, as well as the conquest of Elam, Judah and Phoenician cities.

WHEELED ADVANTAGE
An Assyrian king charges along in his chariot at a lion hunt. Chariots were also used to ride into battle. The Assyrians perfected the art of chariot warfare, which gave them a big advantage over enemies who were fighting on foot.

IN THE BEGINNING
A model of a very early chariot, about 4,000 years old, shows the first wheel designs of solid wood. By the time of the Assyrian Empire, about 900-600 BC, war chariots had spoked wooden wheels with metal rims.

THE KING'S GUARDS
A panel from the palace of the Persian kings at Susa shows a long procession of king's guards. The guards are armed with spears, and carry quivers full of arrows. King Cyrus of Persia conquered Babylon in 539BC.

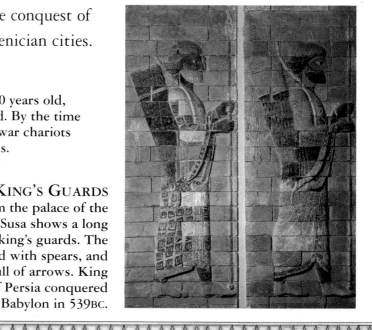

MAKE A CHARIOT
You will need: pen, cardboard, scissors, paints and paintbrushes, flour, water and newspaper to make papier mâché, glue, masking tape, 2 x dowel 16cm long, card tubes, needle, 4 cocktail sticks.

1 Cut four circles about 7cm in width out of the card. Use the scissors to make a hole in the centre of each circle. Enlarge the holes with a pen.

2 Cut out two sides for the chariot 12cm long x 8cm high as shown, one back 9 x 8cm, one front 9 x 15cm, one top 9 x 7cm and one base 12 x 9cm.

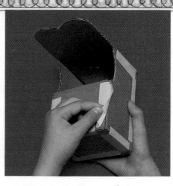

3 Trim the top of the front to two curves as shown. Stick the side pieces to the front and back using masking tape. Stick on the base and top.

SLINGS AND ARROWS

Assyrian foot-soldiers used rope slings and stone balls the size of modern tennis-balls. Others fired arrows while sheltering behind tall wicker shields. They wore helmets of bronze or iron and were protected by metal scale armour and leather boots.

GOING INTO BATTLE

Sumerian chariot drivers charge into battle. A soldier armed with spears stands on the footplate of each chariot ready to jump off and fight. They are all protected by thick leather cloaks and helmets. The chariots were drawn by onegars (wild asses).

STORMING A CITY

Many Assyrian fighting methods can be seen in the palace reliefs at the city of Nimrud. In this scene, the Assyrians storm an enemy city which stands on a hill. A siege engine with spears projecting from the front breaks down the walls. Attacking soldiers would also scale the walls with the help of siege ladders, protected by archers.

Your chariot copies a clay model made in northern Mesopotamia over 4,000 years ago.

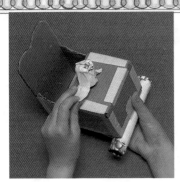

4 Roll up a piece of newspaper to make a cylinder shape 3cm long, and attach it to the chariot. Attach the cardboard tubes to the bottom of the chariot.

5 Mix a paste of flour and water. Dip newspaper strips into the paste to make papier mâché. Cover the chariot with layers of papier mâché. Leave to dry.

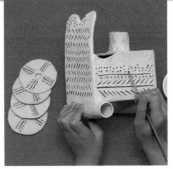

6 Paint the whole chariot cream. Add detail using brown paint. Paint the wheels, too. Make a hole with the needle in each end of the dowels.

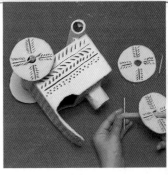

7 Insert a cocktail stick in the dowel, add a wheel and insert into the tube. Fix another wheel and stick to the other end. Repeat with the other wheels.

Palace Builders

A MESOPOTAMIAN PALACE was not just built as the king's residence but also as a centre of government. Many were impressive buildings where the kings received ambassadors.

Most information about palace buildings comes from the Assyrian palaces at Nimrud, Nineveh and Khorsabad. King Ashurnasirpal built a magnificent palace at Nimrud on the River Tigris in the 900s BC. He knocked down the old city and built a huge platform of 120 layers of mud-bricks as a foundation. On that platform, he wrote, 'I built my palace with seven beautiful halls roofed with boxwood, cedar, cypress and terebinth wood. I decorated the doors with bands of bronze. I carved and painted the walls with vivid paint showing my victories.' The king had lapis lazuli coloured glazed bricks specially made and set them in the walls above the gates.

HAULING WOOD
Workers drag heavy pieces of cedar wood to the building site of the palace at Nimrud. The timber for the palace roof and the imposing doors at the entrance was imported from Lebanon, which was famous for its pine and cedar wood. It came by boat along the Mediterranean coast. Once the ships were unloaded, the timber was hauled overland to the city.

MIGHTY BEASTS
Lamassus were huge statues that stood at palace entrances to frighten evil spirits away from the palace and the king. They were carved from a single block of gypsum, a soft stone that was easy to carve, and weighed several tonnes. They have five limbs so that they have four legs when seen from the side. The extra leg was so that they did not appear one-legged if seen from the front.

EXOTIC SETTING
Assyrian palaces were often set in exotic gardens. At Nimrud in 970BC, King Ashurnasirpal took pride in his garden where he planted all kinds of seeds and plants brought back from his campaigns in foreign countries. He had vines, nut trees and fruit trees. He wrote: 'Pomegranates glow in my garden of happiness like stars in the sky. In my garden the plants vie with each other in fragrance. The paths are well kept and there are canals so the plants can be watered.'

YOU HAVE BEEN WARNED

Palace walls were decorated with carved reliefs designed to impress visitors, and to show that the king was fulfilling the role given to him by the gods. In this relief at Ashurnasirpal's palace at Nimrud, the king is depicted heroically fighting a snarling lion, proving that he is the protector of his people. Other scenes showed the king victorious in battle, as a warning to anyone considering rebellion against Assyria.

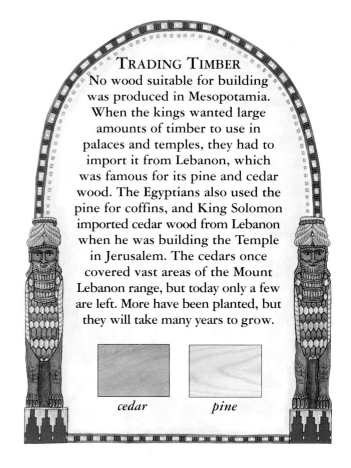

TRADING TIMBER

No wood suitable for building was produced in Mesopotamia. When the kings wanted large amounts of timber to use in palaces and temples, they had to import it from Lebanon, which was famous for its pine and cedar wood. The Egyptians also used the pine for coffins, and King Solomon imported cedar wood from Lebanon when he was building the Temple in Jerusalem. The cedars once covered vast areas of the Mount Lebanon range, but today only a few are left. More have been planted, but they will take many years to grow.

cedar   *pine*

WEALTH AND SPLENDOUR

Henry Layard, the archaeologist who excavated the city of Nimrud in the 1840s, imagined the city looked like this at the height of its powers. His picture was based on his excavations, but it may not be entirely accurate. However, it gives an idea of the splendour and wealth of an Assyrian capital city. Archaeologists found the remains of several palaces and temples at Nimrud. They had been built by various kings in the 8th and 9th centuries BC.

Furnishing the Palace

The Assyrian kings loved the luxury of ivory furniture. They filled their palaces with ivory beds, armchairs, footstools and tables. No complete pieces of ivory furniture have survived to modern times, but Henry Layard found part of an ivory throne at Nimrud in the 1840s. He also found some whole tusks of elephant ivory and a great many small, carved ivory plaques that were once attached to the wooden framework of pieces of furniture. The Assyrians were free to use as much ivory as they liked because elephants were not then an endangered species. No textiles have survived but palaces would probably have been made more comfortable with cushions and woollen rugs. Stone entrances to the palace rooms carved in the form of floral-patterned carpets show us what the rugs may have looked like.

Woman in a Window
The Phoenicians were very skilful at ivory carving. This piece, showing a woman looking out of a window, is typical of their work. The holes were used to attach it to a mirror handle.

Inside the Palace
Palaces were built from mud-brick, but the lower interior walls were decorated with carved and painted slabs of stone. Teams of sculptors and artists produced scenes showing the king's military campaigns and wild bull and lion hunts. The upper walls were plastered and painted with similar scenes to glorify the king and impress foreign visitors. Paints were ground from minerals. Red and brown paints were made from ochres, blues and greens from copper ores, azurite and malachite.

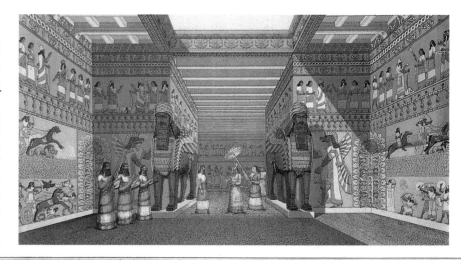

Make a Bronze and Ivory Mirror

You will need: pencil, strong white and reflective card, ruler, scissors, thick dowel, masking tape, flour, water and newspaper for papier mâché, sandpaper, paints and brushes, glue.

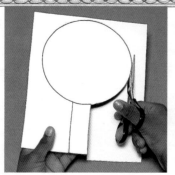

1 Using a pencil, draw a circle 12cm across on to the strong white card. Add a handle about 6cm long and 2.5cm wide as shown. Cut out.

2 Take a length of dowel about 20cm long. Fix the dowel to the handle using masking tape. Bend the card round the dowel as shown in the picture.

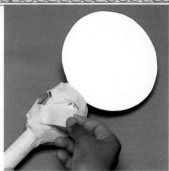

3 Scrunch up a piece of newspaper into a ball. Attach the newspaper ball to the top of the handle with masking tape as shown.

LUXURY IN THE GARDEN

King Ashurbanipal and his wife even had luxurious ivory furniture in the palace gardens at Nineveh. In this picture, the king is reclining on an elaborate ivory couch decorated with tiny carved and gilded lions. The queen is sitting on an ivory chair with a high back and resting her feet on a footstool. Cushions make the furniture more comfortable. Ivory workers used drills and chisels similar to those used by carpenters. The ivory plaques had signs on them to show how they should be slotted together.

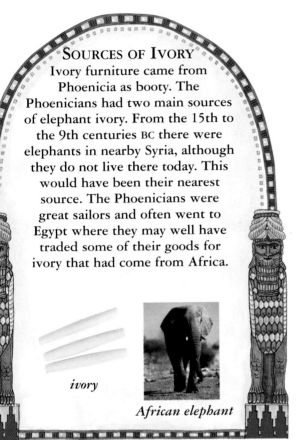

SOURCES OF IVORY

Ivory furniture came from Phoenicia as booty. The Phoenicians had two main sources of elephant ivory. From the 15th to the 9th centuries BC there were elephants in nearby Syria, although they do not live there today. This would have been their nearest source. The Phoenicians were great sailors and often went to Egypt where they may well have traded some of their goods for ivory that had come from Africa.

ivory

African elephant

Polished bronze was used for mirrors in ancient times. A mirror with a carved ivory handle would have belonged to a wealthy woman.

BOY-EATER

This furniture plaque shows a boy being eaten by a lioness. The boy's kilt is covered with gold leaf, and his curly hair is made of tiny gold pins. There are lotus flowers and papyrus plants in the background, inlaid with real lapis lazuli and carnelian. Sometimes ivory was stained or inlaid with paste to imitate jewels.

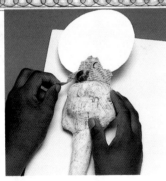

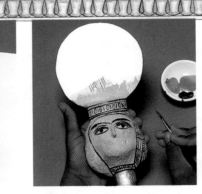

4 Make a paste with flour and water, and dip strips of newspaper in it. Cover the handle with several layers, allowing each layer to dry.

5 Use newspaper to make the nose and ears. Add a strip of papier mâché at the top of the head for the crown. Leave to dry, then sandpaper until smooth.

6 Paint a base coat of grey paint on the face and bronze on the handle. Then add the details of the face and crown in black using a fine paintbrush.

7 Cut out a circle of reflective card to match the mirror shape. Glue the reflective card carefully on to the white card. This is your bronze mirror.

Marvellous Sculptures

From the beginning of the civilization in Mesopotamia, sculpture was an important art. The earliest sculptors were good at making small statues and figurines. Some were made of stone, but others were of painted clay. Apart from boulders found in rivers there was no stone in Sumer, so most of the materials for sculpture had to be imported. In Assyria, further north, there were quarries near the modern town of Mosul, where a kind of gypsum was found. This is a fairly soft stone which can be carved in great detail. Large pieces of gypsum were cut with pickaxes and sawn with two-handled saws. The slabs were then put on carts and taken to the river where they were transferred on to rafts and floated to the building site. The slabs were carved and painted after they were placed in position.

PROTECTIVE GENIE

Many rooms in the palace King Ashurnasirpal built at Nimrud in the 900s BC were decorated with genies. These creatures have human bodies but the wings, heads and beaks of birds of prey. They were carved to protect the king and the courtiers from evil spirits. The genie shown here is carrying a cone and a bucket and seems to be using them for some kind of ritual. He was possibly blessing the king.

OFF TO WORK

Men go to work at a gypsum quarry near to the modern city of Mosul on the River Tigris. It was not far from the ancient Assyrian cities of Nimrud and Nineveh. The workers are carrying pickaxes to hack out massive blocks of stone. The two-handled saws will be used to slice the blocks into thinner slabs to be fixed to the walls of a palace before they are carved and painted by teams of artists.

GLAZED BRICKS FROM BABYLON

Babylonian kings decorated their city with beautiful sculptures made of glazed bricks. This panel comes from the Ishtar Gate at Babylon. It shows the mushushshu (snake dragon) of the city god Marduk. The gate also featured bulls. The animals were made from glazed bricks formed in special moulds so that they stood out from the wall as if they had been carved.

CHOSEN BY ASHUR

In this carved relief from the throne room in Ashurnasirpal's palace, the king is shown twice. He is standing in front of a sacred tree. Above the tree is a winged disc containing the figure of a god. He seems to be pointing at Ashurnasirpal to indicate he is the god's choice. The god could be Ashur.

MONSTER GUARDIAN

Assyrian palace entrances were guarded by lamassus, immense statues three metres high or more. When a sculpture was complete, it was painted to make it more lifelike. Lamassus were strange monsters with the bodies of lions or bulls, the wings of mighty birds, human heads and caps with horns to show they had divine powers. They combined all the most powerful forces of heaven and earth and were supposed to prowl up and down warding off evil spirits from the palaces. They are symbols of pent-up supernatural fury.

PUBLIC DISPLAY

Assyrian kings liked to be seen as faithful servants of the gods. They often ordered a stela (stone slab) to be set up in a public place and carved with pictures. This stela was set up outside the temple of Ninurta, the war god, at Nimrud. It shows King Ashurnasirpal showing respect to the gods. The symbols represent different gods – the goddess Ishtar (star), Adad the storm god (forked lightning), Sin the moon god (crescent Moon), Shamash the sun god (disc with flames), and Ashur (horned cap).

RELIEF WORK

Stone was cut into large slabs on the quarry site using tough, two-handled saws. The slabs were taken to the palace or temple. Workers joined them together by hammering lead dowels and clamps into them with mallets. Teams of sculptors would then carve the figures in outline with big bronze or iron chisels. They would use finer ones for details of face, hair, jewellery and dress. The carved surface was polished with sand or painted.

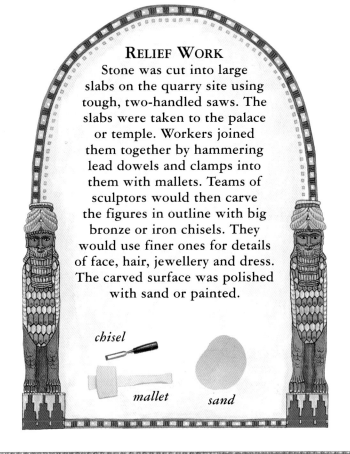

chisel

mallet   *sand*

The Lion Hunt of the King

FROM EARLIEST TIMES, Mesopotamian kings hunted lions, because lions represented evil and it was the duty of the king to protect his people. The first known picture of a king doing this is on a stela (stone slab) from the ancient Sumerian city of Uruk and is over 5,000 years old. Most of our information about royal lion hunts comes from reliefs in a sloping corridor of the palace of the Assyrian king Ashurbanipal (669-631BC) at Nineveh, which show every stage of a hunt. When the lion had been killed, the king poured a libation of oil or wine over the body, and offered it to the gods.

AFRICAN LION
Mesopotamian mountain lions were smaller than the African lion shown here but were just as dangerous. They came from the mountains and attacked the villagers of the plain and their farm animals. The mountain lions are extinct now but lived in Mesopotamia until the 1800s.

LION ARENA
A hungry snarling lion has been released from its cage. The kings did not hunt lions in open country but in special arenas heavily guarded by soldiers, gamekeepers and fierce dogs. The royal hunting ground was just outside Nineveh, and lions were brought there in strong cages. Local people sometimes climbed nearby hills to get a good view.

HUNTING FOR FOOD
The Mesopotamians were good farmers, growing barley and other crops and raising sheep and goats, but they also had to go hunting for meat to supplement their diet. These men have shot a deer using a bow and arrow and trapped a rabbit in a snare. Sometimes, they caught birds using nets, and they collected locusts. Marsh scenes carved on the palace walls show men and boys fishing from boats or sitting on inflated animal skins.

MAKE A ROYAL TUNIC
You will need: coloured cotton fabric 90cm by 230cm, white pencil, tape measure, scissors, pins, needle and thread, white cotton fabric 50cm by 24cm, pencil, fabric paints and paintbrushes, glue, sponge.

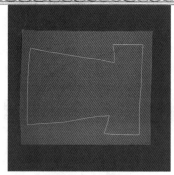

1 Fold the coloured cloth in two. Using the white pencil, draw a tunic shape as shown. It should be roughly 90 cm across and 115 cm long.

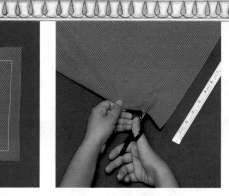

2 Cut out the tunic shape, making sure that you are cutting through both layers of material. Be careful to cut the lines as smoothly as you can.

3 Pin around the edges of the two tunic shapes. Then sew down the sides and across the top, making sure you leave holes for your head and arms.

PROTECTOR OF THE PEOPLE

Hunters were heavily armed. Here King Ashurbanipal's arrows have only injured the lion. When the lion attacks his horse, the king plunges his spear into it. Eventually, the lion is worn out, and the king dismounts and runs it through with his sword. The king is not just hunting for sport, but because the lion symbolized evil to the Mesopotamians. It is the king's religious duty to protect his people from such evil.

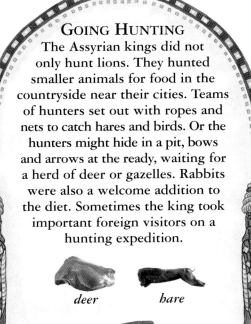

GOING HUNTING

The Assyrian kings did not only hunt lions. They hunted smaller animals for food in the countryside near their cities. Teams of hunters set out with ropes and nets to catch hares and birds. Or the hunters might hide in a pit, bows and arrows at the ready, waiting for a herd of deer or gazelles. Rabbits were also a welcome addition to the diet. Sometimes the king took important foreign visitors on a hunting expedition.

deer   *hare*

rabbit

Royal robes were made from fine woollen material. Patterns were woven into the fabric or embroidered later. The most highly prized cloth was imported from the Phoenician cities, where it was coloured purple with dye from murex shellfish.

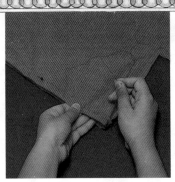

4 Neaten the edges of the arms and around the bottom by turning in a small amount of material to make a hem. Pin the hem, then sew it as shown.

5 Draw strips about 3cm wide on the white material. Paint brightly coloured decorative designs along the strips with the fabric paints.

6 When the paint is dry, cut out the decorative strips, keeping the lines as straight as you can. Glue the strips on to the tunic across the chest and arms.

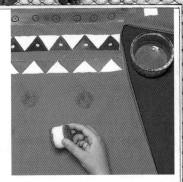

7 Use the sponge to make decorative patterns on the rest of the tunic. Dip the sponge into fabric paint and press it lightly on to the fabric.

Kingship

THE KINGS OF MESOPOTAMIA considered themselves to have been chosen by the gods. For example, Ur-Nanshe of Lagash (2480BC) said that he was granted kingship by Enlil, chief of the gods, and Ashurbanipal (669BC) claimed he was the son of the Assyrian god, Ashur, and his wife, Belit. The Mesopotamian kings ran the state on the god's behalf. Even in the Assyrian Empire, when the kings had grand titles such as 'King of the Universe', they still felt they were responsible to the gods for the well-being of their people. Another of their titles was 'Shepherd'. This meant they had to look after their people, just as a shepherd tends his flock.

AUTHORITY
This onyx mace belonged to the Babylonian kings. It was a symbol of authority. At the New Year festival, the king placed his mace before the statue of the chief god, Marduk. He was later given back the mace so that he could reign for another year.

SUN GOD TABLET FROM SIPPAR
Kings had to see that temples and statues of the gods were kept in good repair. This tablet shows King Nabu-apla-iddina of Babylon being led into the presence of the god Shamash. The story on the tablet tells us that the king wanted to make a new statue of the god. He was meant to repair the old one but it had been stolen by enemies. Fortunately a priest found a model of the statue that could be copied.

MAKE A FLY WHISK

You will need: calico fabric, pencil, ruler, PVA glue and brush, scissors, thick card, paints and paintbrushes, newspaper.

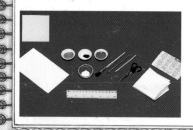

1 Draw long leaf shapes about 45cm long on to the calico fabric with the pencil. Paint the shapes with watered down PVA glue. Leave to dry.

2 Cut out the leaf shapes. Make a card spine for the centre of each leaf as shown, thicker at the bottom than at the top, and glue them on.

3 Paint the leaves in gold, yellow and red paints on both sides. Add fine detail by cutting into the edge of each leaf using the scissors.

FIGHTING FOR THE GODS

Kings believed that they were commanded by the gods to conquer in their name. In this relief, King Sennacherib is sitting on his throne receiving the booty and prisoners taken after the city of Lachish had fallen. The king devoted a whole room in his palace at Nineveh to the story of this siege. He also made war on Babylon and completely devastated the city. In 612BC the Babylonians had their revenge. They destroyed Nineveh and hacked out Sennacherib's face on this sculpture.

EXPLORATION AND DISCOVERY

Another mark of good kingship was the expansion of knowledge. King Shalmaneser III sent an expedition to find the source of the River Tigris pictured here. When his men found it, they set up a stela to record the event and made offerings to the gods to celebrate. Many of the Mesopotamian kings were learned men. Kings such as Ashurbanipal collected clay tablets to make great libraries. Others collected exotic plants and animals.

Fly whisks made of long thin leaves or feathery reeds kept the flies away from the king. They could also be used as a fan to keep him cool.

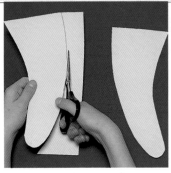

4 Draw two identical handle shapes on to the stiff card. They should be about 22cm long and 10cm wide at the top. Cut out the shapes with the scissors.

5 Tear up newspaper strips and dip into glue. Wrap the strips around the edges of the two handles to fasten them together. Leave the top of the handle unglued.

6 Decorate the handle with gold paint. Leave to dry. Paint decorative details on to the gold with black paint using a fine paintbrush.

7 Glue the bottoms of the leaves and push them into the top of the handle, between the two pieces of cardboard. Spread the leaves well apart.

Royal Libraries and Museums

WHAT THE FUTURE HOLDS
Clay models of sheep's livers were used for divining what the future might hold. They were divided into zones with names such as Station, Path, Finger and Palace Gates. The diviners used these to interpret what they saw in the livers of sacrificed animals. If the Palace Gates were open, for example, this could mean attack by an enemy, or famine. If they were together, it was a good sign.

IN THE MID-700s BC, King Ashurbanipal decided to found a great library at Nineveh. Every temple in the land had a library, so he sent his scribes round all the temples of Babylonia with instructions to bring him anything that looked interesting. If the priests were reluctant to let a tablet go, the scribes were told to make a copy. The library at Nineveh eventually contained over 25,000 clay tablets, and most of what is known about Mesopotamian learning comes from there.

In the Nineveh library were ancient myths and legends such as the *Epic of Gilgamesh* and the *Birth Legend of Sargon of Agade*, dictionaries, mathematical problems, and texts on astronomy, astrology and medicine. There were collections of clay models of sheep's livers and lists of weather omens for predicting future events. For example, if it was foggy in a particular month, the land was expected to go to ruin.

The Babylonian king, Nebuchadnezzar II, founded a museum, which had statues, a stela of a Mari governor who introduced bee-keeping into Mesopotamia, and objects and clay tablets that went back to Sumerian times.

WRITING TO GODS
If a king wanted to build a temple or go on a campaign, he asked the gods about it first. The Assyrian king, Esarhaddon, wrote letters to the sun god, Shamash, which were kept in the library at Nineveh. He wrote a question on a clay tablet and asked for a clear answer. The tablet was then placed in front of the god's statue. An animal was slaughtered and the liver examined. The diviners (fortune-tellers) could tell by looking at it whether or not the god approved.

WORK IT OUT
King Ashurbanipal, founder of the library at Nineveh, collected many mathematical tablets. The Babylonians were the world's first mathematicians, and worked out many processes that are still used today. The library had a number of mathematical tables that made it easier for people to divide and multiply numbers. Clay tablets included tables showing reciprocals, square numbers and square roots.

DISCOVERY

Before the discovery of the 4,000-year-old library at Ebla, no one knew that libraries existed at such an early date. The city was mentioned in Sumerian texts but its location was not known. The mound at Tell Mardik in northern Syria was first excavated in the 1960s by Italian archaeologists. Proof that it was the ancient city of Ebla came with the discovery of the royal library, and a royal statue inscribed with the words 'Ibbit-Lim, King of Ebla.'

LOOK IT UP

The oldest library found in the world so far dates from the 3rd millennium BC and was discovered at Ebla in north Syria. The city lay beyond Mesopotamia, but the people used similar writing, and kept records just like the Sumerians. This library was found in the palace at Ebla. Tablets were in heaps on the floor, but the excavators could see marks on the walls where shelves had once been. Librarians kept all the tablets about a particular subject together on one part of the shelves. Small tablets were stored in baskets.

MAP OF THE WORLD

A unique map of the world was found in the library of Ashurbanipal at Nineveh, although it was originally drawn up in Babylon. It shows the world as the Babylonians saw it. The earth is a flat disc surrounded by ocean. Babylon is named in the box inside the circle. The River Euphrates flows through the middle. Mysterious regions lie to the north, south, east and west. The north is described as 'the land where the Sun is never seen'. Few people had ever been there, but the text says Sargon of Agade had. He is known from his own records to have conquered distant regions, and was still regarded as a hero hundreds of years later.

Maths, Medicine and Astronomy

THE MESOPOTAMIANS liked working things out. They had two number systems, one using 10 as a base and the other, 60. The Sumerians were the first to calculate time in hour-long units of 60 minutes, and their astronomers worked out a calendar based on 12- and 28-day cycles and 7-day weeks from studying the moon and the seasons. In particular, the Babylonians were especially interested in studying the heavens, and their astronomers could predict events such as eclipses, solstices and equinoxes.

Mesopotamian doctors did not really understand how the body works, but made lists of patients' symptoms. Their observations were passed on to the Greeks hundreds of years later and so became one of the foundations of modern medicine.

HEAVY COUGH CURE
This tablet suggests mixing balsam (a herb) with strong beer, honey and oil to cure a cough. The mixture was taken hot, without food. Then the patient's throat was tickled with a feather to make him sick. Other prescriptions used mice, dogs' tails and urine.

BAD OMEN
Eclipses were considered a bad sign. However, an eclipse that was obscured by cloud did not count. When an eclipse could not be seen in a royal city, the king was told it had nothing to do with him or his country and he should not worry about it.

MEDICINAL BREW
Servants are distilling essence of cedar, a vital ingredient for a headache cure. Cedar twigs were put into a pot, and heated to give off a vapour. It condensed against the cooler lid and trickled into the rim of the pot from where it was collected. The essence was mixed with honey, resin from pine, myrrh and spruce trees, and fat from a sheep's kidney.

MAKE A SET OF LION WEIGHTS
You will need: pebbles of various sizes, kitchen scales, modelling clay, cutting board, cocktail stick, paints and paintbrushes.

1 Weigh a pebble and add modelling clay to make it up to a weight of 225g. Once the clay has dried out, the final weight will be only about 200g.

2 Take a portion of the weighed modelling clay and shape it into a rectangle roughly 12cm by 7cm. This will be the base for your weight.

3 Wrap another piece of the weighed modelling clay around the weighed pebble to make the lion's body. Shape the body into a pear shape.

SKY MAP
The sky in this sky map is divided into eight parts and the stars in each section are indicated. The heavens were seen as a source of information about the future, so the kings often consulted astronomers. One astronomer wrote to the king in the 600s BC: 'I am always looking at the sky but nothing unusual has appeared above the horizon'.

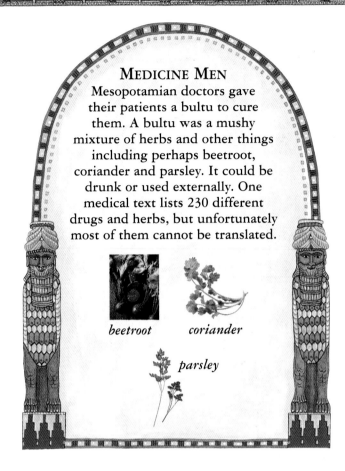

MEDICINE MEN
Mesopotamian doctors gave their patients a bultu to cure them. A bultu was a mushy mixture of herbs and other things including perhaps beetroot, coriander and parsley. It could be drunk or used externally. One medical text lists 230 different drugs and herbs, but unfortunately most of them cannot be translated.

beetroot   *coriander*

parsley

WEIGHTS AND MEASURES
Officials weigh metal objects that have been taken as booty after a victory. The duck-shaped object is a weight. The kings were responsible for seeing that weights and measures were exact and that nobody cheated customers. Prices were fixed by law and calculated in shekels (1 shekel was about 8g of silver).

Bronze lion weights from a set belonging to King Shalmaneser V have been found at Nimrud. Like your weights they were of different sizes.

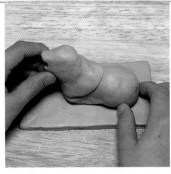

4 Position the pebble and clay on to its base. Add another piece of weighed clay to form the head and mane. Shape the face and jaw with your fingers.

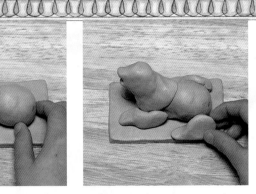

5 Model four pieces of weighed clay to make the lion's four legs and stick them on to the body. Flatten the clay slightly at each end for the paws.

6 Make a tail and ears using up the remaining weighed clay. Using the cocktail stick, add extra detail to the face, mane, paws and tail. Leave to dry.

7 Paint the lion and the base cream. Flick with brown paint for a mottled appearance. Add details to the face, mane and paws. Make more lions for a set.

Babylonian Power

ATTACK ON BABYLON
Assyrian kings usually showed great respect for Marduk, the god of Babylon. But when the Babylonians allowed King Sennacherib's son to be captured, the angry king attacked Babylon and burnt down Marduk's temple. His son and grandson were so worried by this that they decided to rebuild the city and temple as quickly as they could. This stela shows Sennacherib's grandson Ashurbanipal holding a brick-basket for building.

REBUILDING BABYLON
Nabopolassar and his son, Nebuchadnezzar built a new city worthy of Babylon's status as a world power in the 500s BC. The city was constructed on both banks of the River Euphrates with a bridge on stone pillars connecting the two parts of the new Babylon. There were several temples and palaces. A massive 8-km wall surrounded the city. The road on top of the wall was so wide that two four-horse chariots could pass each other.

THE NAME BABYLON means Gateway of the Gods. Although Babylon was quite a small place in Sumerian times, it began to grow in importance from the time of King Hammurabi. It soon became the chief city of the whole of southern Mesopotamia, and this region became known as Babylonia. The main temple of the god Marduk was in Babylon, and the city became a great centre of learning. Many of the texts in King Ashurbanipal's library came from Babylonia, or were copies of Babylonian works. Towards the end of the 600s BC, the Babylonians attacked and destroyed the Assyrian cities of Ashur, Nimrud and Nineveh. The Assyrian Empire came to an end, and for a time Babylon became very powerful under its great king, Nebuchadnezzar II. King Nebuchadnezzar took over many parts of the ancient world that had once belonged to Assyria, including Palestine and Phoenicia. When King Necho of Egypt challenged Nebuchadnezzar and tried to take some of the old Assyrian territory for himself, the Babylonian king promptly chased him back to his country.

GATEWAY TO THE GODDESS

The inner wall of the city of Babylon had several gateways leading into the city, each having the name of an important god or goddess. The most splendid was the Ishtar Gate, named after the goddess of love and war and built in the reign of Nebuchadnezzar II. The gate was decorated with blue-glazed bricks inset with three-dimensional sculptures of moulded bricks. These showed the bull of Adad and the snake dragon of Marduk, the god of Babylon.

A FORMIDABLE ENEMY

King Marduk-apla-iddina was the very first Babylonian king to be mentioned by name in the Bible, where he is called Merodach Baladan. This boundary stone was found in Babylon and shows

him making a grant of land to the governor of Babylon in around 700 BC. Marduk-apla-iddina fought many battles against the Assyrian kings, Sargon and Sennacherib. Even after he had been defeated and forced to retreat to the marshes, he continued to stir up trouble for the Assyrians.

THE WAY OF THE LION

Babylon had a special road for processions. The Processional Way led from the temple of Marduk through the Ishtar Gate on its way out of the city to the temple where the New Year festival was held. The way was decorated with blue-glazed tiles and moulded brick figures of lions. Each year the statues of the gods were carried along here to attend a special ceremony in which the Babylonian Story of Creation was enacted and the king was re-invested with royal power.

WONDER OF THE WORLD

The city of Babylon was famous for its Hanging Gardens. Like the pyramids at Giza in ancient Egypt, they were one of the Seven Wonders of the Ancient World. Tradition says the magnificent gardens were created by one of its kings. He had married a Persian wife who was homesick for the hills of her own country. The king loved her so much he built an artificial mountain and planted it with trees and flowers. Later many people tried to find the gardens but no one has ever succeeded, although strangely one modern scholar thinks they were in Nineveh rather than Babylon.

Bible Links

FLOODS

A tale like the Bible story of Noah's Ark was found in the library at Nineveh. King Utnapishtim was warned that the god Enlil was going to send a flood and told to make a boat and take his family, all the animals and craftworkers on board. It rained for seven days and seven nights. When it stopped, the king sent out birds to see if the water had gone down. The goddess Ishtar put her necklace in the sky as a sign this would never happen again.

THERE ARE MANY LINKS between Mesopotamia and the Bible. Mesopotamian flood stories are remarkably like the story of Noah's Ark. Abraham, the father of the Israelite and Arab nations, lived at the Sumerian city of Ur before he and his family set off for the Promised Land. Several of the laws and customs relating to marriage and adoption mentioned in these stories about Abraham are like those of Mesopotamia. Jonah was instructed by God to go to the Assyrian city of Nineveh, and the Jewish people were exiled from their Promised Land to Babylon. Assyrian records often include kings and events mentioned in the Old Testament.

One Assyrian king, Shalmaneser III, records his victory at the Battle of Qarqar in Syria. He says he fought against twelve kings, one of whom was Ahab of Israel. This is the first time a king of Israel appears in the history of another country. From this time onward, the paths of Assyria and Israel often crossed.

DESERT JOURNEY

Abraham, the father of the Jewish and Arab nations, travels from the Sumerian city of Ur to the country God has promised his people. In this painting of the 1800s, Abraham is leading a wandering existence in a desert landscape with his flock of sheep moving from one area to another in search of grazing ground for his animals. However, people would not have used camels at the time he is thought to have lived, about 2000BC. Camels were not used for transport in Mesopotamia until about 1000BC.

BLACK OBELISK

The man bowing in front of the Assyrian king, Shalmaneser III, could be Jehu, King of Israel. Israel had been an enemy of Assyria, but Jehu has decided to change sides and become an ally of Assyria. The picture appears on the Black Obelisk, which tells of Shalmaneser III's conquests at war. The writing says that the gifts of the Israelite king are being presented to show his loyalty and win Shalmaneser's approval.

WAR CORRESPONDENTS

The Bible reports that the Assyrian king Sennacherib laid siege to Jerusalem when Hezekiah was king of Judah. It says he withdrew from the siege when an angel attacked his army. In Sennacherib's version of events on this clay prism (a hollow tablet), he does not say he was defeated or that he captured Jerusalem. All he says is he shut Hezekiah up like a bird in a cage.

EXILE IN BABYLON

The great Babylonian king of the 500s BC was Nebuchadnezzar II, who took over many parts of the ancient world that had formerly been part of the Assyrian Empire. In 597BC he attacked Jerusalem, the chief city of the kingdom of Judah, a scene imagined here by a medieval painter. At the end of a successful siege, he took the king, his courtiers, the army and all the craftworkers to Babylon. There they spent many years far from home, a time known among Jewish people as the Exile. Nebuchadnezzar took treasures from the temple in Jerusalem as booty. He appointed another king, Zedekiah, to rule in Jerusalem. Nebuchadnezzar returned some years later when Zedekiah rebelled, and punished him severely.

ANCIENT INDIA

India is a land of high mountains and mighty rivers, of beautifully decorated temples and teeming cities. Religion has played an important part in Indian culture for thousands of years. This land is the home of Hinduism and the birthplace of Buddhism, and Islam became widely accepted there. Secrets of Indian civilization include epic tales of Hindu gods and the art of the emperors from gorgeous clothing to marvellous carpets.

DAUD ALI

CONSULTANT: NICK ALLEN

The Glory of Ancient India

THE INDIAN SUBCONTINENT IS HOME to one of the world's most ancient and varied civilizations because many different groups of people have travelled over the Himalayan mountains and settled there. From the arrival of Aryan tribes about 3,000 years ago until the invasion of the Mughals in the 1500s, each new wave of people brought fresh ideas and ways of life. As a result, India's religious and artistic life became very rich and mixed.

Two major world religions – Hinduism and Buddhism – developed in ancient India, and for hundreds of years, India was also at the heart of Muslim life in Asia. These three religions shaped the course of India's history, and led to the building of magnificent monuments, many of which still stand.

With its Hindu and Buddhist temples and sculptures, and the sumptuous palaces of the Muslim rulers, India is full of amazing treasures from the past.

DAWN OF INDIAN CIVILIZATION
Ancient stone buildings, such as the Great Bath at Mohenjo-Daro in the Indus Valley, tell archaeologists a great deal about the dawn of civilization in India. Fewer buildings of later times have been excavated, partly because later houses were made of mud, thatch and wood, none of which has survived.

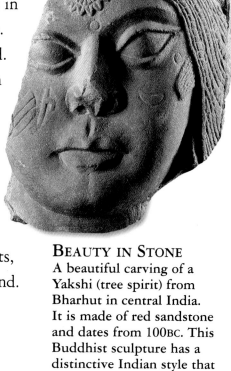

BEAUTY IN STONE
A beautiful carving of a Yakshi (tree spirit) from Bharhut in central India. It is made of red sandstone and dates from 100BC. This Buddhist sculpture has a distinctive Indian style that you can see in sculptures from much later periods. Buddhism was the first religion in India to inspire people to build monuments and make sculptures.

TIMELINE 6000BC–AD400

From early times until the coming of the British in 1757, India was divided into many kingdoms. It was never a single state. The regions of Ancient India were linked by a common culture, rather than by politics, religion or language.

statue of priest king from Indus valley

c. 6000BC Neolithic settlements in Baluchistan.

c. 2800–2600BC Beginnings of settlements in the Indus Valley region.

rice cultivation

c. 1700BC Sudden and mysterious decline of the Indus Valley civilization.

c. 1500–1200BC Immigration of Vedic Aryans into north-western India.

c. 2300–1700BC The great cities of the Indus Valley (Mohenjo-Daro and Harappa), the Punjab (Kalibangan) and Gujarat (Lothal) flourished.

c. 1200–600BC The Vedic texts are composed.

c. 800BC Use of iron for weapons and the spread of Aryan culture into the Gangetic plains.

c. 500–300BC Rice cultivation and the introduction of iron for the use of agriculture in the eastern Gangetic plains lead to the formation of more complex societies, cities and states.

fragment of pot with brahmi inscription

6000BC   2500BC   1200BC   500BC

TEMPLE OF THE SUN
A huge carved stone wheel forms a panel on the wall of the Sun Temple at Konarak on India's east coast. This part of the temple is carved in the shape of a gigantic twelve-wheeled chariot, drawn by seven stone horses. It dates from the 1200s, when medieval Hindu kings built magnificent temples to their gods.

GRAND ENTRANCE
The Alamgiri Gate is one of three magnificent entrances built by the Mughal emperor Aurangzeb to the Shahadra fort at Lahore (in modern-day Pakistan). The fort doubled as a luxurious palace.

LIFE STORY
A limestone frieze dating from AD100 shows a good deed carried out by the spiritual leader, Buddha. The frieze comes from Amaravati, in south-eastern India, which was an important Buddhist site from 300BC. Stories of the Buddha's past lives, called jatakas, were popular in ancient India.

A COUNTRY OF MOUNTAINS AND PLAINS
India is bounded to the north by the Himalayan mountains. The central Deccan plateau is framed by mountain ranges known as the Eastern and Western Ghats. The first settlements grew up near rivers on the fertile plains in the north.

c. 500–400BC Inscribed fragments of pots from Sri Lanka discovered.

c. 478–400BC Life of the Buddha. He is born a prince but leaves his family to live in poverty.

coin of Alexander the Great

327–325BC Alexander the Great arrives in north-western India.

320BC The rise of the Magadhan empire under the Maurya family, founded by King Chandragupta I.

268–233BC King Ashoka, the grandson of Chandragupta I, issues the first royal edicts on pillars and rocks throughout the subcontinent.

c. 50BC–AD100 Intensive trade connections with the Roman Empire.

AD50–AD200 Kushanas and Shakas (tribes from Central Asia) set up kingdoms and adopt Indian religions. Indian dynasty of Satavahanas arises in southern India.
Ashokan pillar

c. AD150 Kushana and Shaka kings in the north and west adopt Sanskrit as the courtly language.

c. AD200–400 *Ramayana*, *Mahabharata* and the *Bhagavad-Gita* Hindu epic poems are composed in their final form.

AD400 Nearly all courts are using Sanskrit.

gateway to Buddhist stupa

300BC

AD100

AD400

The Land of Ancient India

INDIA IS ISOLATED FROM THE main continent of Asia by the world's highest mountains, the Himalayas. The mountains made it difficult for people to invade. The easiest overland route, taken by the earliest settlers from Asia, is from the north-west (present-day Afghanistan) through the Karakoram mountains. However, it was still a difficult journey. Once people had arrived in India, they tended to stay.

The first people settled in the bare mountain foothills, and survived by keeping herds of animals such as sheep and goats. People gradually moved south of the Himalayas, to areas where mighty rivers run through huge, fertile plains. Here, the climate enabled them to grow various crops.

India's climate is dominated by the monsoon, a wind that brings alternating seasons of hot, dry weather and heavy rain and flooding. In the drier west and north, wheat was the main crop from very early times, while higher rainfall in the east and south was ideal for growing rice. Rice cultivation was so successful in the plains around the Ganges river that many people settled there. This led to the growth of cities from around 300BC. Later, cities developed along rivers farther south.

From the 1st century AD, people no longer needed to make the overland journey into India. They came by ship from as far away as the Mediterranean Sea to ports on the west coast, in search of trade.

TRADING NATION
From 200BC, ancient India traded with the outside world by sea. They also bought and sold goods by land along the Silk Road – a route that cut across the Himalayas and through Central Asia to Samarkand and beyond.

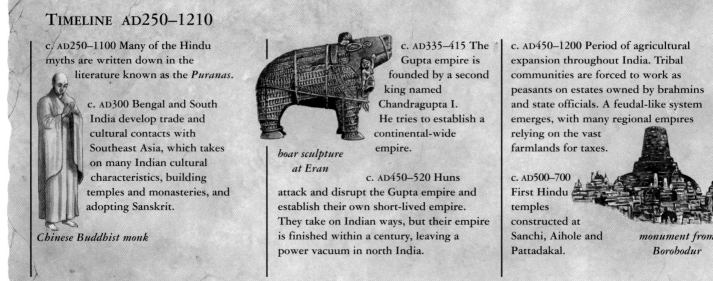

TIMELINE AD250–1210

c. AD250–1100 Many of the Hindu myths are written down in the literature known as the *Puranas*.

c. AD300 Bengal and South India develop trade and cultural contacts with Southeast Asia, which takes on many Indian cultural characteristics, building temples and monasteries, and adopting Sanskrit.

Chinese Buddhist monk

boar sculpture at Eran

c. AD335–415 The Gupta empire is founded by a second king named Chandragupta I. He tries to establish a continental-wide empire.

c. AD450–520 Huns attack and disrupt the Gupta empire and establish their own short-lived empire. They take on Indian ways, but their empire is finished within a century, leaving a power vacuum in north India.

c. AD450–1200 Period of agricultural expansion throughout India. Tribal communities are forced to work as peasants on estates owned by brahmins and state officials. A feudal-like system emerges, with many regional empires relying on the vast farmlands for taxes.

c. AD500–700 First Hindu temples constructed at Sanchi, Aihole and Pattadakal.

monument from Borobodur

AD250   AD330   AD500   AD600

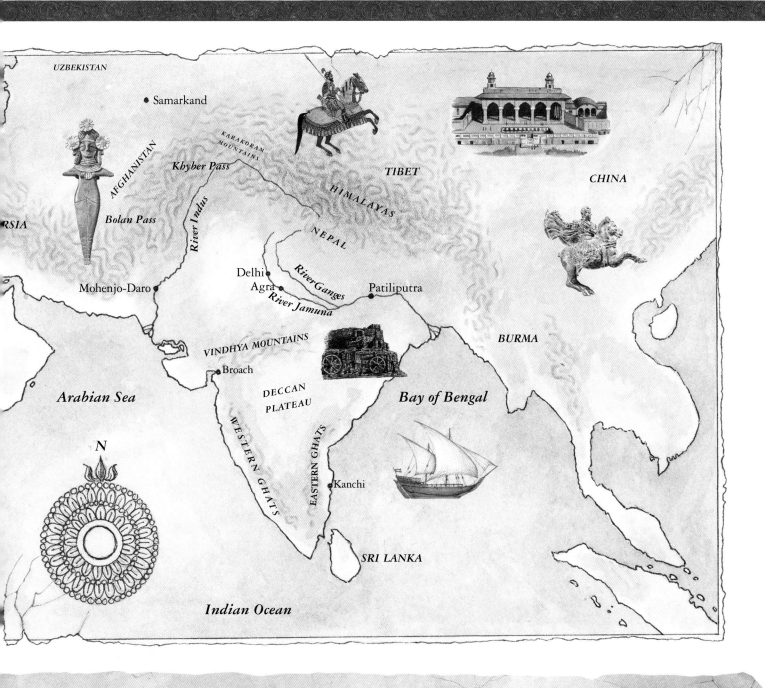

UZBEKISTAN

• Samarkand

AFGHANISTAN

KARAKORAM MOUNTAINS

Khyber Pass

TIBET

HIMALAYAS

CHINA

PERSIA

Bolan Pass

River Indus

NEPAL

Mohenjo-Daro •

Delhi
Agra
River Ganges
Patiliputra

River Jamuna

BURMA

VINDHYA MOUNTAINS

Broach •

Arabian Sea

DECCAN PLATEAU

Bay of Bengal

N

WESTERN GHATS

EASTERN GHATS

Kanchi •

SRI LANKA

Indian Ocean

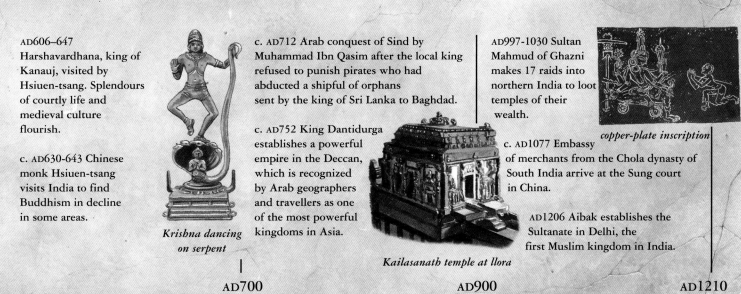

AD606–647 Harshavardhana, king of Kanauj, visited by Hsiuen-tsang. Splendours of courtly life and medieval culture flourish.

c. AD630-643 Chinese monk Hsiuen-tsang visits India to find Buddhism in decline in some areas.

Krishna dancing on serpent

c. AD712 Arab conquest of Sind by Muhammad Ibn Qasim after the local king refused to punish pirates who had abducted a shipful of orphans sent by the king of Sri Lanka to Baghdad.

c. AD752 King Dantidurga establishes a powerful empire in the Deccan, which is recognized by Arab geographers and travellers as one of the most powerful kingdoms in Asia.

Kailasanath temple at Ilora

AD997-1030 Sultan Mahmud of Ghazni makes 17 raids into northern India to loot temples of their wealth.

copper-plate inscription

c. AD1077 Embassy of merchants from the Chola dynasty of South India arrive at the Sung court in China.

AD1206 Aibak establishes the Sultanate in Delhi, the first Muslim kingdom in India.

AD700

AD900

AD1210

History Makers

MANY OF THE REMARKABLE FIGURES of Indian history who shaped the country's destiny were great leaders. Ashoka was a powerful ruler in the 3rd century BC, who encouraged the spread of Buddhism. Babur, a warlord from Samarkand in Central Asia, founded the Mughal Empire in India in the early 1500s. His grandson, Akbar, was a gifted politician and soldier who ruled for 49 years. The Mughal period was a time of huge development in the arts. Some Mughal rulers built magnificent cities, and many of their fine monuments and royal tombs can still be seen today.

From the time of the ancient civilization of the Aryans in the Indus Valley, religious teachers and scholars were respected. This may be because poverty and suffering have always been problems in India, which led people to think about why life was so difficult, and to seek ways of coping. Two of the most famous religious leaders are Gautama Buddha, who established the Buddhist way of life, and Guru Nanak, who founded the Sikh religion.

AN INFLUENTIAL LEADER
A statue of Gautama Buddha seated on a lotus flower. He founded Buddhism, which shaped life in India for thousands of years. Buddhism eventually died out in India, but it spread through many other parts of Asia. This created a link between India and many different eastern peoples and cultures.

TIMELINE AD1290-1875

AD1293 Marco Polo visits South India. A flourishing trade is conducted throughout the Indian Ocean in silks, fabrics, spices and other luxuries.

AD1334-1370 The sultanate of Madurai, the southernmost Muslim kingdom, established briefly in south India before being defeated by southern kingdoms.

stone chariot from Vijayanagar

c. AD1346–1565 The last great Hindu empire of Vijayanagar founded in south India.

c. AD1360 Vedic and Hindu revival by the brothers Sayana and Madhava at the Vijayanagar court.

AD1398 The Mongol Timur devastates Delhi.

tomb from the Sultanate period

c. AD1440 Death of the Bhakti saint Kabir at Gorakhpur, where both Hindus and Muslims claim him as a great teacher.

AD1469-1539 Life of Guru Nanak, founder of Sikhism.

AD1498 Portuguese explorer Vasco da Gama visits Calicut.

AD1510 The Portuguese conquer Goa.

Qutb Minar marble fountain

AD1290   AD1340   AD1400   AD1520

ROYAL HANDWRITING

This signature of Emperor Harsha (AD606–647) is carved in copper. Harsha was a patron (supporter) of arts and literature, and during his reign, the richness and elegance of the court reached new heights.

A SAINTLY LIFE

A statuette of Karaikal Ammaiyar, a woman who lived in southern India around AD600. She was so devoted to the god Shiva that she left her home and family, and gave her life entirely to him. She fasted as a symbol of her faith and became incredibly thin. Karaikal Ammaiyar is revered as a saint even today in southern India.

ASHOKA'S PILLAR

An edict (order) of Ashoka, the ruler of India's first empire, is inscribed on this pillar. He published his edicts on pillars and rockfaces throughout the land. Ashoka was a Buddhist. He claimed to have improved the lives of humans and animals, and had helped to spread justice.

ART LOVER

Shah Jahan was one of the greatest statesmen of the Mughal Empire. He extended Mughal power south into the Deccan plateau and north into Afghanistan. However, he did not fulfil the Mughal dream of capturing the trading city of Samarkand, the 'blue pearl of the Orient', in Central Asia. Shah Jahan was a great patron of architecture.

AD1526 Babur, the Mongol, defeats the Sultan of Delhi and founds the Mughal empire.

AD1556-1605 Reign of Akbar, the most enlightened Mughal emperor.

Mongol horseman

AD1739 Nadir Shah sacks Delhi and carries off the Peacock Throne.

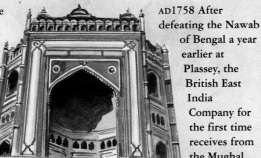

palace at Phata Pursi

AD1758 After defeating the Nawab of Bengal a year earlier at Plassey, the British East India Company for the first time receives from the Mughal rulers the right to collect land taxes in Bengal.

AD1857–8 British crown imposes direct rule and the East India Company is dissolved.

AD1870 Construction of Red Sea telegraph brings direct link with Britain.

farman (order) of Mughal emperor to East India Company

AD1750   AD1850   AD1875

The First Indian Civilization

IN THE 1920s, archaeologists made an astonishing discovery. They found the remains of two great cities near the Indus River in north-western India. The cities were called Mohenjo-Daro and Harappa. Before this, no one had known very much at all about India's earliest history, but it was now clear that there had been a vast urban civilization in the area as far back as 2600BC, and that it had lasted for nearly a thousand years.

These ancient cities were very well organized. They had drainage systems, a network of roads, granaries, water tanks and canals, as well as raised citadels (fortresses) where the rulers lived. It is clear that the city dwellers traded with other civilizations, too, because Indus valley objects have been found as far away as Egypt and Mesopotamia. For some reason, this bustling culture declined after 1700BC. It is possible that the climate became drier, causing crops to fail, or that the people destroyed their own environment, perhaps by overgrazing. No one is sure.

LOST CITY

Ruins of the citadel at Mohenjo-Daro. Like all the cities of the Indus Valley civilization, Mohenjo-Daro had a lower city and a high citadel. It was probably the largest of the Indus Valley cities. The raised stump at the back of the picture is the remains of a stupa – a monument containing relics of the Buddha. The stupa was erected long after the city declined.

TRADING TOKEN

Seals cast from soft soapstone may have been used as tokens for trading goods. This one shows a humped bull, or zebu. It comes from Mohenjo-Daro, and is over 4,000 years old. The symbols on the seal may have identified traders.

MAKE A CLAY SEAL

You will need: rolling pin, modelling clay, board, ruler or measuring tape, blunt knife, scrap paper, pencil, modelling tool, PVA glue, paintbrush, white paint, string, plastic oven-drying modelling material.

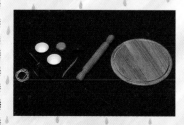

1 Use the rolling pin to roll out the modelling clay. When you have finished, you should have a rectangle-shaped slab of clay about 2 cm thick.

2 Carefully trim away the edges of the slab of clay so that they are neat and even. Your rectangle should now measure 10 x 7 cm.

3 Draw an animal shape on to the clay. (Practise drawing the shape on scrap paper first.) Carefully cut the pattern into the clay using a modelling tool.

CLAY WOMAN

A terracotta figurine from Mohenjo-Daro shows a woman in a headdress. The headdress looks as if it was made up of two baskets – a way of carrying heavy loads in India even today. The statue may have been a mother goddess or a doll or toy. Archaeologists have found groups of clay figurines like this that show people doing things in and around the home.

DESERTED VALLEY

Today, the Indus Valley is no longer a fertile place in which people grow crops, but an arid (dry) landscape of bare soil. Around 1700BC, the cities of the Indus Valley were suddenly and rapidly depopulated. It is believed that a change in the course of the Indus River may have disturbed the primitive irrigation system, and led to a collapse in agriculture.

STORING FOOD

Large storage jars were used to keep and distribute food that was grown around Mohenjo-Daro. The fact that its people were able to store surplus food shows how settled and organized the society was.

INDUS VALLEY DANCER

This copper statuette shows a dancer from Mohenjo-Daro. The dancer has an elaborate hairstyle, necklaces and lots of arm bangles. Thousands of years later, hairstyles and jewellery like this are still the ideal of what makes a woman look beautiful in India.

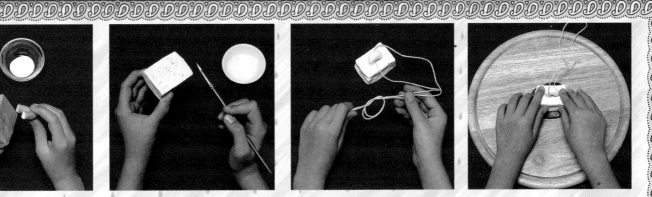

4 Roll out a 2–3 cm sausage-shaped piece of modelling clay. Bend it into a curved handle shape. Glue the handle to the slab.

5 Paint the clay slab with a single coat of white paint. This will give your seal a clean surface that will not stain or leave any dirty marks.

6 Loop the string through the handle of your seal. Knot the string to secure. Mould the plastic oven-drying modelling material into a slab shape.

7 Press the seal into the modelling material. Your pattern appears raised in reverse. Bake the material, following the instructions on the packet.

The Noble People

A KING AND HIS PRIESTS
A raja (king) consults his Brahmin priests near a sacrificial fire. The relationship of the Brahmin and the raja became very close in the time of the Vedic hymns. Brahmins performed the sacrifice for the raja in order to bring him wealth, prosperity and sons. When empires began to form after about 350BC, the Brahmins became the ministers of the king's government because of their important role.

ABOUT 400 YEARS after the decline of the Indus Valley civilization, a new wave of people arrived in India from the north-west, probably from central Asia. They were known as the Aryans, or 'noble people'. They lived in small groups or larger tribes. Gradually they moved farther into India and took over the part of the plains between the Indus and the Ganges rivers. At first, the Aryans lived by herding animals, but as they settled, they started growing crops instead.

The Aryans divided society into three castes (classes). These were made up of priests (Brahmin), warriors (Kshatriya), and property holders (Vaishya). There was a also a fourth caste of servants and labourers called Shudra, made up of the people that the Aryans had conquered. Each of the castes played a different role in an important Aryan custom – the offering of a burnt sacrifice of meat and grains to the gods in return for rains, wealth and sons. The hymns of praise to the gods during this sacrifice were called the Vedas. They were composed in a language that came to be known as Sanskrit, meaning refinement. These Aryan customs and writings formed the basis of the Hindu religion.

OFFERING CUP

You will need: Plastic drinking cup, scissors, piece of medium card, PVA glue or tape, modelling clay, rolling pin, board, modelling tools, dark brown and red-brown paint, paintbrushes, kitchen towel, non-toxic varnish.

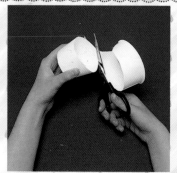

1 Cut off the top half of the plastic cup. Roll the piece of card into a tube shape. It should be wide enough for the bottom of the cup to sit into it neatly.

2 Overlap the edges of the rolled-up card. Glue or tape the edges to hold them in place. Fit the trimmed cup into the card tube, right side up.

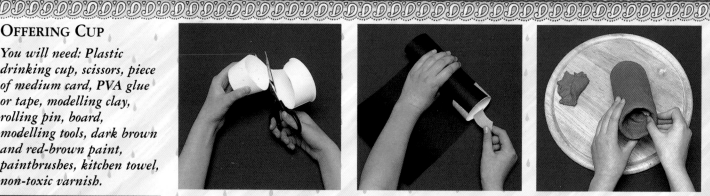

3 Roll out the modelling clay. Cover the card tube with the clay. Use some of the clay to cover the plastic drinking cup, too. Leave the clay to dry.

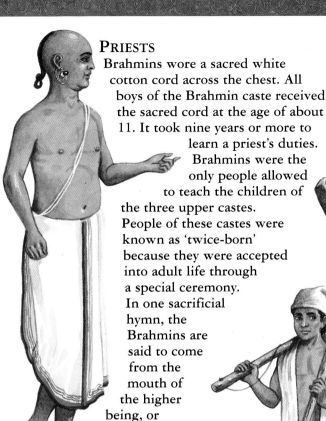

PRIESTS

Brahmins wore a sacred white cotton cord across the chest. All boys of the Brahmin caste received the sacred cord at the age of about 11. It took nine years or more to learn a priest's duties. Brahmins were the only people allowed to teach the children of the three upper castes. People of these castes were known as 'twice-born' because they were accepted into adult life through a special ceremony. In one sacrificial hymn, the Brahmins are said to come from the mouth of the higher being, or Cosmic Man.

WARRIORS

The warrior noble, or Kshatriya, was the next highest caste after the Brahmin. The raja, who was the protector of society, came from the Kshatriya class. It was his duty to safeguard the position of each caste and to give money to the Brahmins. The Kshatriyas were thought to be the arms of the Cosmic Man.

ORDINARY PEOPLE

The Vaishyas were the common people of the Aryan clans. They were large in number and rich in wealth. They practised agriculture and trade, and were thought to be the 'thighs' of the Cosmic Man. They were above the peasants and people of no caste, who were considered 'impure'.

Offering cups were an important part of the ritual of the sacrifices that the Aryans made to the gods. The cups were always the same shape, and would have been filled with holy water.

4 Using a wooden modelling tool, carefully start to carve your chosen design into the modelling clay on the cup.

5 Finish carving the picture. Cut lines into the clay to add texture. This will help make your finished cup look as if it has been made from wood.

6 Paint the cup with dark brown paint. While it is still wet, wipe some of the paint off with kitchen towel, to give it a streaked look. Leave to dry.

7 Paint the cup with red-brown paint. The darker paint will still show through in places. Leave to dry, then brush the cup with two coats of varnish.

Buddhist India

THE CUSTOMS AND TEACHINGS of the Aryan people meant that the highest born Brahmins (priests) were the only ones who could be saved from life's suffering. People of other castes were not happy with this, and by 500BC new religious practices began to develop. Siddharta Gautama was born into the warrior caste, but left his family at the age of 30 to seek spiritual enlightenment (freedom). He gained many followers during his lifetime and became known simply as the Buddha, which means enlightened. He taught what he called a 'Middle Way' between pleasure and suffering, which everyone could follow regardless of caste.

The Buddha's followers evolved into an order of monks called the sangha, who wandered from place to place with a begging bowl and survived on people's donations. Many important people, including kings and merchants, gave generously to the sangha and built monasteries for them to live in. After the Buddha's death, his followers honoured him by building large domed monuments, called stupas.

From 272BC, King Ashoka encouraged the spread of Buddhism. Ashoka is said to have built an incredible 80,000 stupas, each with its own monastery.

RECORDED IN STONE
This relief from the AD500s shows events from Buddha's life. Scenes, such as his departure from his father's palace and his enlightenment under the bodhi tree, were recorded on monuments. There, they could be read by many people.

GIFTS TO THE BUDDHA
The stupa at Sanchi was built by Ashoka and added to by later monarchs. The dome is surrounded by a beautifully carved railing that shows scenes from the Buddha's life. At this stupa and several others at Sanchi, nearly 900 short inscriptions have been found. Each one records the gifts of monks and ordinary people.

CAVE MONASTERY

In western India, cave monasteries were built among the rocks to house communities of monks. Buddhist monks needed to be alone in order to meditate and follow the path to enlightenment.

ANCIENT AND MODERN

Modern monks in Sri Lanka worship an ancient statue of the Buddha. Buddhism was brought to Sri Lanka by Ashoka's son, Mahinda. The very oldest form of Buddhism, called Theravada, is still practised in Sri Lanka today.

TIBETAN PRAYER HANGING

A painting of the Buddha on a prayer hanging in Tibet has a face that is more Central Asian than Indian. In Tibet, Buddhism grew into a new form called Vajrayana. This tradition often included secret teachings about rituals.

RELICS OF THE BUDDHA

A limestone carving at the great stupa in Nagarjunakonda, in eastern India, shows gods and men venerating (worshipping) the Buddha's relics. The relics are encased in the central mound of every stupa. Relics are pieces of bone or hair that Buddhists believe have come from the body of the Buddha.

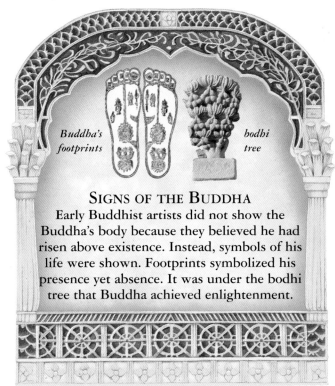

Buddha's footprints

bodhi tree

SIGNS OF THE BUDDHA

Early Buddhist artists did not show the Buddha's body because they believed he had risen above existence. Instead, symbols of his life were shown. Footprints symbolized his presence yet absence. It was under the bodhi tree that Buddha achieved enlightenment.

Hindu Gods and Goddesses

Buddhism remained the dominant religion in India until about AD200, but the religion of the Aryan people did not disappear. Instead, it evolved into new forms, which together became known as Hinduism. Many of the beliefs were the same, but Hinduism discouraged the Vedic practice of making animal sacrifices, and introduced new gods to replace the Aryan deities. Gradually, Hinduism took over from Buddhism, and has remained India's dominant religion ever since.

In the two main types of Hinduism – Vaishnavism and Shaivism – Hindus believe that one god (Vishnu or Shiva) rules the universe. From about AD1000, some worshipped the goddess Devi instead. In each version, the Cosmic Man (the god's representation on earth) takes on different forms depending on the task, so that Hindu mythology seems to have lots of gods. In fact, they are versions of Vishnu, Shiva or Devi.

TERRIBLE GOD
Shiva appears in the form of a terrifying being wielding a trident. At times, Shiva is associated with the destructive forces of the universe and commands demonic beings, called ganas.

HAPPY GOD
The conch shell and the discus are the symbols of the god Vishnu, who is often shown with blue skin. Vishnu mostly brings happiness, preservation and kingship. He stands on a lotus flower.

MAKE A GARLAND OF FLOWERS

You will need: Tissue paper in orange, yellow, red, pink and white, pencil, scissors, PVA glue, paintbrush, length of string, darning needle.

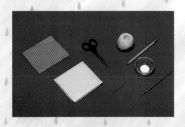

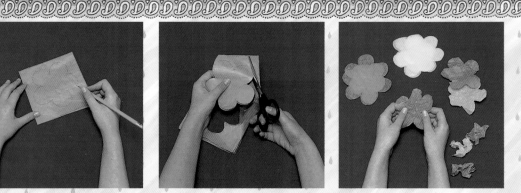

1 Draw simple flower shapes on to sheets of coloured tissue paper. If you like, you can lay the sheets of paper in layers, one on top of the other.

2 Using scissors, cut out your flower shapes. Take care not to tear the tissue paper. Cut the same number of flowers in each colour.

3 Scrunch up the tissue flower shapes with your hands. Then uncrumple them, but don't smooth them out too much.

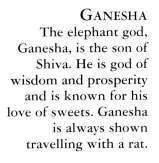

GANESHA

The elephant god, Ganesha, is the son of Shiva. He is god of wisdom and prosperity and is known for his love of sweets. Ganesha is always shown travelling with a rat.

KRISHNA AND RADHA

The god Krishna was an incarnation of Vishnu on earth. Krishna was born as a cowherder. In his youth, he is said to have been adored by many women, but his favourite was Radha. The love of Radha and Krishna is the theme of many Hindu religious songs.

GODDESS OF DEATH AND WAR

Shiva's wife had many forms. The fiercest was Kali, goddess of death. Here, she holds an array of weapons in her many arms. Kings often worshipped Kali before going into battle.

Hindus make garlands of fresh flowers to wear at festivals to honour their gods.

4 Glue the flower shapes together loosely in layers to make larger, single flowers. Use eight layers of tissue paper for each finished flower.

5 Now gently fluff up the layers of tissue paper with your fingers. This will make your flowers look much more impressive.

6 Measure a length of string that is long enough to go around your neck. Start to thread the flowers on to the string to make a garland.

7 Thread all the tissue flowers on to the length of string. When you have secured all the flowers, tie a double knot in the string to finish.

Epic Tales of the Gods

A DECISIVE BATTLE
Prince Arjuna and Krishna face the Kauravas on the battlefield. It is here that Krishna (painted blue) reveals that he is a god to Arjuna, and sings a song that instructs him on how to behave properly. Krishna's song is known as the *Bhagavad-Gita*.

BROTHERS IN ARMS
The five Pandava brothers are honoured in this shrine. They are the heroes of the *Mahabharata* story. They struggle with the Kauravas to regain their kingdom, and are aided by Krishna. Each brother is known for a noble quality, such as heroism.

THE MOST IMPORTANT ancient stories of the Hindus are told in two great epics (long poems) called the *Ramayana* and the *Mahabharata*. No one is sure exactly who wrote them or when, but they were written down in their present form by AD500. In both, the god Vishnu appears in different incarnations (forms) to save the earth from destruction and to tell people about right and wrong.

In the *Ramayana*, Vishnu takes the form of the exiled prince Rama. His wife, Sita, is abducted by the demon Ravana and taken to a fortress in Lanka (present-day Sri Lanka). Rama rescues Sita with the help of the monkey god, Hanuman.

The *Mahabharata* is a much longer story, with many subplots. It tells of a bitter struggle between two families, the Pandavas and the Kauravas. Krishna, another human version of Vishnu, helps the Pandavas to defeat the Kauravas. Part of the *Mahabharata* is Krishna's advice on morality to the Pandava prince, Arjuna. It is known as the *Bhagavad-Gita*, and is given just before the last battle, which the Pandavas finally manage to win.

MAKE A RAMAYANA HEADDRESS

You will need: ruler, pencil, 2 x A2 sheet of thin red card, scissors, sticky tape, strips of corrugated cardboard, red paint, paintbrushes, string, drawing pin, brightly coloured paints, PVA glue, coloured foil sweet wrappers.

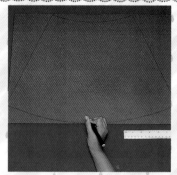

1 Use a ruler and pencil to draw two straight lines at an angle as shown, onto card. Join these lines with curved lines, as shown. Cut out the shape.

2 Roll the card into a shape that is narrower at the top. The bottom of the card should be wide enough to fit your head. Fix the edges with tape.

3 Tape a strip of corrugated cardboard around the base of your headdress shape, but leave a gap at the back where the seam is.

RAMA ON THE ATTACK

With the help of Hanuman and his army of monkeys, and an army of bears, Rama attacks the forces of the demon Ravana in Lanka. Rama is victorious in his battle and kills Ravana. He is then reunited with his wife, Sita.

MONKEY KING

Hanuman, leader of the monkeys of the forest, became Rama's most faithful follower. As Rama searched desperately for his wife, Sita, it was Hanuman who found her in Ravana's palace in Lanka. Hanuman led Rama and his monkey forces to Sita's rescue.

THE DOOMED DEMON

Ravana, the demon king, leads his demon generals. In the *Ramayana*, Ravana was the all-powerful king of the island of Lanka. However, a prophecy foretold that he would lose his life because of a woman. That woman turned out to be Sita.

Hindus wear headdresses to act out scenes from the story of Rama and Sita.

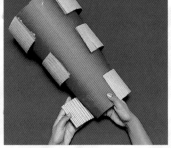

4 Tape corrugated card strips around the middle and the top of your hat shape, again leaving a gap at the back. Paint the strips with red paint.

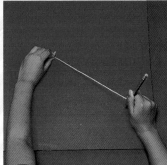

5 Measure the height of your headdress. Using string tied to a drawing pin and a pencil, draw a circle with a diameter that matches the height of your headdress.

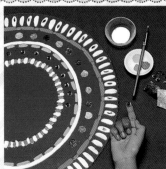

6 Carefully cut out the circle. Now use brightly coloured paints and foil sweet wrappers to decorate your headdress in all the colours of the rainbow.

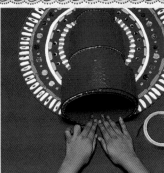

7 Leave the decorated circle to dry thoroughly. Then glue or tape it to the back of your headdress. Finally, decorate the headdress.

Houses of the Gods

A HINDU TEMPLE IS RATHER like a palace that has been built for a god to live in. In the old Aryan Vedic religion, people believed that the gods lived in the skies and were fed by the sacrificial fires. After each sacrifice, the altar was taken down. When Hinduism evolved, it adopted the Buddhist practice of building places of worship called stupas. Shaivas and Vaishnavas built beautiful temples and invited their gods to come and live in them in the form of images, such as statues. Brahmin priests looked after the statues, tending to their every need. The gods were woken, bathed, dressed, entertained and fed each day. This practice of honouring a god's image is called puja, and is still central to Hinduism today.

By AD500, temples were common. As kings converted to Hinduism, they built many huge temples across India and lavished donations of money and tax revenue from farmlands upon them. By AD1000, most Hindu temples were not only places of worship but places where country people traded goods.

HONOURING THE BUDDHA
This frieze is from a 2,000-year-old stupa at Amaravati, a Buddhist site in south India. It shows men and gods honouring the feet of the Buddha. Puja (worship) was first practised by Buddhists. It later became popular among Hindus as well.

TEMPLE TOWER
The temple to Shiva at Bhubaneshwar in Orissa was built in the AD800s. The tower is the home of a linga, or symbol of Shiva. The tower itself is a mix of north and south Indian styles of temple. The central tower of another temple can be seen in the background of the picture. Kings often built several temples close to one another.

A SHRINE IN THE HOME
A man makes an offering at a shrine in his home. From early times, Hindus worshipped gods in the household, as well as in the temple. Most Hindus do not pray together, but privately, alone.

A PORTABLE SHRINE

This cloth was used as a portable shrine for worshipping the god Pabuji. Pabuji was a hero of the 1300s who was converted into a god. The pictures surrounding the figure of Pabuji represent scenes from his life as told in a folk story. Folk priests in the northern state of Rajasthan went from village to village carrying cloths like these, to use as temples.

SYMBOL OF POWER

A gopuram (gate tower) at the Shiva temple at the city of Madurai, in Tamil Nadu. Gopurams were built by kings as symbols of power, each king trying to outdo his rivals. This gopuram is so huge, it is larger than the shrine inside the temple itself. Gopurams are covered in painted carvings and can be seen from afar.

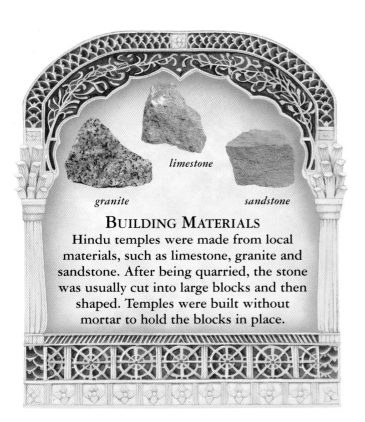

granite *limestone* *sandstone*

BUILDING MATERIALS

Hindu temples were made from local materials, such as limestone, granite and sandstone. After being quarried, the stone was usually cut into large blocks and then shaped. Temples were built without mortar to hold the blocks in place.

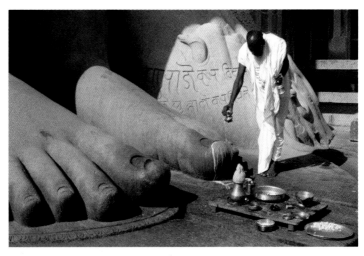

AT THE FEET OF THE SAINT

A worshipper performs puja (worship) to a saint in south India. His image is so huge that the priests can only reach his toes to place flower and coconut offerings. When the image is bathed, scaffolding is erected to reach the head.

The Coming of Islam

THE MUSLIM RELIGION, called Islam – which means submission to God – was founded in Arabia (present-day Saudi Arabia) by a man named Mohammed in AD622. It spread quickly into the countries around Arabia, but it took nearly 400 years for Islam to reach India.

In AD1007 Sultan Mahmud, the Muslim leader of the city of Ghazni in Afghanistan, started a series of attacks on northern India to loot the rich temples there. More Islamic leaders followed his example, and by AD1206, Muslim Turks from Central Asia had founded a new kingdom, or Sultanate, based in the city of Delhi. The Delhi Sultanate ruled the region for 300 years.

Islam gradually spread among ordinary people. Islamic sufis (mystics) played an important role in spreading the message of God's love for all people. They worshipped in a very emotional style at their countryside shrines, in a way that the Hindu peasants could understand. By the 1700s, nearly a quarter of India's population was Muslim. They showed great tolerance to other religions and cultures, especially the Hindu faith.

BEAUTIFUL WRITING
This page is from a Persian commentary on the holy book of Muslims, the *Quran*. Muslims were not allowed to represent images, such as humans, animals or flowers, in art. Instead they developed calligraphy (the art of beautiful writing).

SEAFARING SETTLERS
The Indian Ocean was controlled by Muslim traders from about AD700. They arrived along the south-western coast of India on their way to Indonesia and China, and were among the earliest Muslims to settle in India. These traders followed Muslim law. Different Muslim laws spread in India through further Muslim invasions from Turkey and Afghanistan in the 1100s and 1200s.

FROM TEMPLE TO MOSQUE

The Quwat al-Islam, a large mosque in Delhi, was built out of parts of destroyed temples of older faiths. It has two architectural features that were introduced to India by Islam. One feature is the arch, the other is the use of mortar for sticking bricks together. The mosque was built by the Delhi Sultanate in 1193.

HOLY MEN

Sufis (mystics) gather together to pray. Sufism was a type of Islam that preached that people's souls can communicate to God through ecstatic music, singing and dancing. Sufism came into prominence in Persia in the AD900s. By about 1100 it had also gained a foothold in the north-west of India.

FAMILY TOMB

A man cycles towards a tomb of one of the later Sultans of Delhi. The tomb is in the gardens of the Lodi family, the last rulers of the Delhi Sultanate. The last Lodi Sultan was defeated in battle by the Mughal prince Babur, in 1526.

SUFI SHRINE

This tomb-shrine, or dargah, in Rajgir, honours a famous sufi saint. Sufi teachers were called pirs, or shaikhs. They often had a large number of followers.

The Sikh Society

As islam spread through northern India, Hinduism and Islam existed side by side. In the Punjab region of northern India, a new religion emerged that had elements of both. It was called Sikhism, and was founded by a man called Guru (teacher) Nanak (1469–1539). Sikhism rejected the strict Hindu caste system and adopted the Islamic idea that all people are equal before God, but kept many aspects of Hindu ritual. Sikhs worshipped in temples called gurdwaras (abode of the gurus). After Nanak, there were nine more gurus. The fifth, Arjan, founded the Golden Temple at Amritsar, which later became the holiest of all gurdwaras. He also wrote the Sikh holy book, or *Adi Granth*.

In the 1600s, the Muslim Mughal rulers in Delhi became concerned about the growth of this new religion. They began to persecute the Sikhs and killed Arjan and another guru. The tenth guru, Gobind Singh, decided that Sikhs should protect themselves and founded a military order called the khalsa. Members carried a comb and dagger, wore a steel bangle, breeches, and did not cut their hair. Sikh men took the title Singh (lion). After the death of Gobind Singh in 1708, there were no more gurus, but Sikhs continued to live by the teachings of the *Adi Granth*.

LETHAL TURBAN
A Sikh war turban is decorated with weapons that could be removed and used against the enemy during battle. Metal throwing rings could slice heads off, while 'claws' were for disembowelling people.

THE GOLDEN TEMPLE
The greatest Sikh temple is the Golden Temple in the Sikh holy city of Amritsar. The temple was built by Guru Arjan Singh (1581-1606). Its white marble walls and domes are decorated with gold. The city of Amritsar is named after the lake that surrounds the temple. Sikhs worship in their temples in large congregations (groups). Free kitchens are attached to Sikh temples, where all can eat.

SYMBOLIC COMB

This close-up picture of a Sikh turban shows the kangha, a comb that is pinned to the centre. The kangha is one of the five signs of the Sikh religion. Sikh men do not cut their hair – another sign of Sikhism.

THE SACRED BOOK

The *Adi Granth* is the sacred book of the Sikhs. Its text was compiled by Guru Arjan Singh in the late 1500s. After the death of the last teacher, Guru Gobind Singh, Sikhs came to accept these scriptures as the symbol of God. They took over the role of the teacher from the Gurus.

A MILITARY MAHARAJA

The Maharaja Ranjit Singh (1799–1838) holds court. The water tank of the Golden Temple can be seen in the background. Ranjit Singh led the Sikh army to victory against Afghan warlords and the collapsing Mughal Empire. He established a separate Sikh kingdom in the Punjab region of India.

AN ABLE WARRIOR

A Sikh soldier sits on a cushion in this portrait from the 1800s. When the British ruled India, they recruited many Sikhs into their army. Sikhs were regarded as one of India's most warlike peoples.

The Mughal Empire

Ⓘ N 1526, A PRINCE from the area now called Uzbekistan invaded India from the north-west. His name was Babur. He swept across the country with a powerful army and soon arrived in Delhi, where he defeated the Sultanate and founded a new empire. His successors came to be known as the Mughals. The Mughal Empire was the last important dynasty of India before the British arrived in the 1700s.

Babur's grandson, Akbar, who ruled from 1556 to 1605, was a great Mughal leader. Although he was Muslim, he was tolerant of other religions and took Hindu princesses as his wives. Forty years later, the warlike Mughal ruler Aurangzeb returned to a stricter form of Islam and expanded the empire. The Mughals were patrons of the arts, and built glorious

palaces, gardens and tombs. Many of India's most precious works of art date from this era. Persian was the language of their court, but they also spoke Urdu, a mixture of Persian, Arabic and Hindi.

ORDERLY COURTIERS
Mughal nobles had to take part in court rituals. They had to arrive punctually at court, and line up in rows. Their dress and posture were very important. The cummerbund tied around the waist and the turban were signs of self-control. Courtiers guarded the palace strictly in turn.

THE FIRST MUGHAL EMPEROR
Babur defeats Ibrahim Lodi, the last sultan of Delhi, at the Battle of Panipat in 1526. Babur invaded India because he was unable to recapture his own homeland in Samarkand.

MAKE A LACQUERED STORAGE BOX

You will need: pencil, ruler, sheets of card, scissors, sticky tape, newspaper, wallpaper paste or flour and water, bowl, fine sandpaper, paint in white and bright colours, paintbrushes, non-toxic varnish.

1 Scale up the shape shown here to the size you want your box to be and copy the shape on to card. Cut out the shape and fix the edges with sticky tape to form a box.

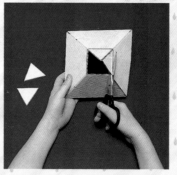

2 Draw 4 card triangles with sides the same length as the top of the box. Tape the triangles together to form a pyramid and cut off the top.

3 Add newspaper strips to the paste, or flour and water, to make papier mâché. Cover the box and lid with three layers of papier mâché. Dry between layers.

A POEM IN STONE

The emperor Shah Jahan commemorated his wife Mumtaz Mahal (who died in childbirth) by building this magnificent mausoleum. It was built between 1631 and 1648, and came to be known as the Taj Mahal. It is built of white marble from Rajasthan. The Taj Mahal is one of the most magnificent buildings in the world, and is the high point of Mughal art.

JADE HOOKAH

This Mughal period hookah (pipe) is made from precious green jade. During Mughal times, the culture of the court reached a high point in Indian history, with many fine pieces like this being made.

RED PALACE

The Red Fort in Agra is one of the palaces built by Akbar. The Mughal emperors broke with the tradition of kings living in tents, and built sumptuous residences in their capital cities.

Lacquered boxes were popular with women of the royal court for storing jewellery.

4 When the papier mâché is dry, smooth any rough edges with sandpaper. Add squares of cardboard as feet. Paint the box and the lid white.

5 Allow the painted box and lid to dry. Draw a pattern on to the box and lid. You could copy the pattern shown here, or use your own design.

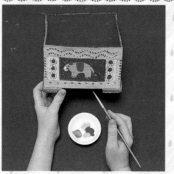

6 Paint the lid and the box, including the feet, with brightly coloured paints. Use the pattern that you have drawn as a guide. Leave to dry.

7 To finish, paint the box and lid with a coat of non-toxic varnish. Leave to dry completely, then add a final coat of varnish. Your storage box is now finished.

The Symbols of Royalty

OVER THE CENTURIES, kings of many different religions ruled India. The titles that they took and the objects that surrounded them often had symbolic significance and tell us a lot about their role as leaders. From the time of Ashoka, around 250BC, the ruler of the empire was called cakravartin (wheel-turner). The wheel was a Buddhist symbol for the world, so this suggested that the king made the world go round. Objects that were symbols of royalty included sceptres, crowns and yak-tail fly whisks. The most important object was the chatra (umbrella), which signified the king's protection of his realm.

Later, Hindu kings (called maharajadhirajas) developed the idea that the god Vishnu lived within them. When Islam arrived, the sultans showed their obedience to the caliph, the head of Islam in Baghdad, by taking titles such as nasir (helper). Mughals took Persian titles such as padshah, which simply means emperor.

DISPLAY OF POWER
A Mughal emperor rides through the city on top of an elephant, a symbol of royalty. Kings often processed through their cities to display their power and majesty. They were always followed by attendants and courtiers.

THE MARKS OF A KING
A picture of the man/god Rama's foot depicts the lotus, conch shell, umbrella, fly whisk and other royal symbols. People thought that a world-ruling king was born with special features. Among these were unique marks on the soles of his feet and palms of his hands, which foretold that he would be emperor.

MAKE A CHAURI
You will need: strip of corrugated cardboard measuring 3cm x 25cm, raffia, scissors, sticky tape, PVA glue, 20 cm length of dowel, modelling clay, paint in gold and a contrasting colour, paintbrushes, foil sweet wrappers.

1 Put the strip of card on a covered, flat surface. Cut strips of raffia. Carefully tape the strands of raffia to the card. Leave your chauri to dry.

2 Wrap the card and raffia around the dowel, and glue it in place. Keep the card 2 cm from the top, so that the dowel supports the raffia.

3 Tape the card and raffia band firmly in place to make sure that it will not come undone when you use your whisk. Leave the whisk to dry.

A KING'S HALO

The king in this procession has a halo surrounding his head. From Mughal times, rulers were thought to be blessed with the divine light of wisdom. This was represented in pictures by a halo.

ROYAL CUSHION

Raja Ram Singh of Jodhpur sits with his nobles. Only the king may sit on a cushion. The Rajputs were the kings of northern India, who fought against Muslim invaders but later became their most important military allies under the Mughals.

ROYAL RAMA

Rama, the human form of the god Vishnu, sits with his wife Sita and his brothers. He holds a bow, a symbol of courage. Also seen are other symbols of royalty – an umbrella and a yak-tail whisk.

The fly whisk was a symbol of a Hindu king's power.

4 Make lots of small beads from modelling clay. Glue these on to the dowel in a circle, about 2.5 cm below the strip of card. Leave to dry.

5 Paint the dowel and beads with two coats of gold paint. Leave it to dry. Then paint a pattern on the strip of card and the dowel, in different colours.

6 When the paint is dry, glue bits of coloured foil paper to your chauri. The more decorations you add, the more it will look like a real chauri.

Ententainments

THE ROYAL COURTS OF Mughal India were places of marvellous entertainment. Courtiers listened to poetry and music every day. They loved riddles and word games, and in contests, poets were given half a verse and asked to complete it. Different art forms were connected to one another. For example, the *Natyashastra*, an ancient text on dance and drama, includes a long section on music. Dancers were also storytellers, using hand gestures to show meaning.

North and south India developed their own musical traditions – Hindustani in the north and Karnatak in the south. Islam introduced new instruments, such as the sitar (a stringed instrument) and the tabla (a drum). Outside the courts, religion played a part in the development of singing. Muslim mystics sang and played musical pieces called qawwali, while Hindus sang songs to Krishna.

JOYFUL OCCASION
Drummers and trumpeters at the Mughal court joyfully proclaim the birth of Akbar's son, Prince Salim. Music was often used to announce celebrations. Though they enjoyed royal patronage and were often renowned for their talent, musicians, dancers and actors were generally considered to be of low social standing.

INSTRUMENTAL BIRD
An instrument called a sarangi has been finely carved in the shape of a peacock. The sarangi was played with a bow and usually accompanied the dance performances of courtesans during late Mughal times.

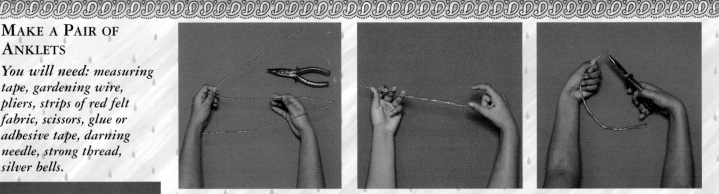

MAKE A PAIR OF ANKLETS
You will need: measuring tape, gardening wire, pliers, strips of red felt fabric, scissors, glue or adhesive tape, darning needle, strong thread, silver bells.

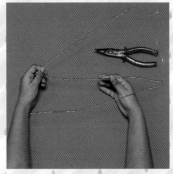

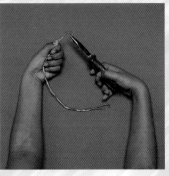

1 Measure the diameter of your ankle. Multiply this figure by three, then add 4 cm for a loop. Use the pliers to cut two pieces of wire to this length.

2 Loop the first cut piece of wire around itself about three times. Twist it tightly as you go. Then twist the second piece of wire in the same way.

3 Using the pliers, bend one end of each strip of twisted wire to form a loop. Bend the other end to form a hook. These act as a fastener.

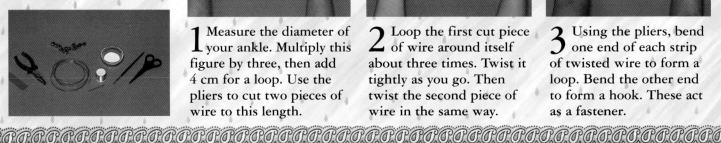

FOLK DANCING

A decorative border shows figures linking hands in a Punjabi folk dance. Ordinary village people danced to celebrate births, weddings and many other special occasions. Each dance usually involved lots of dancers.

ON A STRING

A woman from Rajasthan plays with a yo-yo. Games with balls and strings were not expensive, so they could be enjoyed by both rich and poor people. Many other kinds of games were afforded only by the wealthy.

ENTERTAINING AT COURT

Dancers perform the style of dance known as a Kathak for the great Mughal emperor Akbar. Dance was a popular form of entertainment at court. Many of the complicated dance styles known in India today originated at the courts of kings in ancient times. The dances performed at court often told a story.

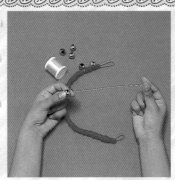

Anklets were worn by dancers who performed at ceremonies in the royal courts of the Mughals.

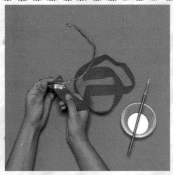

4 Cut out two strips of felt fabric that are slightly longer than your strips of wire. Glue or tape a felt strip on to the end of the twisted wire.

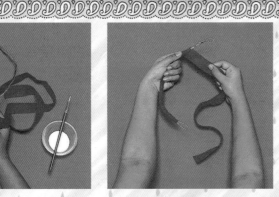

5 Wrap the felt around the wire, overlapping the edges of the felt. Glue the end of the felt to the place where you began. Wrap the second wire strip.

6 Thread a darning needle with sewing thread. Sew lots of tiny silver bells to the felt fabric covering your wire loops.

7 Repeat your stitches several times to make sure that the bells stay firmly in place. Add more bells, so that you cover both anklets completely.

Games and Sports

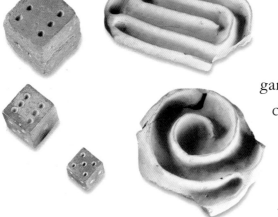

MANY GAMES DEVELOPED in the royal courts, where people had leisure time on their hands. One of these games, called caturanga, developed into the modern game of chess. Caturanga referred to the four parts of the army – the infantry, chariots, cavalry and elephants. It had different rules from modern chess, though it is not known exactly what these rules were. The game was played with dice, and up to four players may have taken part at once.

Outdoor sports were usually associated with shikar (hunting), and included archery, falconry (hunting with birds of prey) and horsemanship. Muslim rulers brought the game of polo, played on horseback, from Persia.

Religious fairs and festivals gave ordinary people the chance to play games, too. Cockfighting, ramfighting and wrestling were important. Spring was the season of playfulness. The ancient spring festival, Holi, is associated with love and play, and people had great fun throwing coloured powders and water over each other. Social roles were relaxed during the games of Holi, and people from different castes mixed freely. Holi is still celebrated today.

IMPORTANT PIECES
Sandstone and terracotta dice and other game pieces were discovered in the Indus valley. We cannot be certain what games these dice were used for. However, later Indian literature has recorded the importance of dice in playing games.

BOARD GAME
Archaeologists have found board games, such as the one pictured above, and toy animals in the Indus valley. These show that the Indus people must have enjoyed playing with toys and games.

A DANGEROUS SPORT
Wrestling was a favourite sport as long ago as 1000BC, and many kings had the title malla (wrestler). Wrestlers endured strict diets and physical training in camps known as akharas. Wrestling could be a highly dangerous activity. One inscription tells of a wrestler who was accidentally killed during a match.

PLAYING AT WARFARE

Mughal nobles play a game of polo. First played in Persia, polo was introduced to India by Muslim conquerors in the 1200s. The game was originally intended to train cavalry (soldiers on horseback) as it developed good horse-handling skills and taught riders how to manoeuvre at close quarters. Under the Mughals, polo became a popular sport among the nobility. However, it has never lost its military associations, and the Indian army maintains a polo team to this day.

DEER HUNTER

A Mughal king hunts deer. Hunting was an important activity. Like battle, it was an occasion to display the manhood of the king. The preferred prey were lions, tigers, boars and deer. In Mughal times, the emperor would hold secret meetings, and put his closest servants to the test during the hunt.

FLYING A KITE

A Mughal woman flies a kite. Kite-flying was a favourite sport in Mughal times. Competitions were so fierce that kite-fliers would dip the strings of their kites in crushed glass in order to cut down rival kites from the sky.

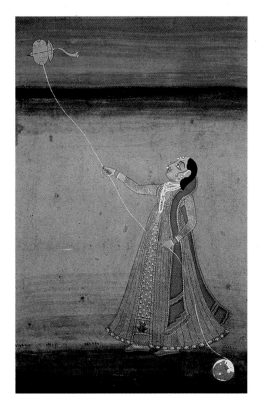

A GAME OF STRATEGY

A Mughal period chess set of painted ivory from Rajasthan. Chess was used to educate princes, ministers and nobles at court, and sharpen their planning skills. The most important chess board piece – the king – has the least power, as he acts through those around him. This was similar to how Indians viewed their own king.

The Importance of Animals

ANIMALS WERE PART OF everyday life throughout Indian history. Cows, oxen, water buffaloes, camels, horses and elephants carried loads, were used for transport and helped with farming. Hindus came to see the cow as the source of all life, and therefore the most important animal of all. It became protected and holy, and to this day Hindus are forbidden to harm them.

People kept pets as well, especially birds. They had peacocks in their gardens, and caged parrots, which were often taught how to speak. Muslim nobles also kept pigeons.

Animals played an important part in Hindu myths. For example, the god Vishnu incarnated himself as a turtle and a boar to save the world. Shiva's son Ganesha had an elephant's head, and the man god Rama's most faithful companion was Hanuman, king of the forest monkeys. In the *Pancatantra* fables, each animal symbolized a human virtue or vice. Lions, tigers and elephants were considered powerful, noble, brave and proud, but dogs were seen as unclean creatures with no self-respect. Jackals and herons were greedy and cunning, while the monkey was playful and foolish.

SYMBOL OF ROYALTY

Lions became the most common symbol of courage and nobility in India. They feature on this Ashokan pillar dating from around 250BC. This pillar was adopted as the symbol of the Indian republic in 1948.

MYTHICAL MAKARA

The makara is one of the mythical animals of India. It was a cross between an alligator and a tortoise. Makaras were a favourite of artists and appear frequently as decorations on stupas and temples.

MIGHTY ELEPHANTS

Elephants were seen as strong and supporting, no doubt because they were often used to carry heavy loads. It was believed that at the end of the earth were heavenly elephants that held up the sky. Elephants were also thought to be fierce and violent, and were favoured for use in battle. The best elephants were from Orissa, in eastern India, and from Sri Lanka.

CHARMING THE SNAKES

A snake charmer coaxes a cobra from a basket to amuse the Hindu god Shiva. Snake charmers were known for their ability to lure and mesmerize snakes. They did this, not through the noise of their flute, but by using the movement of their hands and body to hold the reptile's attention. Snake charmers are still popular in India today.

CAT AND MOUSE

A cat sits inside a palace, while a mouse escapes across the roof. Cats were not usually treated as pets, but were tolerated as part of the household because they played an important role in controlling vermin, such as rats.

parrot

TALKATIVE PARROTS

Parrots and other talking birds were kept by wealthy people in cities in India. The birds were trained to speak by the people of the court. Since medieval times, many stories tell of parrots who blurted out the secrets of the palace in front of visitors!

BEAUTIFUL GUARDIANS

Peacocks were kept in gardens to help ward off snakes and to add to the beauty of the surroundings. They were also exported to the courts of emperors in Rome, China and Persia as exotic gifts. The peacock's brilliant plumage inspired the design of many textile patterns in India.

Writing and Language

THE EARLIEST KNOWN WRITING IN INDIA has been found on some seals from the ancient civilization of the Indus valley, but no one has yet been able to work out what the symbols mean. Later, when the Aryan people arrived, they brought a language with them that then developed into a number of different regional languages. There was one formal version of all these, which was called Sanskrit.

In about 300BC, a new form of script (writing) appeared, called Brahmi. The Buddhist king Ashoka used this script to inscribe proclamations on rocks and pillars all over his empire, and by about 100BC, Brahmi was used throughout India.

Early Indian documents were written on sheaves of palm leaf or bark, which were then threaded together. Important documents, that needed to last for a long time, were engraved on copper plates. The coming of Islam brought the Persian language to India, along with Arabic writing, which was developed into an art form called calligraphy. By Mughal times, paper and ink were replacing older methods of record keeping.

A WOODEN INSCRIPTION
This wooden tablet contains a Buddhist text written in a script known as Kharosthi. It was the script of a group of people who lived in north-west India from the first to the third centuries AD. The kings who ruled them wanted their people to follow Buddhism.

CARVED IN STONE
A stone inscription of AD900 on the pedestal of a Buddhist image from eastern India is written in Sanskrit. The image was given by a Buddhist monk for the benefit of his parents and teacher. The inscription is in an eastern form of nagari, the script used for modern Hindi.

MAKE A SUTRA
You will need: two 30 x 9 cm pieces of balsa wood or thick card, dark brown paint, paintbrushes, clear non-toxic varnish, A2 sheet of white paper, cold tea, scissors, ruler, pencil or bradawl, large darning needle, string or twine.

1 Brush the two 30 x 9 cm rectangular pieces of balsa wood or card with brown paint so that they look like dark wood. Leave to dry.

2 Varnish your painted book covers. Leave them to dry. Give them a second coat, and a third. The extra coats will give the book a laquered finish.

3 Scrunch up the sheet of paper so that it wrinkles. Unscrunch it, lay it out flat and paint it with cold tea. Leave it to dry. This makes it look old.

MUGHAL PAINTER AND SCRIBE

A young painter from the Mughal court, named Manohar, sits with the scribe Mohammad Husain al-Kashmiri surrounded by inkwell, pen box, books and letters. They are writing in Persian, the language of the Mughal court and administration.

A MUGHAL WRITING SET

A jewel-inlaid box dating from Mughal times contains writing materials. These include a letter opener, a pen, a spoon and an in-built inkwell.

INSCRIBED TOWER

An extract from the *Quran*, the Muslim holy book, decorates the Qutb Minar, a 72-metre-high tower in Delhi. The tower was built in the AD1200s by Qutb-ud-Din Aibak, the first Muslim sultan of Dehli, to celebrate his victory over the Hindu kings. The art of beautiful writing, or calligraphy, was highly developed in Islamic cultures.

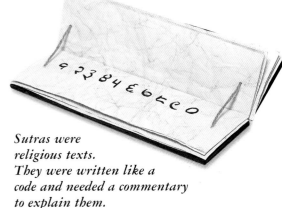

Sutras were religious texts. They were written like a code and needed a commentary to explain them.

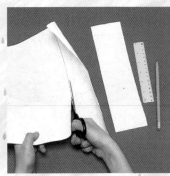
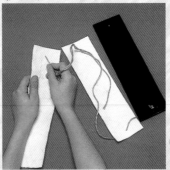
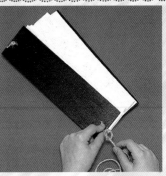

4 When it is completely dry, cut the crinkled paper into rectangular pieces measuring 29 x 8 cm. These will be the pages of your book.

5 Mark a point in the centre of each book cover, about 2 cm from each short edge. Use a pencil or bradawl to make holes in the book covers.

6 Put the paper pages between the two book covers. Use a large needle to thread string or twine through the paper and the book covers.

7 Knot the ends of the string or twine firmly. Make sure that the knot is bigger than the hole in the book cover, so that the pages stay in place.

Homes of Rich and Poor

Houses in India differed according to social class. Poor people made their homes out of mud, clay and thatch. Materials such as these do not last long, so few of these houses have survived. By about 600BC, wealthier people were building homes made of brick and stone. It is thought that people's caste determined not only the part of a town or city that they lived in, but also what colour they painted their homes. The Brahmins of Jodhpur in Rajasthan, for example, painted their houses blue.

A wealthy man's house of about AD400 had a courtyard and an outer room where guests were entertained. Behind this were the inner rooms where the women of the house stayed and where food was cooked. Beyond the house itself there were often gardens and fountains surrounded by an outside wall. Homes like this stayed much the same in design over many centuries.

Royal palaces were more elaborate. They had many courtyards and enclosures surrounded by numerous walls. These were to protect the king from beggars and servants who might make a nuisance of themselves. Unlike ordinary homes, palaces changed in design with each new wave of rulers.

DECORATED DOORSTEP
Pictures in chalk and rice powder were drawn on the doorsteps of houses. Over time, they came to signify prosperity and good luck. Making such drawings was one of 64 forms of art that a cultured person was expected to be able to do.

birdcage

mango leaves hung for good luck

water trough

courtyard

MOUNTAIN HOMES
These modern mountain homes made from mud and thatch continue a tradition that is thousands of years old. Unlike valley homes, they have to be well insulated for protection against the colder climate.

THE GOOD LIFE
Life in a rich man's household was divided between the inner area, where he slept and ate, and the outer regions, dominated by a courtyard where he entertained friends, read, listened to music and strolled in the garden. Here, salons (groups) of men would meet to discuss life and politics.

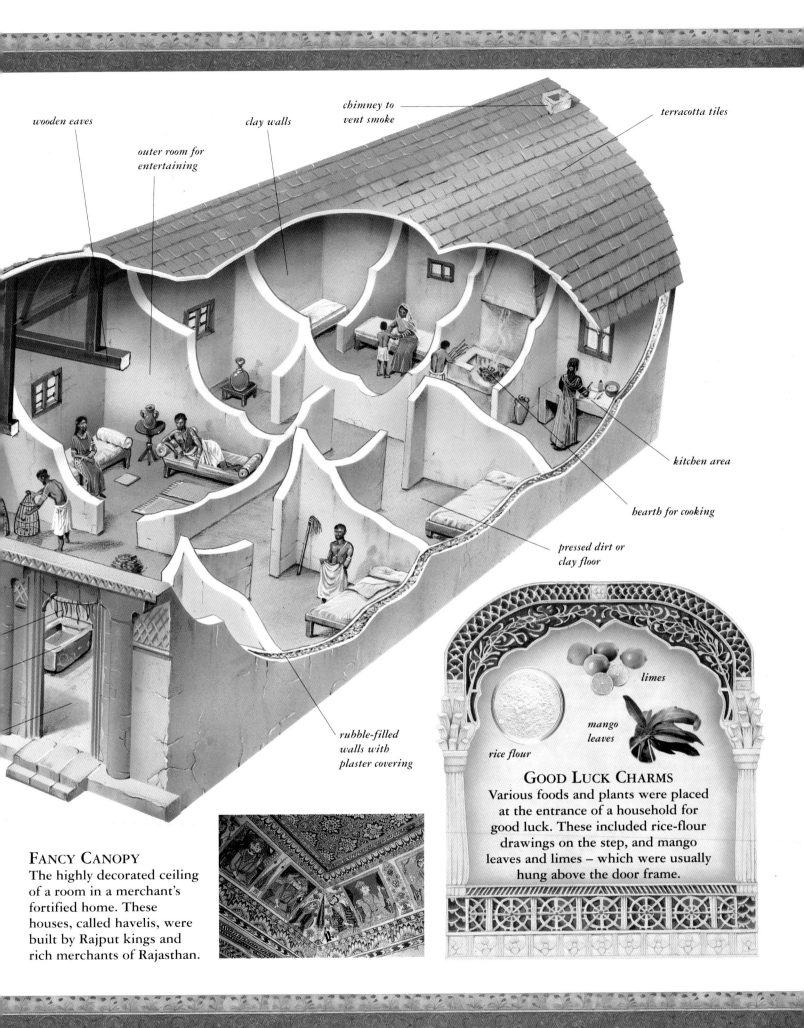

wooden eaves

outer room for entertaining

clay walls

chimney to vent smoke

terracotta tiles

kitchen area

hearth for cooking

pressed dirt or clay floor

rubble-filled walls with plaster covering

FANCY CANOPY
The highly decorated ceiling of a room in a merchant's fortified home. These houses, called havelis, were built by Rajput kings and rich merchants of Rajasthan.

GOOD LUCK CHARMS
Various foods and plants were placed at the entrance of a household for good luck. These included rice-flour drawings on the step, and mango leaves and limes – which were usually hung above the door frame.

limes

mango leaves

rice flour

A Woman's Place

ORDINARY WOMEN did not have an easy life in India. They toiled in the fields and threshed the wheat. In some parts of India and among Muslims, women had to dress very modestly and some were not allowed to go out at all. Women from rich families were symbols of a man's wealth. The more wives he had the better, as it showed that he was rich enough to look after them. Kings had several wives, too, because marrying women from different regions was a way of forming alliances. Very occasionally, queens became leaders. Queen Raziya, for example, was sultan in the 1200s.

For nearly 2,000 years in Indian art and literature, women ideally have had long hair, almond-shaped eyes, a sweet birdlike voice and a shy manner. Sometimes they were portrayed as romantic heroines, such as Rama's virtuous wife Sita in the *Ramayana*. Hinduism also had many goddesses. Saraswati was the goddess of learning, Lakshmi the goddess of wealth and Durga the goddess of warfare.

IDEAL BEAUTY
This woman is shown with large, almond-shaped eyes – the ideal of beauty in ancient India. Women lined their eyes with a black paste called collyrium, to accentuate the almond shape.

QUEST FOR KNOWLEDGE
Female Hindu ascetics (who practise self-denial) surround their leader in a holy hermitage. Rarely could women abandon worldly life for spiritual pursuits, as men did. Usually, only widows were allowed to take the spiritual path.

TIE A SARI
You will need: silky or cotton fabric measuring 4 x 1 m, large safety pin. To make a decorated border for your sari, dip a cork into gold paint and print a pattern along one long edge of the fabric. Leave to dry.

1 Hold one corner of the fabric to your stomach with the decorated border on the outside. Wrap the long side of the fabric once around your waist.

2 Make a number of pleats where the fabric comes back to the front again. Make them as even as you can. The pleats act as the sari's underskirt.

3 Tuck the pleated section into the waist of the underskirt. You could hold the pleats in place with safety pins, while you practise tying the sari.

MORE THAN ONE WIFE
Mughal emperor Shah Jahan is shown with one of his wives, Qudsia Begum. Both Hindu and Muslim men of rank often took more than one wife. Though this increased the chance of producing heirs, it could also create jealousy within the royal household.

COVERED HAIR
These women from Rajasthan cover their hair with their saris. The spread of Islam influenced the habits of Hindu women in northern India. They had to dress according to what was considered modest by Muslims.

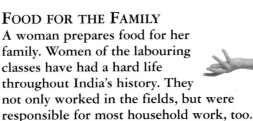

HARD DAY'S WORK
Female labourers pick tea in north-eastern India. Though tea was not drunk in India, women laboured in the fields to cultivate other crops. Low-caste peasant women formed the most exploited class in society.

A sari is a single large cloth covering both the upper and lower body. Saris were first worn in eastern India over a 1,000 years ago.

FOOD FOR THE FAMILY
A woman prepares food for her family. Women of the labouring classes have had a hard life throughout India's history. They not only worked in the fields, but were responsible for most household work, too.

4 Take the excess length of fabric in your left hand and pass it all the way around your back. Take care that the pleats don't come out.

5 Now take the rest of the fabric in your right hand and lift it up so that it is level with your shoulders. Do this in front of a mirror, if possible.

6 Swing the fabric over your left shoulder. The fabric should fall in gentle folds from your shoulder, across your body, to your waist.

7 Carefully pin the fabric to the shoulder of your tee-shirt, to keep it in place. Look in a mirror, to see if it fits well. If it doesn't, try again!

Village India

A VILLAGE HOME
Cane houses with thatched roofs have been typical of villages in eastern India for hundreds of years. The stone foundation raises the floor of this house above light flooding levels. Other building materials for village structures include mud, clay and wood.

THROUGHOUT HISTORY, most people in India have lived in the country rather than in towns, so village life has always been an essential part of Indian civilization. This worked in one of two ways. Some villages were tribal, which meant that the villagers organized their own lives and were independent from other rulers. In other villages, the people were peasants, which meant that they were controlled by local rulers or emperors, and had to pay taxes.

From medieval times onwards, more and more villagers became peasants. Whether they were peasants or tribal, however, people had plenty of contact with towns and cities, because they provided city-dwellers with food. The taxes demanded by rulers were often in the form of food, too.

Villagers farmed differently depending upon where they lived. In drier and higher regions it was difficult to grow crops. Villagers in these areas grew a few crops and kept animals. They often remained tribal. In the fertile plains and river basins, rice cultivation supported densely populated and complex societies, which grew into great empires.

A CRUCIAL CROP
Terraced paddy fields in the hills of eastern India have been flooded with water. Rice cultivation requires elaborate irrigation techniques, as the plant's root must be submerged in water. Rice cultivation was the dominant agricultural activity in central, eastern and southern India in the past, as now. Rice was a high-yield crop, and it could feed large numbers of people. This in turn gave rise to advanced societies and massive empires.

BULLOCK CART
A villager and his bullock arrive at the construction site of a Mughal palace. Bullock carts were the most common vehicles in villages. They carried heavy loads of grain and rice, and building materials, too.

WASHING CLOTHES
A village dhobi (washerman) cleans clothes in a river. He scrubs the clothes on stone slabs beside the river. Behind the dhobi, men are working on a building site.

THE MARKET
A Mughal period painting shows food being sold at a village market. Milk is being drawn from a cow, and rice and water are being sold. Each village or cluster of villages had a street market where produce was bought and sold.

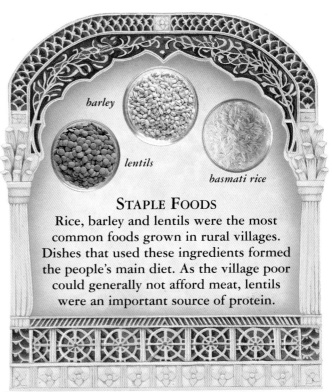

barley

lentils

basmati rice

STAPLE FOODS
Rice, barley and lentils were the most common foods grown in rural villages. Dishes that used these ingredients formed the people's main diet. As the village poor could generally not afford meat, lentils were an important source of protein.

TYPICAL VILLAGE LIFE
A caravan (a group of merchants travelling together) passes by a river near Murshidabad with three villages nearby. Villagers bathe by the river and plough the fields. Horses and camels can be seen in a horse market. In the foreground an ascetic receives visitors.

Dress and Accessories

CLOTHING HAS ALWAYS BEEN quite simple in India. Noble people, both men and women, usually wore a single piece of fabric that was draped around the hips, drawn up between the legs, then fastened securely again at the waist. Women wore bodices above the waist, but men were often barechested. Although their clothes were simple, people had elaborate hairstyles that included flowers and other decorations. Men and women also wore a lot of jewellery, such as earrings, armbands, breastplates, noserings and anklets. The Hindu male garment was called the dhoti, and the female garment gradually evolved into the sari – a single large cloth draped around the body, with a bodice worn underneath.

When Islam arrived, tailored garments became widespread in northern India. People wore sewn cotton trousers called paijama or shalwar, with a long tunic called a kamiz or kurta. For men, turbans became popular. Muslim women were expected to dress modestly, so they began to wear veils, a practice that Hindu women also adopted.

SETTING THE TREND
Bangles and ear studs from the Indus Valley are among the earliest ornaments found in India. They are more than 4,000 years old. The styles of these pieces of jewellery, and the designs on them, were used again in later forms of decoration.

ANCIENT BEAUTY AIDS
This mirror, collyrium applicator and hair pin are over 4,000 years old. Large dark eyes were considered a sign of beauty, so women drew attention to their eyes by outlining them with collyrium, a black substance.

ANCIENT DRESS
A painted fragment of a pillar shows a woman wearing a long red skirt and jewellery. The pillar is about 2,000 years old.

MAKE A FLOWER BRACELET

You will need: A5 sheets of thin white card, pencil, scissors, gold paint, paintbrush, A5 sheets of white paper, PVA glue, foil sweet papers, gardening wire, pliers.

1 Draw some simple flower shapes on the white card. They should be about 2 cm in diameter. Give each flower six rounded petals.

2 Carefully cut out each of the flower shapes. Then paint both sides of each flower with gold paint. Leave the flowers to dry.

3 Draw 10 to 12 wedge shapes on the white paper sheets. They should be wider at the bottom than at the top. Cut out the wedge shapes.

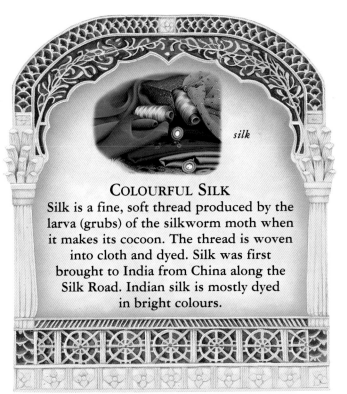

COLOURFUL SILK

Silk is a fine, soft thread produced by the larva (grubs) of the silkworm moth when it makes its cocoon. The thread is woven into cloth and dyed. Silk was first brought to India from China along the Silk Road. Indian silk is mostly dyed in bright colours.

silk

HINDU DRESS

In this detail from a painted panel, a Hindu man and woman wear typical dress – a dhoti for the man and for the woman, a sari. Both men and women liked to wear brightly coloured clothes.

JEWELS FOR ALL

A Rajasthani woman wears traditional jewellery and dress. Nowadays in India, jewellery is still so valued that even the poorer peasants own pieces for special occasions.

Floral designs are common patterns used throughout Indian art.

CLOTHING FOR THE COURT

Courtiers from Mughal times wear a side-fastening coat called a jama. It has a tight body, high waist and flared skirt reaching to below the knees. It is worn over tight-fitting trousers, or paijama, gathered at the ankle. A sash, called a patuka, is tied at the waist. Courtiers also wore a small turban as a mark of respect.

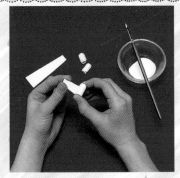

4 Apply glue to the wedge shapes and roll them up to make beads, leaving a hole through the middle. Paint the beads gold and leave to dry.

5 Carefully cut out tiny circles from the coloured foil paper. Make sure you have enough to stick on to the centre of each flower.

6 Measure gardening wire long enough to go around your wrist. Add 4 cm for a loop. Tape the flowers to the wire and thread on the beads.

7 To finish the flower bracelet, use a pair of pliers to bend back one end of the wire to form a loop and the other end to form a hook.

Textiles and Printing

MAKING TEXTILES HAS ALWAYS BEEN an important activity in India. There are records of ancient Romans buying Indian cloth, so the textile trade must have been well established by then. As fabric does not last very well, there are few examples from before AD900, but sculptures show us the kinds of cotton cloth that were made. In Buddhist and Hindu sculptures, clothing is generally light and draws attention to the shape of the body.

India's textiles show a lot of different influences. Silk originally came from China, but from about AD100 it was produced in India and became an important Indian export. From about AD1100, Turkish and then Persian invaders introduced floral designs. Fine carpets also began to be made following Persian traditions and styles. Some places began to specialize in the production or sale of textiles. In Mughal times, silks and muslin (fine cotton fabric) were produced at Ahmedabad, Surat and Dhaka, while Kanchipuram, near Madras, became known for its fine silk saris. The Coromandel coast, Gujarat and Bengal all became textile export centres.

DRAPED GARMENT
A red sandstone figure from Jamalpur dates from about AD400, and shows the Buddha dressed in a fine muslin garment. Many clothes in ancient India were draped and folded rather than sewn.

SPINNING WHEEL
A woman sits at her spinning wheel. Weavers were important because Indian fabrics were in great demand in Europe.

MAKE A PRINTING BLOCK

You will need: paper, felt-tipped pen, scissors, halved raw potato, blunt knife, 20 x 15 cm piece of beige calico fabric, iron, scrap paper, paints, paintbrush.

1 Copy the pattern shown here on to a sheet of paper. You can invent your own Indian design, if you prefer. Carefully cut out the pattern.

2 Place the cut-out pattern on the cut surface of the halved potato. Draw around the outline of the pattern with a felt-tipped pen.

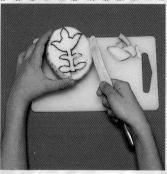

3 Use the knife to cut away the potato around the pattern. Your pattern should be raised about 5 mm above the rest of the potato half.

PERSIAN-STYLE CARPET

This fine, wool carpet is decorated with floral patterns. In Mughal times, many fine carpets like this one were produced in India. Carpet weaving was a skill learned in the north-west of India from Persian craftworkers.

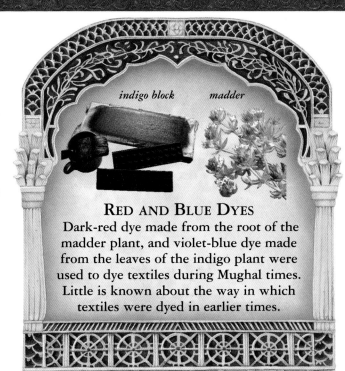

indigo block   *madder*

RED AND BLUE DYES

Dark-red dye made from the root of the madder plant, and violet-blue dye made from the leaves of the indigo plant were used to dye textiles during Mughal times. Little is known about the way in which textiles were dyed in earlier times.

PRINTING COTTON CLOTH

A Punjabi man prints a pattern on to a length of cotton with a printing block. Dyes for cotton cloth were usually made from vegetables.

HUNTING COAT

This satin hunting coat has scenes and animals of the hunt embroidered on it in silk. It is typical of the type of dress worn by Mughal nobles.

Printing blocks were used in Mughal times to decorate fabric for festivals and other special occasions.

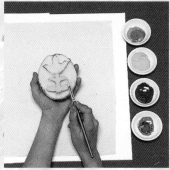
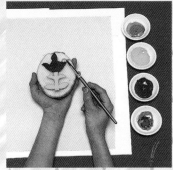

4 Ask an adult to help you to iron the fabric. Lay the ironed fabric on top of scrap paper. Apply paint to part of your printing block with a paintbrush.

5 Brush a different colour of paint on to your printing block. Give the block an even coat of paint that is not too heavy. Do not drench the block.

6 Press the printing block on to the fabric a few times. When the paint design starts to fade, apply more paint to the block with the paintbrush.

7 When the print design has dried, add some colourful details. Try out different colours on your printing block, or alter the pattern on the fabric.

Gardens

THE GARDENS of the Mughals were enclosed spaces filled with pools and flowering plants. As they required constant care and watering, gardens were only for wealthy people who could afford staff. Gardeners worked hard to ensure that parts of the garden were in bloom all year round. Courtiers amused themselves in gardens by playing games such as hide-and-seek, or with cockfighting. For at least 2,000 years, Indians have been especially fond of flowers. The mango blossom, ashoka flower and jasmine all appeared in courtly poetry. The lotus (a kind of water-lily), with its underwater stem system and floating flower, was a symbol of goodness and life. Flowers and leaves were used to make garlands to decorate the body and hair, and to decorate images of Hindu gods in the practice of puja (worship).

For Muslims, gardens had symbolic significance because they were seen as a miniature map of paradise. Muslim rulers divided gardens into four parts called charbhags, separated by water channels that represented the rivers of paradise. Gardens were so important that they inspired the designs on carpets that were made during Mughal times.

FAVOURITE PLANTS

Ponds filled with aquatic plants, such as waterlilies, were favourites in both Hindu and Muslim gardens. Courtly poetry describes many varieties of lotus and waterlily. Some varieties were grown to bloom at night, by moonlight.

MOUNTAIN GARDEN

A garden, at the mountain fortress of Sigiriya in Sri Lanka, dates from around AD400. It contains the remains of enclosures and pavilions. It once had water works, including fountains, an artificial stream and a large central tank. Sigiriya is surrounded by a moat. It is said that the moat once had crocodiles in it to deter intruders.

WATERING THE PLANTS
A group of malis (gardeners) use an elaborate system of water courses intersecting at right angles to irrigate plants, in this Mughal period painting.

PARADISE GARDEN

A Persian-influenced carpet is woven with a design inspired by a garden. In Islam, paradise is imagined as a garden that contains the finest objects in the world. Persian carpets were usually woven into designs based on gardens.

TENDING THE GARDEN

Gardens were popular in the houses of rich and powerful people. If a household had no gardener, the women of the house were responsible for tending the garden. Usually, a garden had a mixture of flowers and useful plants, such as fruits and herbs, growing in it.

DANGEROUS PLACE

An intruder pretending to be a gardener is being threatened by the garden's owner, a noble. The painting is from the Mughal period and dates from the 1600s. In those days, the garden was a place not only of romantic but also of political intrigue. A powerful person's life could be at risk away from the house.

Weapons and Warfare

FROM ARYAN TIMES, when tribes fought among each other and stole each others' cattle, warfare was a fact of life in India. As larger empires came into being, warfare became more elaborate. By the time of the emperor Ashoka in 250BC, armies were divided into four parts – infantry (footsoldiers), cavalry (horses), chariots and elephants. The infantry was the core of all Indian armies, but was often made up of poorly trained peasants. Elephants, on the other hand, were a symbol of royalty and majesty, and gave an army great prestige.

In the 1000s, when Turks invaded, chariots became less important. This was because the Turks had excellent horses and could use bows on horseback. Soon, all Indian armies copied them and began to use high-class cavalry. The first recorded use of gunpowder was in the Deccan plateau, in central India, in the 1400s. Later, the Mughals combined field artillery (guns) with cavalry and elephants.

UNEQUAL CONTEST
A mounted warrior and a footsoldier attack each other. From the 1200s, nobles preferred to fight on horseback. Footsoldiers faced a great disadvantage in fighting men on horseback, who not only used swords, but bows as well.

SUPERIOR WARRIOR
A Mongol warrior draws his bow and aims behind him as he rides. The Mongols were great fighters, especially on horseback. In 1398, they devastated Delhi and took many of its citizens as slaves.

MUGHAL HELMET

You will need: strips of newspaper, flour and water or wallpaper paste, bowl, inflated balloon, scissors, fine sandpaper, thin card, sticky tape or PVA glue, gold and black paint, paintbrushes, 20 x 10 cm piece of black card, ruler.

1 Soak the newspaper in the paste or flour and water. Cover half the balloon with three layers of newspaper. Leave to dry between layers.

2 When dry, burst the balloon and remove it. Smooth edges of helmet with sandpaper. Wrap a strip of card around the base. Fix with tape or glue.

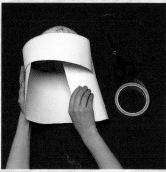

3 Place a longer piece of card inside the helmet. It should be long enough to cover your ears and neck. Glue or tape it into position and trim to fit.

LIGHT PROTECTION

A Hindu warrior on horseback uses a spear. Warriors had little armour besides shields. They often wore ornaments and lucky charms.

FORTIFIED CHAIR

A king at war travels in a fortified howdah (chair) on an elephant's back. The combination of howdah and elephant was like the armoured tank of modern warfare. The best army elephants were captured mainly in eastern and southern India, and in Sri Lanka.

BEST WEAPON

A Hindu footsoldier uses a bow and arrows. These weapons, and swords, were the kinds they preferred. Maces, lances, spears and daggers were also used.

FINE WEAPONRY

This Mughal dagger handle is inlaid with gold and jewels. Weapons were often crafted from the finest materials.

A Mughal warrior wore a plumed helmet to protect his head in battle.

4 Paint the entire helmet with two coats of gold paint, using a medium-sized paintbrush. Allow the paint to dry completely between coats.

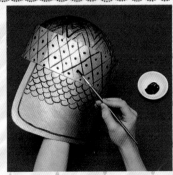

5 Add detail with black paint and a fine paintbrush. You could use a Mughal pattern like the one shown here, or design your own.

6 Cut narrow slits 5 mm apart in the black card. Leave 5 cm uncut at the bottom of the card. Cover this patch with glue and roll the card up tightly.

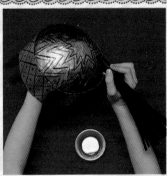

7 When the glue is dry, fix the plume to the top of your helmet with glue, or you can cut a small hole in the helmet and push the plume through.

Transport and Travel

T RAVEL IN INDIA hardly changed from the beginning of the country's history until the middle of the 1800s, and journeys were a great deal longer and harder than they are today. Despite the difficulties, people had many reasons to travel and did so quite a lot. They moved from place to place to trade, to go on pilgrimages, or in times of trouble, such as during wars or famines.

Most people travelled on foot, and used elephants, pack-oxen, horses and camels to carry their goods. Wealthier people had servants to carry loads, too. By the time of King Ashoka, around 250BC, there was a system of paths crossing plains, mountains, rivers and other geographical features. These paths had to weave around difficult or inaccessible terrain. During the monsoon, they became very muddy and sometimes were even washed away.

To overcome some of these transport problems, people used the rivers instead. This happened mainly in northern India, as the rivers in southern India were too rocky. Other people travelled up and down the coasts. For well over 2,000 years, Indians have been very inventive and made many kinds of rafts, floats and sailing vessels.

USING THE RIVERS
Boats like this one were used to travel along rivers in the north of India, such as the Ganges. The boats were steered by a large oar, instead of a rudder. Boats were particularly important for people who were traders. Ocean sailing was not a skill that was heavily developed in India.

TRAVEL BY BULLOCK CART
Carts drawn by bullocks or cows were the most common way of transporting humans and heavy loads over long distances, particularly in the countryside. Wheeled carts have been used for nearly 5,000 years, since the time of the Indus Valley civilization.

BALANCING A LOAD

A pair of women from Rajasthan, in northern India, carry brass pots stacked one on top of the other. They are carrying water from a village well. The pots sit on cloth rings which protect the crest of the head and provide a neat cavity to secure the bottom of the pot. Bearing loads in India long ago, as today, was typically done by balancing heavy objects on the shoulders or head. This made it much easier to carry the weights because the load was spread evenly on top of the body.

MONSOON RIVER FLOOD

Mughal forces struggle to ford a stream that has become swollen by the heavy monsoon (wet season) rains. The monsoon season in India made travel difficult. Because of this, Buddhist monks would wander in the hot dry season and settle in monasteries during the rainy season.

TRAVELLING BY CHAIR

Trumpeters announce the arrival of a Mughal prince and his wife. The royal couple are travelling in an elaborate chair known as a palanquin. Important people often travelled in these chairs, which were carried on the shoulders of slaves or servants.

THE ADAPTABLE CAMEL

Camels were used for transport in hot, dry regions, especially in the deserts of Rajasthan and the hills of north-western India. Camels are very well adapted to extremely hot and dry conditions and are able to travel for long periods without water.

Food and Drink

PEOPLE'S STAPLE (BASIC) FOOD depended on what they could grow. In the wetter areas of eastern, western, southern and central India, rice was the staple diet. In the drier areas of the north and north-west, people grew wheat and made it into different kinds of breads.

Apart from these staple foods, people's diets depended on their religion. Buddhists thought that killing animals was wrong, so they were vegetarians. Most Hindus, particularly the upper castes, became vegetarian too. Because they believed the cow was holy, eating beef became taboo (forbidden). When Islam arrived, it brought with it a new set of rules. Muslims are forbidden to eat pork, although they do eat other meat.

The Indians used a lot of spices in cooking, in order to add flavour and to disguise the taste of rotten meat. Ginger, garlic, turmeric, cinnamon and cumin were used from early times. Chillis were only introduced from the Americas after the 1500s.

CELESTIAL FRUITS
A heavenly damsel offers fruits in this stucco painting from Sri Lanka. From earliest times, Indians ate with their hands rather than with implements. Even so, there were rules to be followed. Generally, they could only eat with the right hand, taking care to use just their fingers.

EVENING DELIGHTS
A princess enjoys an evening party in the garden. She listens to music by candlelight, and is served drinks, sweets and other foods.

MAKE A CHICKPEA CURRY

You will need: knife, small onion, 30ml vegetable oil, wok or frying pan, wooden spoon, 4cm piece fresh ginger root, 2 cloves garlic, ¼tsp turmeric, 450g tomatoes, 225g cooked chickpeas, salt and pepper, 2tbsp finely chopped fresh coriander, plus coriander leaves to garnish, 2tsp garam masala, a lime.

1 Chop the onion finely. Heat the vegetable oil in a wok. Fry the onion in the oil for two to three minutes, until it is soft. Ask an adult to help you.

2 Chop the ginger finely and add to the pan. Chop the garlic cloves and add them, along with the turmeric. Cook gently for another half a minute.

A RICH BANQUET

Babur, the founder of the Mughal Empire in India, enjoys a banquet of exotic fruits. Under the Mughals, a cuisine known as Mughlai developed. It became famous for its rich and sophisticated flavours.

turmeric

black mustard seeds

cardamom

THREE ESSENTIAL SPICES

Turmeric is ground from a root to give food an earthy flavour and yellow colour. Black mustard seed has a smoky, bitter taste. Cardamom – a favourite in northern India – gives a musky, sugary flavour suitable for both sweet and savoury dishes.

LEAF PLATE

In south India, banana leaves were (and are still) used as plates for serving and eating food. South Indian food uses more coconut than the north, and rice-flour is used in several dishes.

DAILY BREAD

Indians eat a variety of baked, griddled or fried breads, such as these parathas. In much of northern and western India, the staple food is wheat, served in the form of unleavened (flat) breads.

Chickpeas are a popular ingredient in Indian cooking. They have been grown in India for thousands of years.

3 Peel the tomatoes, cut them in half and remove the seeds. Then chop them roughly and add them to the onion, garlic and spice mixture.

4 Add the chickpeas. Bring the mixture to the boil, then simmer gently for 10-15 minutes, until the tomatoes have reduced to a thick paste.

5 Taste the curry and then add salt and pepper as seasoning, if it is needed. The curry should taste spicy, but not so hot that it burns your mouth.

6 Add the chopped fresh coriander to the curry, along with the garam masala. Garnish with fresh coriander leaves and serve with slices of lime.

Festivals and Ceremonies

RITUAL CEREMONIES in India go back to Aryan times, when there were fire sacrifices throughout the year. After the growth of Buddhism, the Vedic priests developed a set of rites for important events such as marriages, caste initiations and funerals, which Hindus then used for centuries. Many temple festivals developed too. Some, such as Navaratri and Dasara, honoured fierce goddesses. Diwali was a festival of lights in honour of the goddess Lakshmi. In spring, people played games at the fertility festival of Holi.

Generally, Muslims had fewer and less elaborate rituals. Islamic festivals included Eid al-Fitr after Ramadan, the month of fasting, and Eid al-Adha to mark the sacrifice of the lamb by Abraham. Muslims also adopted some of the customs and practices of the Hindus.

HANDY HENNA
Using henna to mark the hands and feet was a common practice in India, and is still part of marriage ceremonies. Henna is a plant extract that is mixed into a paste with water and used to make patterns on the skin. The paste dyes the skin red.

A FESTIVAL OF FUN
The Vasantotsava (or modern Holi) was a festival of play and courtship which took place in the spring. Men and women threw coloured powders and squirted coloured waters over one another with syringes as they ran about the streets and gardens of the city.

TABLA DRUM

You will need: A2 sheet of thick card, measuring tape, scissors, pair of compasses, pencil, sticky tape, strips of newspaper, flour and water or wallpaper paste, bowl, fine sandpaper, calico fabric, bradawl, red-brown and blue paint, paintbrushes, darning needle, twine, PVA glue.

1 Cut out a card rectangle 55 x 21 cm. Cut slits along both long edges. Use the compasses to measure a card circle with a diameter of 16 cm. Cut out the circle.

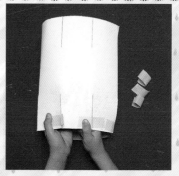

2 Roll the rectangle to form a cylinder with a diameter of 16 cm and tape. Tape the slits so that the drum tapers at each end. Tape the circle to one end.

3 Cover the cylinder with 3 layers of newspaper strips soaked in paste or flour and water. Leave it to dry between layers. Smooth the edges with sandpaper.

CEREMONY AROUND THE FIRE

A bride, with her face covered, is led into the marriage pandal (ceremonial awning), which is covered with mango and lime leaves to bring good luck. The bride will follow her husband around the fire. Hindu marriages still take place in the home around a sacrificial fire, and are administered by a Brahmin priest.

END OF FASTING

Muslim men take part in Eid festivities, in Bombay. Muslim men pray in public congregations at a mosque and give zakat (gifts) to the poor. Then they celebrate with friends and families.

PILGRIMAGE TO MECCA

Muslim pilgrims travel by camel to the city of Mecca, in Arabia (modern Saudi Arabia). Muslims must travel to Mecca once in their lifetime, if possible. The journey is called the haj.

DEATH OF AN IMAM

A passion play with music and drumming is enacted in the streets to celebrate Muharram, the first month of the Muslim calender. For Shia Muslims, the tenth day of Muharram is one of dramatic public mourning to commemorate the death of an imam (spiritual leader) named Husain.

The tabla drum was played at ceremonies and festivals.

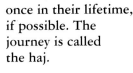

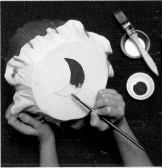

4 Cut a circle of calico with a diameter of 25 cm. Prick holes around the edge with a bradawl. Paint the tabla with two coats of red-brown paint.

5 Thread the needle with a long piece of twine and knot. Place the calico over the tabla's open end. Push the needle and thread through a hole in the calico.

6 Pass the twine across the base and through a hole on the other side of the fabric. Pull the twine tight, to stretch the fabric. Repeat all the way around the tabla.

7 Paint a pattern on to the calico. Then apply a coat of watered down PVA glue. This will help to shrink the calico and pull it tight over the tabla.

Clay and Terracotta Crafts

CLAY AND TERRACOTTA OBJECTS (known as ceramics) have played an important part in the study of Indian history, for two reasons. Making ceramics was one of India's earliest crafts. Many objects have been found at archaeological sites, dating as far back as 5000BC and the Indus Valley civilization. Also, because the objects were fired (baked), they have traces of carbon left on them, which has allowed archaeologists to date them quite accurately using a process called carbon dating.

In the Indus Valley, people made clay storage jars, terracotta seals and terracotta figurines of domestic animals. These clay animals may have been children's toys. People carried on using clay containers throughout India's history. Clay was particularly useful as it kept things cool in the hot climate. Artists also made terracotta figurines of gods and goddesses, though they gradually began to make stone and metal images as well.

RECORD IN CLAY
This terracotta cart found at Mohenjo-Daro is about 4,000 years old. Figurines like this have been found throughout the Indus valley. Although they were probably only toys, they give us information about the way people lived. For example, we can see that they were already using wheeled carts.

PAINTED POTTERY
A painted grey dish made on the Gangetic plains between 1000 and 500BC. Similar pottery was made across the region, which shows that people had contact with each other and shared the same technology.

SIMILAR STYLES
Black and red painted pottery has been found at sites dating from the Indus Valley civilization, and at later sites dating from around 500BC. It is found right across the Indian subcontinent.

MAKE A WATER POT
You will need: inflated balloon, large bowl, strips of newspaper, flour and water or wallpaper paste, scissors, fine sandpaper, strip of corrugated cardboard, sticky tape, terracotta and black paint, paintbrushes, pencil, PVA glue.

1 Cover the balloon with 4 layers of newspaper soaked in paste. When dry, cut a slit in the papier mâché. Remove the balloon. Add more layers to give the pot a tapered top.

2 Roll the corrugated cardboard into a circle shape to fit on to the narrow end of the pot to form a base. Fix the base in place with sticky tape.

3 Cover the corrugated cardboard base with four layers of soaked newspaper. Leave to dry beween each layer. Smooth the edges with sandpaper.

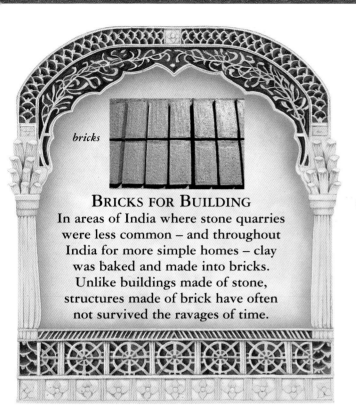

BRICKS FOR BUILDING

bricks

In areas of India where stone quarries were less common – and throughout India for more simple homes – clay was baked and made into bricks. Unlike buildings made of stone, structures made of brick have often not survived the ravages of time.

TERRACOTTA GODDESS

A female terracotta figure found in Mathura, Uttar Pradesh. It may be an image of a mother goddess. Many terracotta images were made during the Mauryan period (400–200BC) and immediately afterwards. They were cheaper versions of the stone sculptures that were built at the imperial court.

THROWING A POT

A village potter shapes a clay vessel as it spins on his potter's wheel. Pottery was an important part of the ancient urban and village economies and is still practised in India today. Clay used for making pottery is available in most parts of the land.

Clay water pots that are 4,000 years old have been found in the Indus Valley. People carried the pots on their heads.

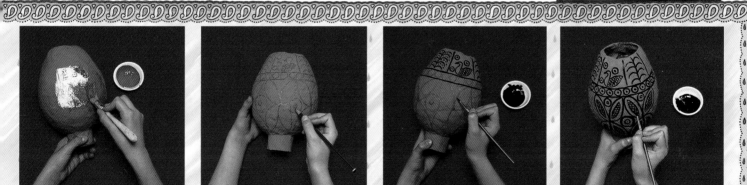

4 When it is dry, paint the water pot with two coats of terracotta paint, to make it look as though it is made of terracotta. Leave to dry between coats.

5 Draw some patterns on the water pot with a pencil. Copy the ancient Indian pattern shown here, or create your own individual design.

6 Carefully paint your designs using black paint and a fine paintbrush. Keep the edges of your lines neat and clean. Leave to dry.

7 Add final details, again using a fine paintbrush. When the paint is dry, seal the surface of the water pot with a coat of watered down PVA glue.

CLAY AND TERRACOTTA CRAFTS 127

THE CHINESE EMPIRE

Between the ancient civilizations of Europe and China lay vast distances, and the world's most impenetrable mountains and deserts. The Chinese civilization developed in isolation. It was amazingly inventive, introducing fine ceramics, silk, gunpowder and paper centuries before these skills were mastered in the West.

PHILIP STEELE

CONSULTANT: JESSIE LIM

An Ancient Civilization

IMAGINE YOU COULD travel back in time 5,000 years and visit the lands of the Far East. In northern China you would come across smoky settlements of small thatched huts. You might see villagers fishing in rivers, sowing millet or baking pottery. From these small beginnings, China developed into an amazing civilization. Its towns grew into huge cities, with palaces and temples. Many Chinese became great writers, thinkers, artists, builders and inventors. China was first united under the rule of a single emperor in 221BC, and continued to be ruled by emperors until 1912.

China today is a modern country. Its ancient past has to be pieced together by archaeologists and historians. They dig up ancient tombs and settlements, and study textiles, ancient books and pottery. Their job is made easier because historical records were kept. These provide much information about the long history of Chinese civilization.

REST IN PEACE
A demon is trodden into defeat by a guardian spirit. Statues like this were commonly put in tombs to protect the dead against evil spirits.

ALL THE EMPEROR'S MEN
A vast model army marches again. It was dug up by archaeologists in 1974, and is now on display near Xian. The lifesize figures are made of terracotta (baked clay). They were buried in 210BC near the tomb of Qin Shi Huangdi, the first emperor of all China. He believed that they would protect him from evil spirits after he died.

TIMELINE 7000BC–110BC

Prehistoric remains of human ancestors dating back to 600,000BC have been found in China's Shaanxi province. The beginnings of Chinese civilization may be seen in the farming villages of the late Stone Age (8000BC–2500BC). As organized states grew up, the Chinese became skilled at warfare, working metals and making elaborate pottery and fine silk.

*c.*7000BC Bands of hunters and fishers roam freely around the river valleys of China. They use simple stone tools and weapons.

Banpo hut

*c.*3200BC Farming villages such as Banpo produce pottery in kilns. This way of life is called the Yangshao culture.

*c.*2100BC The start of a legendary 500-year period of rule, known as the XIA DYNASTY.

*c.*2000BC Black pottery is made by the people of the so-called Longshan culture.

Shang bronze vessel

*c.*1600BC Beginning of the SHANG DYNASTY. Bronze worked and silk produced. The first picture-writing is used (on bones for telling fortunes).

1122BC Zhou ruler Wu defeats Shang emperor. Wu becomes emperor of the WESTERN ZHOU DYNASTY.

Zhou spearheads

7000BC   2100BC   1600BC

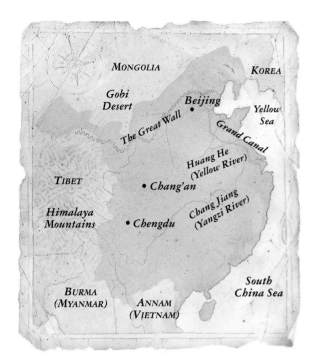

A HEAVENLY HALL

The Hall of Prayer for Good Harvests *(shown right)* is part of Tiantan, the Temple of Heavenly Peace in Beijing. It was originally built in 1420, but had to be rebuilt in the 1890s after it was destroyed by lightning. Buildings like these tell us about traditional technology and design, as well as about Chinese religious beliefs.

THE HAN EMPIRE (206BC–AD220)

China grew rapidly during the Han dynasty. By AD2 it had expanded to take in North Korea, the southeast coast, the southwest as far as Vietnam and large areas of Central Asia. Northern borders were defended by the Great Wall, which was extended during Han rule.

THE JADE PRINCE

In 1968, Chinese archaeologists excavated the tomb of Prince Liu Sheng. His remains were encased in a jade suit when he died in about 100BC. Over 2,400 pieces of this precious stone were joined with gold wire. It was believed that jade would preserve the body.

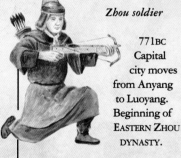

Zhou soldier

771BC Capital city moves from Anyang to Luoyang. Beginning of EASTERN ZHOU DYNASTY.

*c.*604BC Birth of the legendary Laozi, founder of Daoism.

551BC Teacher and philosopher Kong Fuzi (Confucius) born.

513BC Iron-working develops.

453BC Break-up of central rule. Small states fight each other for 200 years. Work begins on Grand Canal and Great Wall.

221BC China unites as a centralized empire under Zheng (Qin Shi Huangdi). Great Wall is extended.

213BC Qin Shi Huangdi burns all books that are not "practical".

Chinese writing

210BC Death of Qin Shi Huangdi. Terracotta army guards his tomb, near Chang'an (modern Xian).

206BC QIN DYNASTY overthrown. Beginnings of HAN DYNASTY as Xiang Yu and Liu Bang fight for control of the Han kingdom.

202BC The WESTERN HAN DYNASTY formally begins. It is led by the former official Liu Bang, who becomes emperor Gaozu.

200BC Chang'an becomes the capital city of the Chinese empire.

terracotta warrior and horse

112BC Trade with the peoples of Western Asia and Europe begins to flourish along the Silk Road.

780BC   550BC   210BC   140BC   110BC

The Middle Kingdom

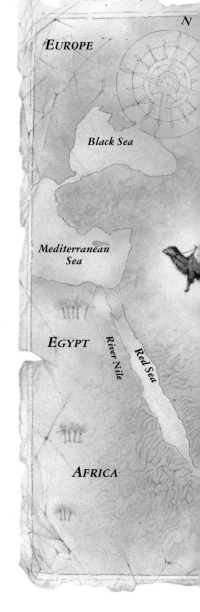

CHINA IS A VAST COUNTRY, about the size of Europe. Its fertile plains and river valleys are ringed by many deserts, mountains and oceans. The ancient Chinese named their land Zhongguo, the Middle Kingdom, and believed that it was at the centre of the civilized world. Most Chinese belong to a people called the Han, but the country is also inhabited by 50 or more different peoples, some of whom have played an important part in Chinese history. These groups include the Hui, Zhuang, Dai, Yao, Miao, Tibetans, Manchus and Mongols.

The very first Chinese civilizations grew up around the Huang He (Yellow River), where the fertile soil supported farming villages and then towns and cities. These became the centres of rival kingdoms. Between 1700BC and 256BC Chinese rule spread southwards to the Chang Jiang (Yangzi River), the great river of Central China. All of eastern China was united within a single empire for the first time during Qin rule (221–206BC).

The rulers of the Han dynasty (206BC–AD220) then expanded the empire southwards as far as Vietnam. The Chinese empire was now even larger than the Roman empire, dominating Central and Southeast Asia. The Mongols, from lands to the north of China, ruled the empire from 1279 to 1368. They were succeeded by the Ming dynasty, which was in turn overthown by the Manchu in 1644. In later centuries, China became inward-looking and unable to resist interference from Europe. The empire finally collapsed, with China declaring itself a republic in 1912.

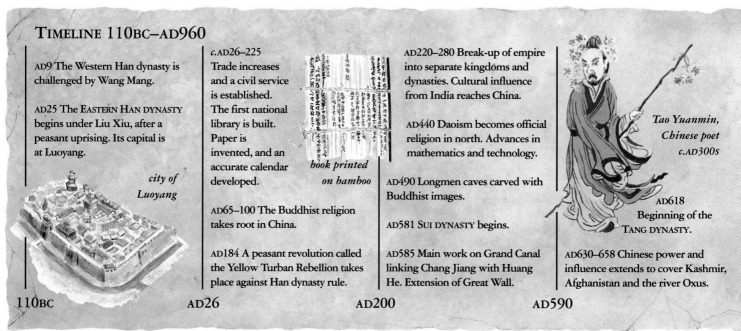

TIMELINE 110BC–AD960

AD9 The Western Han dynasty is challenged by Wang Mang.

AD25 The EASTERN HAN DYNASTY begins under Liu Xiu, after a peasant uprising. Its capital is at Luoyang.

city of Luoyang

c.AD26–225 Trade increases and a civil service is established. The first national library is built. Paper is invented, and an accurate calendar developed.

book printed on bamboo

AD65–100 The Buddhist religion takes root in China.

AD184 A peasant revolution called the Yellow Turban Rebellion takes place against Han dynasty rule.

AD220–280 Break-up of empire into separate kingdoms and dynasties. Cultural influence from India reaches China.

AD440 Daoism becomes official religion in north. Advances in mathematics and technology.

AD490 Longmen caves carved with Buddhist images.

AD581 SUI DYNASTY begins.

AD585 Main work on Grand Canal linking Chang Jiang with Huang He. Extension of Great Wall.

Tao Yuanmin, Chinese poet c.AD300s

AD618 Beginning of the TANG DYNASTY.

AD630–658 Chinese power and influence extends to cover Kashmir, Afghanistan and the river Oxus.

110BC   AD26   AD200   AD590

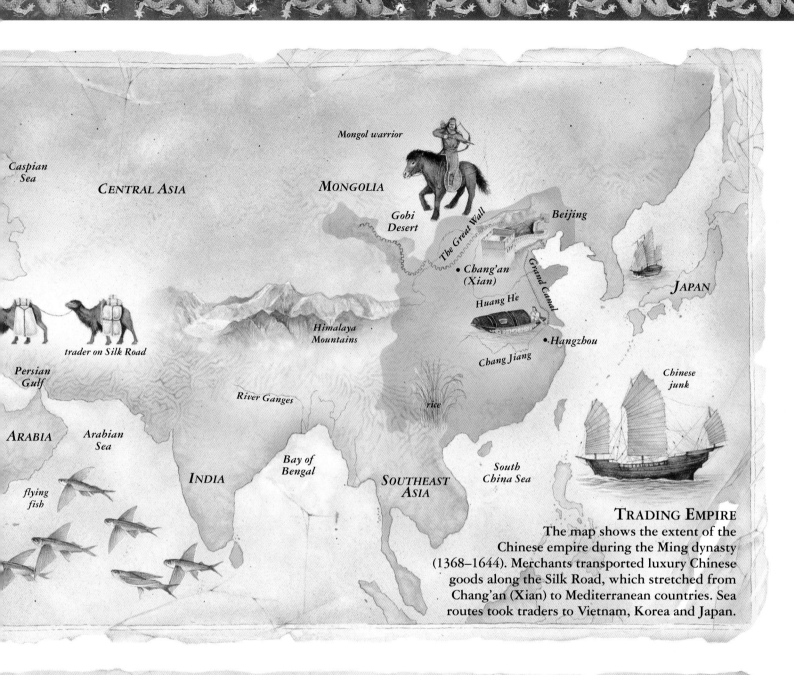

Caspian
Sea

CENTRAL ASIA

MONGOLIA

Mongol warrior

Gobi
Desert

Beijing

The Great Wall

Chang'an
(Xian)

Huang He

Grand Canal

JAPAN

trader on Silk Road

Persian
Gulf

Himalaya
Mountains

Hangzhou

Chang Jiang

Chinese
junk

River Ganges

rice

ARABIA

Arabian
Sea

Bay of
Bengal

SOUTHEAST
ASIA

South
China Sea

flying
fish

INDIA

TRADING EMPIRE

The map shows the extent of the
Chinese empire during the Ming dynasty
(1368–1644). Merchants transported luxury Chinese
goods along the Silk Road, which stretched from
Chang'an (Xian) to Mediterranean countries. Sea
routes took traders to Vietnam, Korea and Japan.

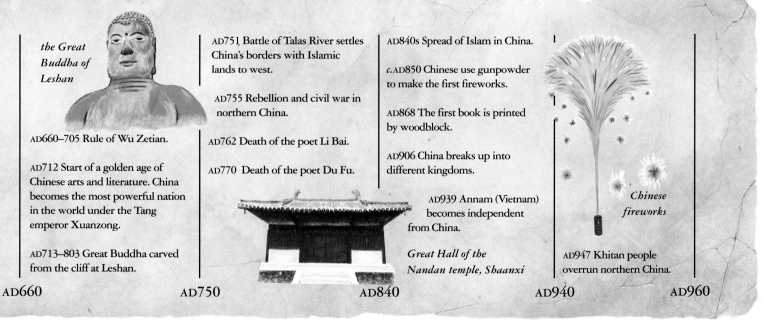

*the Great
Buddha of
Leshan*

AD660–705 Rule of Wu Zetian.

AD712 Start of a golden age of
Chinese arts and literature. China
becomes the most powerful nation
in the world under the Tang
emperor Xuanzong.

AD713–803 Great Buddha carved
from the cliff at Leshan.

AD751 Battle of Talas River settles
China's borders with Islamic
lands to west.

AD755 Rebellion and civil war in
northern China.

AD762 Death of the poet Li Bai.

AD770 Death of the poet Du Fu.

*Great Hall of the
Nandan temple, Shaanxi*

AD840s Spread of Islam in China.

c.AD850 Chinese use gunpowder
to make the first fireworks.

AD868 The first book is printed
by woodblock.

AD906 China breaks up into
different kingdoms.

AD939 Annam (Vietnam)
becomes independent
from China.

*Chinese
fireworks*

AD947 Khitan people
overrun northern China.

AD660   AD750   AD840   AD940   AD960

Makers of History

GREAT EMPIRES ARE made by ordinary people as much as by their rulers. The Chinese empire could not have been built without the millions of peasants who planted crops, built defensive walls and dug canals. The names of these people are largely forgotten, except for those who led uprisings and revolts against their rulers. The inventors, thinkers, artists, poets and writers of imperial China are better known. They had a great effect on the society they lived in, and left behind ideas, works of art and inventions that still influence people today.

The royal court was made up of thousands of officials, artists, craftsmen and servants. Some had great political power. China's rulers came from many different backgrounds and peoples.

Many emperors were ruthless former warlords who were hungry for power. Others are remembered as scholars or artists. Some women also achieved great political influence, openly or from behind the scenes.

LAOZI (born *c*.604BC)
The legendary Laozi is said to have been a scholar who worked as a court librarian. It is thought that he wrote the book known as the *Daodejing*. He believed people should live in harmony with nature, and his ideas later formed the basis of Daoism.

KONG FUZI (551–479BC)
Kong Fuzi is better known in the West by the Latin version of his name, Confucius. He was a public official who became an influential teacher and thinker. His views on family life, society, and the treatment of others greatly influenced later generations.

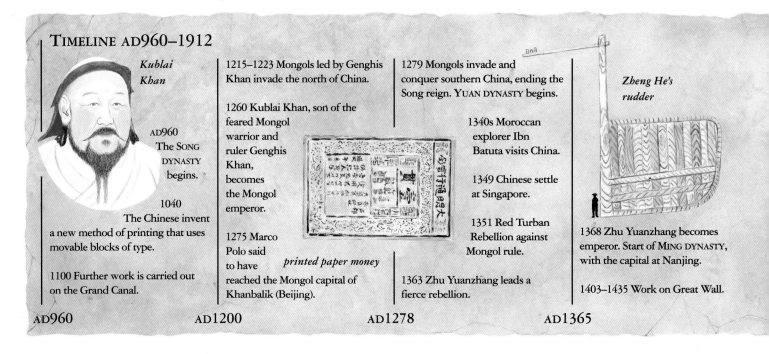

TIMELINE AD960–1912

Kublai Khan

AD960 The SONG DYNASTY begins.

1040 The Chinese invent a new method of printing that uses movable blocks of type.

1100 Further work is carried out on the Grand Canal.

1215–1223 Mongols led by Genghis Khan invade the north of China.

1260 Kublai Khan, son of the feared Mongol warrior and ruler Genghis Khan, becomes the Mongol emperor.

1275 Marco Polo said to have reached the Mongol capital of Khanbalik (Beijing).

printed paper money

1279 Mongols invade and conquer southern China, ending the Song reign. YUAN DYNASTY begins.

1340s Moroccan explorer Ibn Batuta visits China.

1349 Chinese settle at Singapore.

1351 Red Turban Rebellion against Mongol rule.

1363 Zhu Yuanzhang leads a fierce rebellion.

Zheng He's rudder

1368 Zhu Yuanzhang becomes emperor. Start of MING DYNASTY, with the capital at Nanjing.

1403–1435 Work on Great Wall.

AD960   AD1200   AD1278   AD1365

QIN SHI HUANGDI (256–210BC)

Scholars plead for their lives before the first emperor. Zheng came to the throne of a state called Qin at the age of nine. He went on to rule all China and was given his full title, meaning First Emperor of Qin. His brutal methods included burying his opponents alive.

HAN GAOZU (256–195BC)

In the Qin dynasty (221–206BC) Liu Bang was a minor public official in charge of a relay station for royal messengers. He watched as the centralized Qin empire fell apart. In 206BC he declared himself ruler of the Han kingdom. In 202BC he defeated his opponent, Xiang Yu, and founded the Han dynasty. As emperor Gaozu, he tried to unite China without using Qin's harsh methods.

EMPRESS WU ZETIAN (AD624–705)

The emperor Tang Gaozong enraged officials when he replaced his legal wife with Wu, his concubine (secondary wife). After the emperor suffered a stroke in AD660, Wu took control of the country. In AD690 she became the only woman in history to declare herself empress of China.

KUBLAI KHAN (AD1214–1294)

The Venetian explorer Marco Polo visits emperor Kublai Khan at Khanbalik (Beijing). Kublai Khan was a Mongol who conquered northern, and later southern, China.

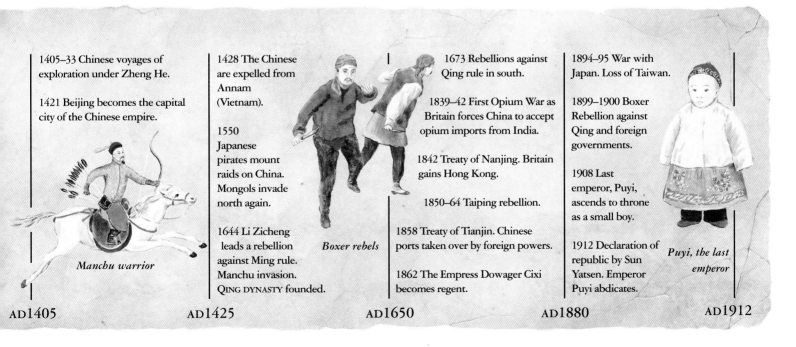

1405–33 Chinese voyages of exploration under Zheng He.

1421 Beijing becomes the capital city of the Chinese empire.

Manchu warrior

1428 The Chinese are expelled from Annam (Vietnam).

1550 Japanese pirates mount raids on China. Mongols invade north again.

1644 Li Zicheng leads a rebellion against Ming rule. Manchu invasion. QING DYNASTY founded.

Boxer rebels

1673 Rebellions against Qing rule in south.

1839–42 First Opium War as Britain forces China to accept opium imports from India.

1842 Treaty of Nanjing. Britain gains Hong Kong.

1850–64 Taiping rebellion.

1858 Treaty of Tianjin. Chinese ports taken over by foreign powers.

1862 The Empress Dowager Cixi becomes regent.

1894–95 War with Japan. Loss of Taiwan.

1899–1900 Boxer Rebellion against Qing and foreign governments.

1908 Last emperor, Puyi, ascends to throne as a small boy.

1912 Declaration of republic by Sun Yatsen. Emperor Puyi abdicates.

Puyi, the last emperor

AD1405   AD1425   AD1650   AD1880   AD1912

The Sons of Heaven

THE FIRST CHINESE RULERS lived about 4,000 years ago. This early dynasty (period of rule) was known as the Xia. We know little about the Xia rulers, because this period of Chinese history has become mixed up with ancient myths and legends. Excavations have told us more about the Shang dynasty rulers of over 3,000 years ago, who were waited on by slaves and had fabulous treasures.

During the next period of rule, the Zhou dynasty, an idea grew up that the Chinese rulers were Sons of Heaven, placed on the throne by the will of the gods. After China became a powerful, united empire in 221BC, this idea helped keep the emperors in power. Rule of the empire was passed down from father to son. Anyone who seized the throne by force had to show that the overthrown ruler had offended the gods. Earthquakes and natural disasters were often taken as signs of the gods' displeasure.

Chinese emperors were among the most powerful rulers in history. Emperors of China's last dynasty, the Qing (1644–1912), lived in luxurious palaces that were cut off from the world. When they travelled through the streets, the common people had to stay indoors.

WHERE EMPERORS PRAYED
These beautifully decorated pillars can be seen inside the Hall of Prayer for Good Harvests at Tiantan in Beijing. An emperor was a religious leader as well as a political ruler, and would arrive here in a great procession each New Year. The evening would be spent praying to the gods for a plentiful harvest in the coming year.

TO THE HOLY MOUNTAIN
This stele (inscribed stone) is located on the summit of China's holiest mountain, Taishan, in Shandong province. To the ancient Chinese, Taishan was the home of the gods. For over 2,000 years the emperors climbed the carved steps to the temple to offer prayers.

IN THE FORBIDDEN CITY
The vast Imperial Palace in Beijing is best described as "a city within a city". It was built between 1407 and 1420 by hundreds of thousands of labourers under the command of Emperor Yongle. Behind its high, red walls and moats were 800 beautiful halls and temples, set amongst gardens, courtyards and bridges. No fewer than 24 emperors lived here in incredible luxury, set apart from their subjects. The Imperial Palace was also known as the Forbidden City, as ordinary Chinese people were not even allowed to approach its gates.

"WE POSSESS ALL THINGS"
This was the message sent from Emperor Qianlong to the British King George III in 1793. Here the emperor is being presented with a gift of fine horses from the Kyrgyz people of Central Asia. By the late 1800s, Chinese rule took in Mongolia, Tibet and Central Asia. All kinds of fabulous gifts were sent to the emperor from every corner of the empire, as everyone wanted to win his favour.

RITUALS AND CEREMONIES
During the Qing dynasty, an emperor's duties included many long ceremonies and official receptions. Here in Beijing's Forbidden City, a long carpet leads to the ruler's throne. Officials in silk robes line the steps and terraces, holding their banners and ceremonial umbrellas high. Courtiers kneel and bow before the emperor. Behaviour at the royal court was set out in the greatest detail. Rules decreed which kind of clothes could be worn and in which colours.

CARRIED BY HAND
The first Chinese emperor, Qin Shi Huangdi, is carried to a monastery high in the mountains in the 200s BC. He rides in a litter (a type of chair) that is carried on his servants' shoulders. Emperors always travelled with a large following of guards and courtiers.

Religions and Beliefs

"THREE TEACHINGS FLOW INTO ONE" is an old saying in China. The three teachings are Daoism, Confucianism and Buddhism. In China they gradually mingled together over the ages.

The first Chinese peoples believed in various gods and goddesses of nature, in spirits and demons. The spirit of nature and the flow of life inspired the writings which are said to be the work of Laozi (born *c.*604BC). His ideas formed the basis of the Daoist religion. The teachings of Kong Fuzi (Confucius) come from the same period of history but they stress the importance of social order and respect for ancestors as a source of happiness. At this time another great religious teacher, the Buddha, was preaching in India. Within 500 years Buddhist teachings had reached China, and by the Tang dynasty (AD618–906) Buddhism was the most popular religion. Islam arrived at this time and won followers in the northwest. Christianity also came into China from Persia, but few Chinese were converted to this religion until the 1900s.

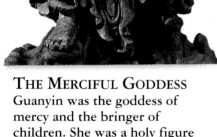

THE MERCIFUL GODDESS
Guanyin was the goddess of mercy and the bringer of children. She was a holy figure for all Chinese Buddhists.

DAOISM – A RELIGION OF HARMONY
A young boy is taught the Daoist belief in the harmony of nature. Daoists believe that the natural world is in a state of balance between two forces – yin and yang. Yin is dark, cool and feminine, while yang is light, hot and masculine. The two forces are combined in the black and white symbol on the scroll.

PEACE THROUGH SOCIAL ORDER
Kong Fuzi (Confucius) looks out on to an ordered world. He taught that the well-being of society depends on duty and respect. Children should obey their parents and wives should obey their husbands. The people should obey their rulers, and rulers should respect the gods. All of the emperors followed the teachings of Confucianism.

ISLAM IN CHINA

This is part of the Great Mosque in Xian (ancient Chang'an), built in the Chinese style. The mosque was founded in AD742, but most of the buildings in use today date from the Ming dynasty (1368–1644). Islam first took root in China in about AD700. Moslem traders from Central Asia brought with them the Koran, the holy book of Islam. It teaches that there is only one god, Allah, and that Muhammad is his prophet.

FREEDOM FROM DESIRE

Chinese monks carved huge statues of the Buddha from rock. Some can be seen at the Mogao caves near Dunhuang, where temples were built as early as AD366. The Buddha taught that suffering is caused by our love of material things. Buddhists believe that we are born over and over again until we learn to conquer this desire.

TEMPLE GUARDIANS

Gilded statues of Buddhist saints ward off evil spirits at Puningsi, the Temple of Universal Peace, near Chengde. The temple was built in 1755 in the Tibetan style. It is famed for its Mahayana Hall, a tower roofed in gilded bronze.

Chinese Society

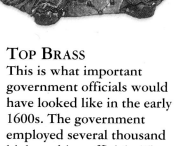

THE RIVER VALLEYS AND COASTS of China have always been among the most crowded places on Earth. Confucius, with his love of social order, had taught that this vast society could be divided into four main groups. At the top were the nobles, the scholars and the landowners. Next came the farmers, including even the poorest peasants. These people were valued because they worked for the good of the whole nation, providing the vast amounts of food necessary to feed an ever-increasing population. In third place were skilled workers and craftsmen. In the lowest place of all were the merchants, because Confucius believed they worked for their own profit rather than for the good of the people as a whole. However, the way in which Chinese society rewarded these groups in practice did not fit the theory at all. Merchants ended up becoming the richest citizens, lending money to the upper classes. In contrast, the highly valued peasants often led a wretched life, losing their homes to floods and earthquakes or starving in years of famine.

TOP BRASS
This is what important government officials would have looked like in the early 1600s. The government employed several thousand high-ranking officials. The civil service was regarded as the most honourable and best rewarded profession. The entry examinations were open to all men. Even the poor could rise to ruling class if they passed the examinations.

THE IDEAL ORDER?
A government official tours the fields, where respectful peasants are happily at work. This painting shows an idealized view of the society proposed by Confucius. The district prospers and flourishes because everybody knows their place in society. The reality was very different – while Chinese officials led comfortable lives, most people were very poor and suffered great hardship. They toiled in the fields for little reward. Officials provided aid for the victims of famine or flood, but they never tackled the injustice of the social order. Peasant uprisings were common through much of Chinese history.

WORKING IN THE CLAYPITS

The manufacture of pottery was one of imperial China's most important industries. There were state-owned factories as well as many smaller private workshops. The industry employed some very highly skilled workers, and also thousands of unskilled labourers whose job was to dig out the precious clay. They had to work very hard for little pay. Sometimes there were serious riots to demand better working conditions.

DRAGON-BACKBONE MACHINE

Peasants enlist the aid of machinery to help work the rice fields. The life of a peasant was mostly made up of back-breaking toil. The relentless work was made slightly easier by some clever, labour-saving inventions. The square-pallet chain pump (*shown above*) was invented in about AD100. It was known as the dragon-backbone machine and was used to raise water to the flooded terraces where rice was grown. Men and women worked from dawn to dusk to supply food for the population.

LIFE BEHIND A DESK

Country magistrates try to remember the works of Confucius during a tough public examination. A pass would provide them with a path to wealth and social success. A failure would mean disgrace. The Chinese civil service was founded in about 900BC. This painting dates from the Qing dynasty (1644–1912). There were exams for all ranks of officials and they were very hard. The classic writings had to be remembered by heart. Not surprisingly, candidates sometimes cheated!

TOKENS OF WEALTH

Merchants may have had low social status, but they had riches beyond the dreams of peasants. They amassed wealth through money-lending and by exporting luxury goods, such as silk, spices and tea. The influence of the merchant class is reflected in the first bronze Chinese coins (*c.*250BC), which were shaped to look like knives, hoes and spades. Merchants commonly traded or bartered in these tools.

knife

hoe

Towns and Cities

Cities grew up in northern China during the Shang dynasty (*c.*1600–1122BC). Zhengzhou was one of the first capitals, built in about 1600BC. Its city wall was seven kilometres long, but the city spilled out far beyond this border. Chinese cities increased in size over the centuries, and by the AD1500s the city of Beijing was the biggest in the world. Some great cities became centres of government, while smaller settlements served as market towns or manufacturing centres.

A typical Chinese city was surrounded by a wide moat and a high wall of packed earth. It was entered through a massive gatehouse set into the wall. The streets were filled with carts, beggars, craft workshops and street markets. Most people lived in small districts called wards that were closed off at night by locked gates. Temples and monasteries were a common sight, but royal palaces and the homes of rich families were hidden by high walls.

The Sound of Bells
Bells were set up at temples and also on towers in the cities. They were struck at daybreak to mark the opening of the gates. Big drums were struck when they were closed at night.

Chinese Skyscrapers
A pagoda (*shown far left*) soars above the skyline of a town in imperial China. Pagodas were graceful towers up to 15 storeys high, with eaves projecting at each level. Buildings rather like these were first seen in India, where they often marked holy Buddhist sites. The Chinese perfected the design, and many people believed that building pagodas spread good fortune over the surrounding land. Sometimes they were used as libraries, where scholars would study Buddhist scriptures.

Make a Pagoda
You will need: thick card, ruler, pencil, scissors, glue and brush, masking tape, corrugated card, 3cm x 1.5cm diameter dowel, embroidery bobbin, half a barbecue stick, paint (pink, terracotta and cream), thick and thin paintbrushes, water pot.

35cm

Roof: *level 1* (35cm x 35cm)

30cm
Side: *level 1* (x4)
Doorway 4cm x 8cm
11.5cm

Spire sides (x4)
2.5cm
4.5cm
7cm

(NB The doorway is 4cm x 8cm for all levels)

Roof: *levels 2–7*

Level 2	32cm x 32cm
Level 3	29cm x 29cm
Level 4	26cm x 26cm
Level 5	23cm x 23cm
Level 6	20cm x 20cm
Level 7	17cm x 17cm

Side (x4): *levels 2–7*

Level 2	27cm x 11.5cm
Level 3	24cm x 11.5cm
Level 4	21cm x 11.5cm
Level 5	18cm x 11.5cm
Level 6	15cm x 11.5cm
Level 7	12cm x 11.5cm

Cut out roof, side and spire pieces from thick card.
Use the measurements shown above (pieces not to scale).

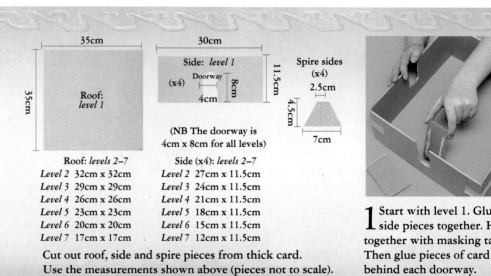

1 Start with level 1. Glue 4 side pieces together. Hold together with masking tape. Then glue pieces of card behind each doorway.

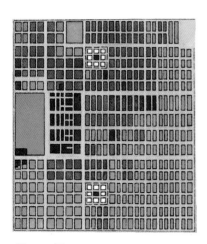

	Lower Class ward
	Middle Class ward
	Upper Class ward
	Government buildings
	Markets
	Offices
	Palace

CITY PLANNING

This grid shows the layout of Chang'an (Xian), the capital city of the empire during the Tang dynasty (AD618–906). The streets were grouped into small areas called wards. The design of many Chinese cities followed a similar pattern.

WESTERN INFLUENCE

The flags of Western nations fly in the great southern port of Guangzhou (Canton) in about 1810. Foreign architectural styles also began to appear in some Chinese cities at this time. In the early 1800s, powerful Western countries competed to take over Chinese trade and force their policies upon the emperor.

LIVING ON THE RIM

Cities around the edge of the empire were unlike those of typical Chinese towns. The mountain city of Lhasa is the capital of Tibet. It stretches out below its towering palace, the Potala. Tibet has had close political links with China since the AD600s. The country did remain independent for most of its history, but was invaded by China in the 1700s and again in 1950.

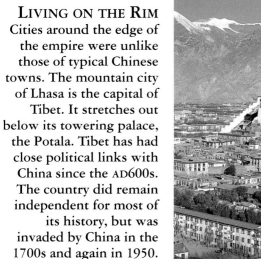

Pagodas were built in China as early as AD523. Some of the first ones were built by Chinese monks who had seen Buddhist holy temples in India. Extra storeys were sometimes added on over the centuries.

2 Glue level 1 roof on top of level 1 walls. Allow to dry. Centre level 2 sides on roof below. Glue down and hold with tape. Add level 2 roof.

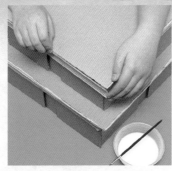

3 Cut four 3cm wide corrugated card strips for each roof. The lengths need to match the roof measurements. Glue to edges of roof and sides.

4 Assemble levels 3 to 7. Glue together spire pieces. Wedge dowel piece into the top. Stick barbecue stick on to bobbin. Then glue bobbin on to dowel.

5 Glue spire on to top level. Use a thick brush to paint the base colour. Paint details, such as terracotta for the roof tiles, with a thin brush.

Houses and Gardens

All buildings in Chinese cities were designed to be in harmony with each other and with nature. The direction they faced, their layout and their proportions were all matters of great spiritual importance. Even the number of steps leading up to the entrance of the house was considered to be significant. House design in imperial China varied over time and between regions. In the hot and rainy south, courtyards tended to be covered for shade and shelter. In the drier climate of the north, courtyards were mostly open to the elements. Poor people in the countryside lived in simple, thatched huts. These were made from timber frames covered in mud plaster. They were often noisy, draughty and overcrowded. In contrast, the spacious homes of the wealthy were large, peaceful and well constructed. Many had beautiful gardens, filled with peonies, bamboo and wisteria. Some of these gardens also contained orchards, ponds and pavilions.

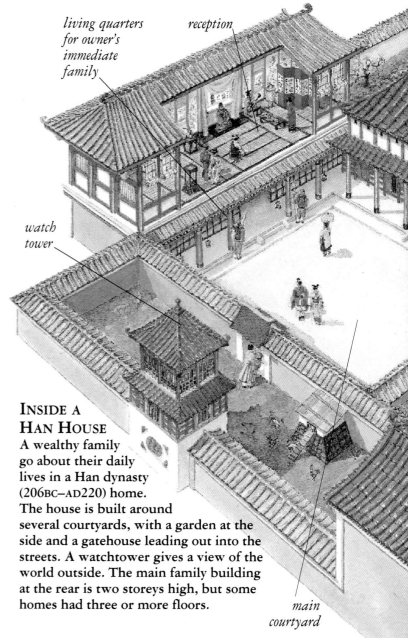

living quarters for owner's immediate family

reception

watch tower

main courtyard

INSIDE A HAN HOUSE
A wealthy family go about their daily lives in a Han dynasty (206BC–AD220) home. The house is built around several courtyards, with a garden at the side and a gatehouse leading out into the streets. A watchtower gives a view of the world outside. The main family building at the rear is two storeys high, but some homes had three or more floors.

MAKE A HOUSE
You will need: thick card, corrugated card, ruler, felt tip pen, scissors, glue and brush, 2.5cm x 0.5cm dowel (x2), masking tape, paint (white, grey, pink), thick and thin paintbrushes, water pot.

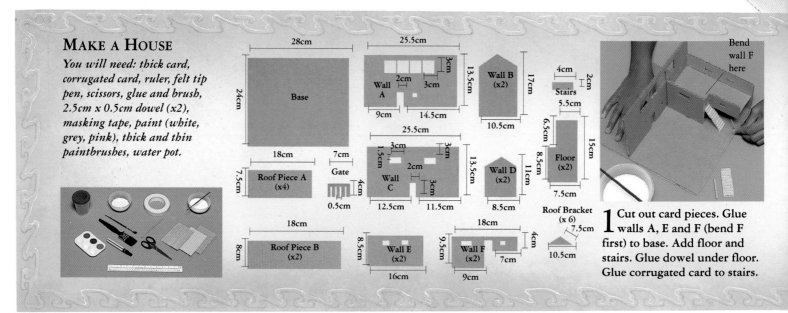

Base — 28cm × 24cm

Wall A — 25.5cm, 3cm, 2cm, 3cm, 9cm, 14.5cm, 13.5cm

Wall B (x2) — 17cm, 10.5cm

Stairs — 4cm, 2cm, 5.5cm, 6.5cm

Wall C — 25.5cm, 3cm, 1.5cm, 2cm, 3cm, 12.5cm, 11.5cm, 13.5cm

Wall D (x2) — 13.5cm, 8.5cm

Floor (x2) — 15cm, 7.5cm, 8.5cm, 11cm

Roof Piece A (x4) — 18cm, 7.5cm

Gate — 7cm, 4cm, 0.5cm

Roof Piece B (x2) — 18cm, 8cm

Wall E (x2) — 8.5cm, 16cm

Wall F (x2) — 18cm, 9.5cm, 4cm, 7cm, 9cm

Roof Bracket (x6) — 7.5cm, 10.5cm

Bend wall F here

1 Cut out card pieces. Glue walls A, E and F (bend F first) to base. Add floor and stairs. Glue dowel under floor. Glue corrugated card to stairs.

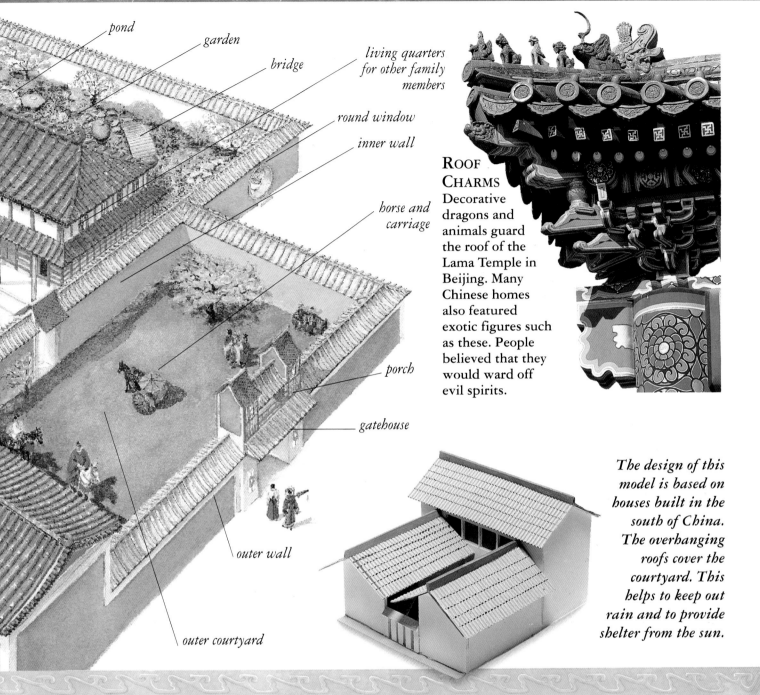

pond

garden

bridge

living quarters for other family members

round window

inner wall

horse and carriage

porch

gatehouse

outer wall

outer courtyard

ROOF CHARMS Decorative dragons and animals guard the roof of the Lama Temple in Beijing. Many Chinese homes also featured exotic figures such as these. People believed that they would ward off evil spirits.

The design of this model is based on houses built in the south of China. The overhanging roofs cover the courtyard. This helps to keep out rain and to provide shelter from the sun.

2 To assemble second side, repeat method described in step 1. If necessary, hold pieces together with masking tape while the glue dries.

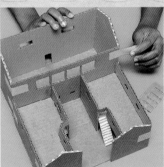

3 Glue B walls to the sides of the base, C wall to the back and D walls to the front. Hold with tape while glue dries. Glue gate between D walls.

4 Assemble A roofs (x2) and B roof (x1). Fix brackets underneath. Glue corrugated card (cut to same size as roof pieces) to top side of roofs.

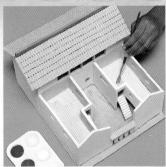

5 Fix a small piece of card over the gate to make a porch. Paint house, as shown. Use a thin brush to create a tile effect on the removable roofs.

Home Comforts

A LARGE HOME in imperial China would include many living rooms for the owner and his wife, their children, the grandparents, and other members of the extended family. There were several kitchens, servants' quarters, and reception rooms where guests would dine. A wealthy scholar's home would even contain its own private library.

Clay stoves provided heat in the cold northern winters. Windows were made of either stiff paper or hemp sacking instead of glass. Walls were tiled, or else decorated with beautiful silk hangings. They could be extended with carved screens. In the early days of the empire, there would be low tables, stools, urns and vases. People slept on low, heated platforms called *kang* in northern China, and the floors of homes would be covered with various mats, rugs and cushions.

Furniture making developed rapidly during the Tang dynasty (AD618–906). Skilled craftsmen began producing beautiful furniture without using nails. Bamboo was widely used in the south. Instead of sitting at floor level, people began to use chairs and high tables. Elaborate furniture was made for the imperial palaces, using rosewood or woods inlaid with ivory or mother-of-pearl. Most people had furniture that was cheaper and simpler in design, but no less beautiful.

BRINGER OF LIGHT
This beautiful lamp is made of gilded bronze, and supported by the figure of a maidservant. It was found in the tomb of Liu Sheng, the Jade Prince. The lamp dates from about 100BC. At that time, homes were lit by oil-lamps or lanterns made of paper, silk or horn.

BEAUTY IN THE HOME
A delicate porcelain plate from the early 1700s shows a young woman standing by a table, leaning on the back of a chair. The neatly arranged books, scrolls and furniture show the importance the Chinese placed on order and harmony in the home. Chairs and tables were put against the walls. There was no clutter or mess, and possessions were always neatly put away.

FURNITURE AND FITTINGS
Richly embroidered hangings and carved tables decorate the office of this Chinese magistrate (*c.* 1600). Wealthy homes and the offices of important people often featured such luxurious decorations and furnishings.

GARDENS OF TRANQUILITY

Chinese gardens offered peace and beauty amidst the hustle and bustle of the city. Bamboo leaves rustled in the wind. Lotus flowers floated gracefully on ponds. Wisteria, with its tumbling blue flowers, wound around the summer houses. There were scented roses, peonies and chrysanthemums. Soft fruits, such as peaches and lychees, were also grown.

lychee

peach

DECORATIVE SCREEN

Standing behind the carved chair is a spectacular folding screen, made in the 1800s. Exotic paintings of landscapes, animals and birds cover its surface, while a glossy lacquer makes it smooth, hard and strong. Many wealthy homes had richly decorated wooden screens, while poorer ones had simpler, carved ones. Screens were used to keep rooms cool in summer and warm in winter.

KEEPING COOL

This wine vessel was made over 3,000 years ago. It was used to store wine for rituals and ceremonies. The vessel was made of bronze, which probably helped to chill the wine. Cooling the wine in this way would improve its flavour.

IMPERIAL AIR CONDITIONING

This beautifully decorated casket was formerly used in the Imperial Summer Palace, near Beijing. Its function was to hold blocks of ice to keep the air cool in the hot season. Its surface is inlaid with gold and other valuable materials. The perforated cover features a gilded bronze dragon design. The casket is supported by legs made in the shape of two kneeling figures.

Family Life

KONG FUZI (CONFUCIUS) taught that just as the emperor was head of the state, the oldest man was head of the household and should be obeyed by his family. In reality, his wife ran the home and often controlled the daily lives of the other women in the household.

During the Han dynasty (206BC–AD220) noblewomen were kept apart from the outside world. They could only gaze at the streets from the watchtowers of their homes. It was not until the Song dynasty (AD960–1279) that they gained more freedom. In poor households women worked all day, spending long, tiring hours farming, cooking, sweeping and washing.

For the children of poorer families, education meant learning to do the work their parents did. This involved carrying goods to market, or helping with the threshing or planting. The children of wealthier parents had private tutors at home. Boys hoping to become scholars or civil servants learned to read and write Chinese characters. They also studied maths and the works of Kong Fuzi.

LESSONS FOR THE BOYS
A group of Chinese boys take their school lessons. In imperial China, boys generally received a more academic education than girls. Girls were mainly taught music, handicrafts, painting and social skills. Some girls were taught academic subjects, but they were not allowed to sit the civil service examinations.

FOOT BINDING
This foot looks elegant in its beautiful slipper, but it's a different story when the slipper is removed. Just when life was improving for Chinese women, the cruel new custom of footbinding was introduced. Dancers had bound their feet for some years in the belief that it made them look dainty. In the Song dynasty the custom spread to wealthy and noble families. Little girls of five or so had their feet bound up so tightly that they became terribly deformed.

CHINESE MARRIAGE
A wedding ceremony takes place in the late 1800s. In imperial China, weddings were arranged by the parents of the bride and groom, rather than by the couples themselves. It was expected that the couple would respect their parents' wishes, even if they didn't like each other!

TAKING IT EASY

A noblewoman living during the Qing dynasty relaxes on a garden terrace with her children (c.1840). She is very fortunate as she has little else to do but enjoy the pleasant surroundings of her home. In rich families like hers, servants did most of the hard work, such as cooking, cleaning and washing. Wealthy Chinese families kept many servants, who usually lived in quarters inside their employer's home. Servants accounted for a large number of the workforce in imperial China. During the Ming dynasty (1368–1644), some 9,000 maidservants were employed at the imperial palace in Beijing alone!

RESPECT AND HONOUR

Children in the 1100s bow respectfully to their parents. Confucius taught that people should value and honour their families, including their ancestors. He believed that this helped to create a more orderly and virtuous society.

THE EMPEROR AND HIS MANY WIVES

Sui dynasty emperor Yangdi (AD581–618) rides out with his many womenfolk. Like many emperors, Yangdi was surrounded by women. An emperor married one woman, who would then become his empress, but he would still enjoy the company of concubines (secondary wives).

Farming and Crops

EIGHT THOUSAND YEARS AGO most Chinese people were already living by farming. The best soil lay beside the great rivers in central and eastern China, where floods left behind rich, fertile mud. As today, wheat and millet were grown in the north. This region was mostly farmed by peasants with small plots of land. Rice was cultivated in the warm, wet south, where wealthy city-dwellers owned large estates. Pears and oranges were grown in orchards.

Tea, later to become one of China's most famous exports, was first cultivated about 1,700 years ago. Hemp was also grown for its fibres. During the 500s BC, cotton was introduced. Farmers raised pigs, ducks, chickens and geese, while oxen and water buffalo were used as labouring animals on the farm.

Most peasants used basic tools, such as stone hoes and wooden rakes. Ploughs with iron blades were used from about 600BC. Other inventions to help farmers were developed in the next few hundred years, including the wheelbarrow, a pedal hammer for husking grain and a rotary winnowing fan.

PIGS ARE FARM FAVOURITES
This pottery model of pigs in their sty dates back about 2,000 years. Pigs were popular farm animals, as they are easy to feed and most parts of a pig can be eaten. They were kept in the city as well as in rural country areas.

FEEDING THE MANY
Rice has been grown in the wetter regions of China since ancient times. Wheat and millet are grown in the drier regions. Sprouts of the Indian mung bean add important vitamins to many dishes.

mung beans

millet

rice

wheat

CHINESE TEAS
Delicate leaves of tea are picked from the bushes and gathered in large baskets on this estate in the 1800s. The Chinese cultivated tea in ancient times, but it became much more popular during the Tang dynasty (AD618–906). The leaves were picked, laid out in the sun, rolled by hand and then dried over charcoal fires.

WORKING THE LAND

A farmer uses a pair of strong oxen to help him plough his land. This wall painting found in Jiayuguan dates back to about 100BC. Oxen saved farmers a lot of time and effort. The Chinese first used oxen in farming in about 1122BC.

KEEPING WARM

This model of a Chinese farmer's lambing shed dates from about 100BC, during the Han dynasty. Sheepskins were worn for warmth, but wool never became an important textile for clothes or blankets in China.

HARVESTING RICE – CHINA'S MAIN FOOD

Chinese peasants pull up rice plants for threshing and winnowing in the 1600s. Farming methods were passed on by word of mouth and in handbooks from the earliest times. They advised farmers on everything from fertilizing the soil to controlling pests.

A TIMELESS SCENE

Peasants bend over to plant out rows of rice seedlings in the flooded paddy fields of Yunnan province, in southwest China. This modern photograph is a typical scene of agricultural life in China's warm and wet southwest region. Little has changed in hundreds of years of farming.

Fine Food

CHINESE COOKS TODAY are among the best in the world, with skills gained over thousands of years. Rice was the basis of most meals in ancient China, especially in the south where it was grown. Northerners used wheat flour to make noodles and buns. Food varied greatly between the regions. The north was famous for pancakes, dumplings, lamb and duck dishes. In the west, Sichuan was renowned for its hot chilli peppers. Mushrooms and bamboo shoots were popular along the lower Chang Jiang (Yangzi River).

For many people, meat was a rare treat. It included chicken, pork and many kinds of fish, and was often spiced with garlic and ginger. Dishes featured meat that people from other parts of the world might find strange, such as turtle, dog, monkey and bear. Food was stewed, steamed or fried. The use of chopsticks and bowls dates back to the Shang dynasty (c.1600–1122BC).

THE KITCHEN GOD
In every kitchen hung a paper picture of the kitchen god and his wife. Each year, on the 24th day of the 12th month, sweets were put out as offerings. Then the picture was taken down and burned. A new one was put in its place on New Year's Day.

A TANG BANQUET
These elegant ladies of the Tang court are sitting down to a feast. They are accompanied by music and singing, but there are no men present – women and men usually ate separately. This painting dates from the AD900s, when raised tables came into fashion in China. Guests at banquets would wear their finest clothes. The most honoured guest would sit to the east of the host, who sat facing the south. The greatest honour of all was to be invited to dine with the emperor.

MAKE RED BEAN SOUP
You will need: measuring jug, scales, measuring spoon, 225g aduki beans, 3 tsp ground nuts, 4 tsp short-grain rice, cold water, tangerine, saucepan and lid, wooden spoon, 175g sugar, liquidizer, sieve, bowls.

1 Use the scales to weigh out the aduki beans. Add the ground nuts and the short-grain rice. Measure out 1 litre of cold water in the jug.

2 Wash and drain the beans and rice. Put them in a bowl. Add the cold water. Leave overnight to soak. Do not drain off the water.

3 Wash and dry the tangerine. Then carefully take off the peel in a continuous strip. Leave the peel overnight, until it is hard and dry.

THAT SPECIAL TASTE

Garlic has been used to flavour Chinese dishes and sauces for thousands of years. It may be chopped, crushed, pickled or served whole. Root ginger is another crucial Chinese taste. Fresh chilli peppers are used to make fiery dishes, while sesame provides flavouring in the form of paste, oil and seeds.

sesame

root ginger

SHANG BRONZEWARE FIT FOR A FEAST

This three-legged bronze cooking pot dates from the Shang dynasty (*c.*1600BC–1122BC). Its green appearance is caused by the reaction of the metal to air over the 3,500 years since it was made. During Shang rule, metalworkers made many vessels out of bronze, including cooking pots and wine jars. They were used in all sorts of ceremonies, and at feasts people held in honour of their dead ancestors.

BUTCHERS AT WORK

The stone carving (*shown right*) shows farmers butchering cattle in about AD50. In early China, cooks would cut up meat with square-shaped cleavers. It was then flavoured with wines and spices, and simmered in big pots over open fires until tender.

Most peasant farmers lived on a simple diet. Red bean soup with rice was a typical daily meal. Herbs and spices were often added to make the food taste more interesting.

4 Put the soaked beans and rice (plus the soaking liquid) into a large saucepan. Add the dried tangerine peel and 500ml of cold water.

5 Bring the mixture to the boil. Reduce the heat, cover the saucepan and simmer for 2 hours. Stir occasionally. If the liquid boils off, add more water.

6 Weigh out the sugar. When the beans are just covered by water, add the sugar. Simmer until the sugar has completely dissolved.

7 Remove and discard the tangerine peel. Leave soup to cool, uncovered. Liquidize the mixture. Strain any lumps with a sieve. Pour into bowls.

Markets and Trade

T HE EARLIEST CHINESE TRADERS used to barter (exchange) goods, but by 1600BC people were finding it easier to use tokens such as shells for buying and selling. The first metal coins date from about 750BC and were shaped like knives and spades. It was Qin Shi Huangdi, the first emperor, who introduced round coins. These had holes in the middle so that they could be threaded on to a cord for safe-keeping. The world's first paper money appeared in China in about AD900.

There were busy markets in every Chinese town, selling fruit, vegetables, rice, flour, eggs and poultry as well as cloth, medicine, pots and pans. In the Tang dynasty capital Chang'an (Xian), trading was limited to two large areas – the West Market and the East Market. This was so that government officials could control prices and trading standards.

CHINESE TRADING
Goods from China changed hands many times on the Silk Road to Europe. Trade moved in both directions. Porcelain, tea and silk were carried westwards. Silver, gold and precious stones were transported back into China from central and southern Asia.

raw silk

Chinese tea

CASH CROPS
Tea is trampled into chests in this European view of tea production in China. The work looks hard and the conditions cramped. For years China had traded with India and Arabia. In the 1500s it began a continuous trading relationship with Europe. By the early 1800s, China supplied 90 per cent of all the world's tea.

MAKE A PELLET DRUM
You will need: large roll of masking tape, pencil, thin cream card, thick card, scissors, glue and brush, 2.5cm x 30cm thin grey card, thread, ruler, needle, bamboo stick, paint (red, green and black), water pot, paintbrush, 2 coloured beads.

1 Use the outside of the tape roll to draw 2 circles on thin cream card. Use the inside to draw 2 smaller circles on thick card. Cut out, as shown.

2 Glue grey strip around one of smaller circles. Make 2 small holes each side of strip. Cut two 20cm threads. Pass through holes and knot.

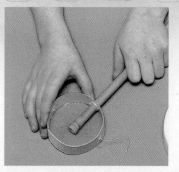

3 Use the scissors to make a hole in the side of the strip for the bamboo stick. Push the stick through, as shown. Tape the stick to the hole.

THE SILK ROAD

The trading route known as the Silk Road developed during the Han dynasty. The road ran for 11,000 kilometres from Chang'an (modern Xian), through Yumen and Kasghar, to Persia and the shores of the Mediterranean Sea. Merchants carried tea, silk and other goods from one trading post to the next.

FROM DISTANT LANDS

A foreign trader rides on his camel during the Tang dynasty. At this time, China's international trade began to grow rapidly. Most trade was still handled by foreign merchants, among them Armenians, Jews and Persians. They traded their wares along the Silk Road, bringing goods to the court at the Tang dynasty capital, Chang'an.

BUYERS AND SELLERS

This picture shows a typical Chinese market in about 1100. It appears on a Song dynasty scroll and is thought to show the market in the capital, Kaifeng, at the time of the New Year festival.

Twist the drum handle to make the little balls rattle. In the hubbub of a street market, a merchant could shake a pellet drum to gain the attention of passers by. He would literally drum up trade!

4 Tape the stick handle down securely at the top of the drum. Take the second small circle and glue it firmly into place. This seals the drum.

5 Draw matching designs of your choice on the 2 thin cream card circles. Cut out a decorative edge. Paint in the designs and leave them to dry.

6 Paint the bamboo stick handle red and leave to dry. When the stick is dry, glue the 2 decorated circles into position on top of the 2 smaller circles.

7 Thread on the 2 beads. Make sure the thread is long enough to allow the beads to hit the centre of the drum. Tie as shown. Cut off any excess.

Medicine and Science

From the empire's earliest days, Chinese scholars published studies on medicine, astronomy and mathematics. The Chinese system of medicine had a similar aim to that of Daoist teachings, in that it attempted to make the body work harmoniously. The effects of all kinds of herbs, plants and animal parts were studied and then used to produce medicines. Acupuncture, which involves piercing the body with fine needles, was practised from about 2700BC. It was believed to release blocked channels of energy and so relieve pain.

The Chinese were also excellent mathematicians, and from 300BC they used a decimal system of counting based on tens. They may have invented the abacus, an early form of calculator, as well. In about 3000BC, Chinese astronomers produced a detailed chart of the heavens carved in stone. Later, they were the first to make observations of sunspots and exploding stars.

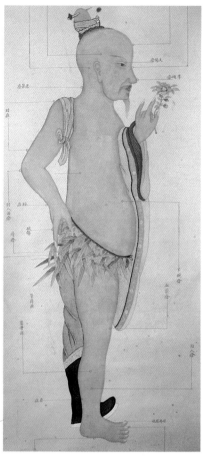

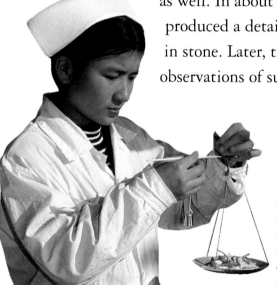

NEW ILLS, OLD REMEDIES
A pharmacist weighs out a traditional medicine. Hundreds of medicines used in China today go back to ancient times. Many are herbal remedies later proved to work by scientists. Doctors are still researching their uses. Other traditional medicines are of less certain value, but are still popular purchases at street stalls.

PRICKING POINTS
Acupuncturists used charts (*shown above*) to show exactly where to position their needles. The vital *qi* (energy) was thought to flow through the body along 12 lines called meridians. The health of the patient was judged by taking their pulse. Chinese acupuncture is practised all over the world today.

MAKE AN ABACUS
You will need: thick and thin card, ruler, pencil, scissors, wood glue and brush, masking tape, self-drying clay, cutting board, modelling tool, 30cm x 0.5cm dowel (x11), paintbrush, water pot, brown paint.

Side A (x2) — 32cm — 3cm

Edge A (x2) — 32cm / 30cm — 0.5cm

Side B (x2) — 16cm — 3cm

Edge B (x2) — 16cm / 15cm — 0.5cm

Base — 32cm x 16cm

Divider — 30cm / Divider edge / 3cm 0.5cm

Using the above measurements, cut out pieces from thick brown card and thin grey card. (pieces not shown to scale).

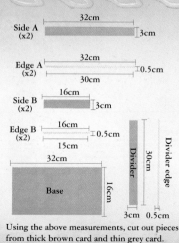

1 Glue sides A and B to the base. Hold the edges with masking tape until dry. Then glue edges A and B to the tops of the sides, as shown.

2 Roll the clay into a 2cm diameter sausage. Cut it into 77 small, flat beads. Make a hole through the centre of each bead with a dowel.

A STREET DOCTOR PEDDLES HIS WARES
This European view of Chinese medicine dates from 1843.
It shows snakes and all sorts of unusual potions being sold on
the streets. The doctor is telling the crowd of miraculous cures.

NATURAL HEALTH
Roots, seeds, leaves and flowers
have been used in Chinese medicine
for over 2,000 years. Today, nine out
of ten Chinese medicines are herbal
remedies. The Chinese yam is used
to treat exhaustion. Ginseng root is
used to help treat dizzy spells,
while mulberry wood is said to
lower blood pressure.

Chinese yam

ginseng root

BURNING CURES
A country doctor
treats a patient with
traditional techniques
during the Song
dynasty. Chinese
doctors relieved pain
by heating parts of the
body with the burning
leaves of a plant called
moxa (mugwort).
The process is
called moxibustion.

*The abacus is an ancient
counting frame that acts as
a simple but very effective
calculator. Using an abacus,
Chinese mathematicians
and merchants could carry
out very difficult
calculations quickly
and easily.*

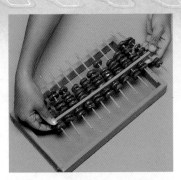

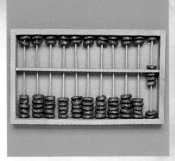

3 Make 11 evenly spaced holes
in the divider. Edge one side
with thin card. Thread a dowel
through each hole. Paint all of
the abacus parts. Leave to dry.

4 Thread 7 beads on to each
dowel rod – 2 on the upper
side of the divider, 5 on the
lower. Carefully fit the beads
and rods into the main frame.

5 Each upper bead on the
abacus equals 5 lower beads
in the same column. Each lower
bead is worth 10 of the lower
beads in the column to its right.

6 Here is a simple sum. To
calculate 5+3, first move
down one upper bead (worth 5).
Then move 3 lower beads in the
same column up (each worth 1).

Feats of Engineering

THE ENGINEERING WONDER of ancient China was the Great Wall. It was known as *Wan Li Chang Cheng*, or the Wall of Ten Thousand *Li* (a unit of length). The Great Wall's main length was an incredible 4,000 kilometres. Work began on the wall in the 400s BC and lasted until the AD1500s. Its purpose was to protect China's borders from the fierce tribes who lived to the north. Despite this intention, Mongol invaders managed to breach its defences time after time. However, the Great Wall did serve as a useful communications route. It also extended the Chinese empire's control over a very long distance.

The Grand Canal is another engineering project that amazes us today. It was started in the 400s BC, but was mostly built during the Sui dynasty (AD581–618). Its aim was to link the north of China with the rice-growing regions in the south via the Chang Jiang (Yangzi River). It is still in use and runs northwards from Hangzhou to Beijing, a distance of 1,794 kilometres. Other great engineering feats were made by Chinese mining engineers, who were already digging deep mine shafts with drainage and ventilation systems in about 160BC.

LIFE IN THE SALT MINES
Workers busily excavate and purify salt from an underground mine. Inside a tower *(shown bottom left)* you can see workers using a pulley to raise baskets of mined salt. The picture comes from a relief (raised carving) found inside a Han dynasty tomb in the province of Sichuan.

MINING ENGINEERING
A Qing dynasty official tours an open-cast coalmine in the 1800s. China has rich natural resources and may have been the first country in the world to mine coal to burn as a fuel. Coal was probably discovered in about 200BC in what is now Jiangxi province. Other mines extracted metals and valuable minerals needed for the great empire. In the Han dynasty engineers invented methods of drilling boreholes to extract brine (salty water) from the ground. They also used derricks (rigid frameworks) to support iron drills – over 1,800 years before engineers in other parts of the world.

HARD LABOUR

Peasants use their spades to dig roads instead of fields. Imperial China produced its great building and engineering works without the machines we rely on today. For big projects, workforces could number hundreds of thousands. Dangerous working conditions and a harsh climate killed many labourers.

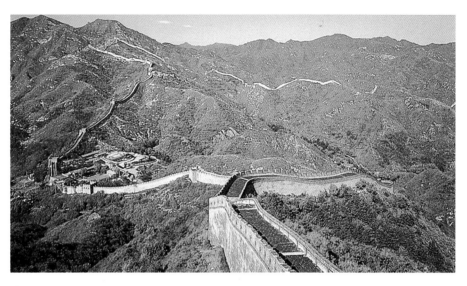

BUILDING THE WALL

The Great Wall snakes over mountain ridges at Badaling, to the northwest of Beijing. The Great Wall and Grand Canal were built by millions of workers. All men aged between 23 and 56 were called up to work on them for one month each year. Only noblemen and civil servants were exempt.

A GRAND OPENING

This painting from the 1700s imagines the Sui emperor Yangdi opening the first stage of the Grand Canal. Most of the work on this massive engineering project was carried out from AD605–609. A road was also built along the route. The transport network built up during the Sui dynasty (AD561–618) enabled food and other supplies to be moved easily from one part of the empire to another.

THE CITY OF SIX THOUSAND BRIDGES

The reports about China supposedly made by Marco Polo in the 1200s described 6,000 bridges in the city of Suzhou. The Baodai Bridge (*shown above*) is one of them. It has 53 arches and was built between AD618 and AD906 to run across the Grand Canal.

Famous Inventions

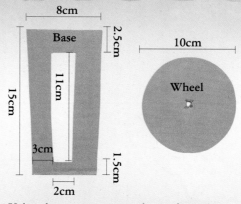

WHEN YOU WALK DOWN a shopping street in any modern city, it is very difficult to avoid seeing some object that was invented in China long ago. Printed words on paper, silk scarves, umbrellas or locks and keys are all Chinese innovations. Over the centuries, Chinese ingenuity and technical skill have changed the world in which we live.

A seismoscope is a very useful instrument in an earthquake-prone country such as China. It was invented in AD132 by a Chinese scientist called Zhang Heng. It could record the direction of even a distant earth tremor. Another key invention was the magnetic compass. In about AD1–100 the Chinese discovered that lodestone (a type of iron ore) could be made to point north. They realized that they could magnetize needles to do the same. By about AD1000, they worked out the difference between true north and magnetic north and began using compasses to keep ships on course.

Gunpowder is a Chinese invention from about AD850. At first it was used to blast rocks apart and to make fireworks. Later, it also began to be used in warfare.

SHADE AND SHELTER
A Qing dynasty woman uses an umbrella as a sunshade to protect her skin. The Chinese invented umbrellas about 1,600 years ago and they soon spread throughout the rest of Asia. Umbrellas became fashionable with both women and men and were regarded as a symbol of high rank.

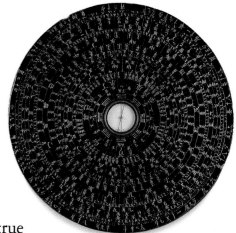

THE SAILOR'S FRIEND
The magnetic compass was invented in China in about AD1–100. At first it was used as a planning aid to ensure new houses faced in a direction that was in harmony with nature. Later it was used to plot courses on long sea voyages.

MAKE A WHEELBARROW

You will need: thick card, ruler, pencil, scissors, compasses, 0.5cm diameter balsa strips, glue and brush, paintbrush, paint (black and brown), water pot, 3.5cm x 0.5cm dowel, 2cm diameter rubber washers (x4).

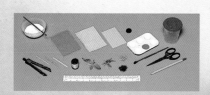

Base — 8cm, 2.5cm, 15cm, 11cm, 3cm, 1.5cm, 2cm

Wheel — 10cm

Using the measurements above, draw the pieces on to thick card. Draw the wheel with the compasses. Cut out pieces with scissors.

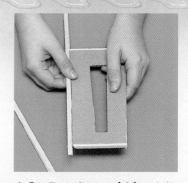

1 Cut 7cm, 8cm and 26cm (x2) balsa strips. Glue 7cm strip to short edge of base and 8cm strip to top edge. Glue 26cm strips to side of base.

SU SONG'S MASTERPIECE

This fantastic machine is a clock tower that can tell the time, chime the hours and follow the movement of the planets around the Sun. It was designed by an official called Su Song, in the city of Kaifeng in AD1092. The machine uses a mechanism called an escapement, which controls and regulates the timing of the clock. The escapement mechanism was invented in the AD700s by a Chinese inventor called Yi Xing.

EARTHQUAKE WARNING

The decorative object shown above is the scientist Zhang Heng's seismoscope. When there was an earthquake, a ball was released from one of the dragons and fell into a frog's mouth. This showed the direction of the vibrations. According to records, in AD138 the instrument detected a earth tremor some 500 kilometres away.

ONE-WHEELED TRANSPORT

In about AD100, the Chinese invented the wheelbarrow. They then designed a model with a large central wheel that could bear great weights. This became a form of transport, pushed along by muscle power.

The single wheelbarrow was used by farmers and gardeners. Traders wheeled their goods to market, then used the barrow as a stall. They would sell a variety of goods, such as seeds, grain, plants and dried herbs.

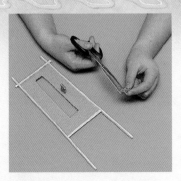

2 Turn the base over. Cut two 2cm x 1cm pieces of thick card. Make a small hole in the middle of each, for the wheel axle. Glue pieces to base.

3 Use compasses and a pencil to draw 1 circle around centre of wheel and 1 close to the rim. Mark on spokes. Paint spaces between spokes black.

4 Paint the barrow and leave to dry. Cut two 7cm balsa strips with tapered ends to make legs. Paint brown. When dry, glue to bottom of barrow.

5 Feed dowel axle between axle supports, via 2 washers, wheel, and 2 more washers. Dab glue on ends of axle, to allow wheel to spin without falling off.

Workers of Metal

THE CHINESE MASTERED THE secrets of making alloys (mixtures of two or more metals) during the Shang dynasty (*c*.1600BC–1122BC). They made bronze by melting copper and tin to separate each metal from its ore, a process called smelting. Nine parts of copper were then mixed with one part of tin and heated in a charcoal furnace. When the metals melted they were piped off into clay moulds. Bronze was used to make objects such as ceremonial pots, statues, bells, mirrors, tools and weapons.

By about 600BC the Chinese were smelting iron ore. They then became the first people to make cast iron by adding carbon to the molten metal. Cast iron is a tougher metal than bronze and it was soon being used to make weapons, tools and plough blades. By AD1000 the Chinese were mining and working a vast amount of iron. Coke (a type of coal) had replaced the charcoal used in furnaces, which were fired up by water-driven bellows. Chinese metal workers also produced delicate gold and silver ornaments set with precious stones.

BEWARE OF THE LION
This gilded *fo* (Buddhist) lion guards the halls and chambers of Beijing's imperial palace, the Forbidden City. It is one of a fearsome collection of bronze guardian figures, including statues of dragons and turtles.

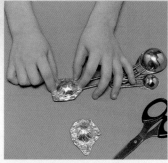

SILVER SCISSORS
This pair of scissors is made of silver. They are proof of the foreign influences that entered China in the AD700s, during the boom years of the Tang dynasty. The metal is beaten, rather than cast in the Chinese way. It is decorated in the Persian style of the Silk Road, with engraving and punching.

MAKE A NECKLACE

You will need: tape measure, thick wire, thin wire, masking tape, scissors, tin foil, measuring spoon, glue and brush, fuse wire.

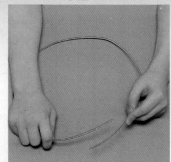

1 Measure around your neck using a tape measure. Ask an adult to cut a piece of thick wire to 1½ times this length. Shape it into a rough circle.

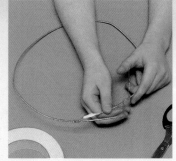

2 Cut two 4cm pieces of thin wire. Coil loosely around sides of thick wire. Tape ends to thick wire. Slide thick wire through coils to adjust fit.

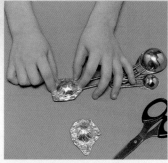

3 Cut out an oval-shaped piece of tin foil. Shape it into a pendant half, using a measuring spoon or teaspoon. Make 9 more halves.

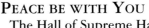

MINERAL WEALTH

The Chinese probably learnt to smelt ore in furnaces from their experience with high-temperature pottery kilns. The land was rich in copper, tin and iron, and the Chinese were very skilled miners. Large amounts of precious metals, such as gold and silver, had to be imported.

gold nugget   silver ore

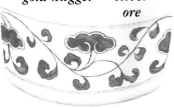

PEACE BE WITH YOU

The Hall of Supreme Harmony in Beijing's Forbidden City is guarded by this bronze statue of a turtle. Despite its rather fearsome appearance, the turtle was actually a symbol of peace.

DECORATIVE PROTECTION

These nail protectors are made of gold, with inlaid feathers. They were worn by the Empress Dowager Cixi in the 1800s to stop her 15-cm-long little fingernails breaking.

GOLDEN FIREBIRDS

Chinese craftsmen fashioned these beautiful phoenix birds from thin sheets of delicate gold. The mythical Arabian phoenix was said to set fire to its nest and die, only to rise again from the ashes. During the Tang dynasty the phoenix became a symbol of the Chinese empress Wu Zetian, who came to power in AD660. It later came to be a more general symbol for all empresses.

4 Glue the 2 pendant halves together, leaving one end open. Drop some rolled-up balls of foil into the opening. Seal the opening with glue.

5 Make 4 more pendants in the same way. Thread each pendant on to the neckband with pieces of thin fuse wire. Leave a gap between each one.

People of all classes wore decorative jewellery in imperial China. The design of this necklace is based on the metal bell bracelets worn by Chinese children.

Porcelain and Lacquer

ALTHOUGH POTTERY FIRST developed in Japan and parts of western Asia, Chinese potters were hard at work over 6,000 years ago. In 3200BC, clay was being fired (baked) in kilns at about 900°C.

By 1400BC, potters were making beautiful, white stoneware, baked at much higher temperatures. Shiny glazes were developed to coat the fired clay. Later, the Chinese invented porcelain, the finest, most delicate pottery of all. It was to become one of China's most important exports to other parts of Asia and Europe. In the English language, the word china is used for all fine-quality pottery.

The Chinese were the first to use lacquer. This plastic-like material is a natural substance from the sap of a tree that grows in China. The sap makes a smooth, hard varnish. From about 1300BC onwards, lacquer was used for coating wooden surfaces, such as house timbers, bowls or furniture. It could also be applied to leather and metal. Natural lacquer is grey, but in China pigment was added to make it black or bright red. It was applied in many layers until thick enough to be carved or inlaid with mother-of-pearl.

ENAMEL WARE
Ming dynasty craft workers made this ornate flask. It is covered with a glassy material called enamel, set inside thin metal wire. This technique, called cloisonné (partitioned), was introduced from Persia.

CHINA'S HISTORY TOLD ON THE BIG SCREEN
This beautifully detailed, glossy lacquer screen shows a group of Portuguese merchants on a visit to China. It was made in the 1600s. Chinese crafts first became popular in Europe at this time, as European traders began doing business in southern China's ports.

FLORAL BOTTLE
This attractive Ming dynasty bottle is decorated with a coating of bright red lacquer. The lacquer is coloured with a mineral called cinnabar. It would have taken many long hours to apply and dry the many layers of lacquer. The bottle is carved with a design of peonies, which were a very popular flower in China.

FISH ON A PLATE

Pictures of fish decorate the border of this precious porcelain plate. It was made during the reign of the Qing emperor Yongzheng (1722–1736), a period famous for its elegant designs. It is coloured with enamel. Porcelain is made from a fine white clay called kaolin (china clay) and a mineral called feldspar. They are fired (baked) to a very high temperature.

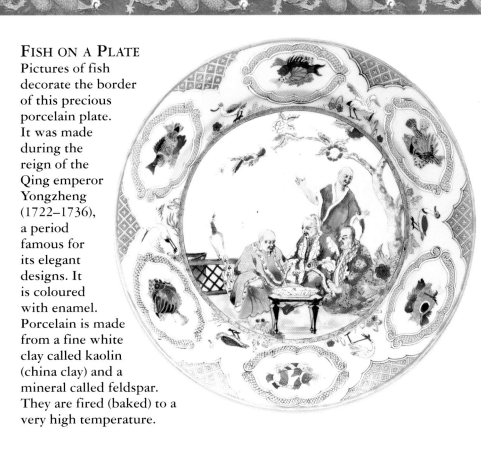

A JUG OF WINE

An unknown Chinese potter made this beautiful wine jug about 1,000 years ago. It has been fired to such a high temperature that it has become glassy stoneware. It is coated with a grey-green glaze called celadon.

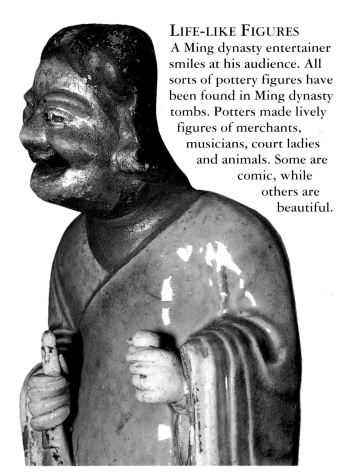

LIFE-LIKE FIGURES

A Ming dynasty entertainer smiles at his audience. All sorts of pottery figures have been found in Ming dynasty tombs. Potters made lively figures of merchants, musicians, court ladies and animals. Some are comic, while others are beautiful.

DEEP BLUE, PURE WHITE

These blue-and-white vases are typical of the late Ming dynasty (1368–1644). In the 1600s large numbers were exported to Europe. Many were produced at the imperial potteries at Jingdezhen, in northern Jiangxi province. These workshops were set up in 1369, as the region had plentiful supplies of the very best clay. Some of the finest pottery ever made was produced there in the 1400s and 1500s.

The Secret of Silk

FOR YEARS, THE CHINESE tried to stop outsiders finding out how they made their most popular export – *si*, or silk. The shimmering colours and smooth textures of Chinese silk made it the wonder of the ancient world. Other countries such as India discovered the secret of silk making, but China remained the producer of the world's best silk.

Silk production probably dates back to late Stone Age times (8000BC–2500BC) in China. Legend says that the process was invented by the empress Lei Zu in about 2640BC. Silkworms (the caterpillars of a type of moth) are kept on trays and fed on the leaves of white mulberry trees. The silkworms spin a cocoon (casing) of fine but very strong filaments. The cocoons are plunged into boiling water to separate the filaments, which are then carefully wound on to reels.

A filament of silk can be up to 1,200 metres long. Several filaments are spun together to make up thread, which is then woven into cloth on a loom. The Chinese used silk to make all kinds of beautiful products. They learned to weave flimsy gauzes and rich brocades, and they then wove elaborate coloured patterns into the cloth in a style known as *ke si*, or cut silk.

PREPARING THE THREAD
A young woman winds silk thread on to bobbins in the late 1700s. Up to 30 filaments of silk could be twisted together to make silk thread for weaving. The Chinese made ingenious equipment for spinning silk into thread. They also built looms for weaving thread into large rolls of fabric. By the 1600s, the city of Nanjing alone had an estimated 50,000 looms.

LOAD THOSE BALES!
Workers at a Chinese silk factory of the 1840s carry large bales of woven silk down to the jetty. From there the woven cloth would be shipped to the city. It might be used to make a costume for a lady of the court, or else exported abroad. The Chinese silk industry reached its peak of prosperity in the mid-1800s.

WINDING SILK

Silk is being prepared at this workshop of the 1600s. The workers are taking filaments (threads) from the cocoons and winding them on to a reel. Traditionally, the chief areas of silk production in imperial China were in the east coast provinces of Zhejiang and Jiangsu. Silk was also produced in large quantities in Sichuan, in the west.

THE DRAGON ON THE EMPEROR'S BACK

A scaly red dragon writhes across a sea of yellow silk. The dragon was embroidered on to a robe for an emperor of the Qing dynasty. The exquisite clothes made for the Chinese imperial court at this time are considered to be great works of art.

MAKING SILK

Raising silkworms is called sericulture. It can be a complicated business. The caterpillars have to be kept at a controlled temperature for a month before they begin spinning their silk cocoons.

adult silkmoth and cocoons

silkmoth larva

MAGIC MULBERRIES

These Han dynasty workers are collecting mulberry leaves in big baskets, over 2,000 years ago. These would have been used to feed the silkworms. Silkworms are actually the larva (caterpillars) of a kind of moth. Like most caterpillars, silkworms are fussy feeders and will only eat certain kinds of plant before they spin cocoons.

Dress and Ornament

CHINESE PEASANTS dressed in simple clothes made from basic materials. They mostly wore cotton tunics over loose trousers, with sandals made of rushes or straw. In the south, broad-brimmed, cone-shaped hats helped to protect the wearer from the hot sun and heavy rain. In the north, fur hats, sheepskins and quilted jackets were worn to keep out the cold. Rich people often dressed in elaborate, expensive clothes. Government officials wore special robes that reflected their rank and status. Beautiful silk robes patterned with dragons (*lung pao*) were worn by court ladies, officials, and the emperor himself.

Court dress varied greatly over the ages. Foreign invasions brought new fashions and dress codes. Under the Manchus, who ruled as the Qing dynasty from AD1644, men had to wear a long pigtail. Rich people grew their little fingernails so long that special nail guards were worn to prevent them from breaking off.

CLOTHES FIT FOR AN EMPEROR
This magnificent imperial robe was made from interwoven, heavy silks in the 1800s. The narrow sleeves, with their horse hoof cuffs, are typical of the Qing dynasty.

MONKEY PENDANT
Wealthy people often wore very expensive, well-crafted jewellery. This beautiful piece from the AD700s is a pendant necklace. It could have been worn by both men and women. The pendant is made from white jade set in a beaded frame of gilded bronze.

FASTEN YOUR BELT
Belt hooks and buckles became an essential part of noblemen's clothing from about the 300s BC. They were highly decorated, and made of bronze.

MAKE A FAN

You will need: masking tape, red tissue paper, thick card base, ruler, pencil, compasses, paint (pink, light blue, cream, light green), thin paintbrush, water pot, scissors, 16cm x 1cm balsa strips (x15), barbecue stick, glue and brush, thin card.

1 Tape tissue paper on to base. Make a compass hole 1cm from the edge. From this mark, draw a 16cm radius semicircle and a 7cm radius semicircle.

2 Place one end of the ruler at compass hole. Mark the point with a pencil. Draw evenly spaced lines 1cm apart between the semi-circles.

3 Draw your design on to the tissue paper. Paint in the details. Allow to dry. Remove paper from base. Cut out fan along edges of the semicircles.

OFFICIAL DRESS

A well-dressed civil servant cools down in the summer heat. Chinese government officials wore elegant clothes that showed their social rank. This picture was painted by a European artist in about 1800. The official is wearing his summer outfit, which consists of a long narrow-sleeved tunic, slippers and a brimmed hat. It is a hot day, so he also carries a fan to provide a cool breeze.

LADIES OF THE COURT

These Tang ladies are dressed in the high fashion of the AD700s. Silk was the material worn by the nobles of the day, and court costume included long robes and skirts, various tunics and sashes. The clothes were often beautifully decorated, with colourful patterns and elaborate designs.

ADDED STYLE

Over the ages, all kinds of accessories became part of Chinese costume. These included elaborate hats and headdresses for men and women, sunshades, fans, belts and buckles. Tiny leather shoes lined with silk were worn by noble women.

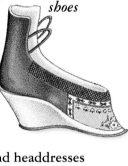

ladies' shoes

fans

earring

The earliest Chinese fans were made of feathers or of silk stretched over a flat frame. In about AD1000 folding fans were introduced into China, probably from Japan.

back of fan

4 Using scissors, cut each balsa strip 1cm narrower (0.5cm each side) for half of its length. Make a compass hole at the base of each strip.

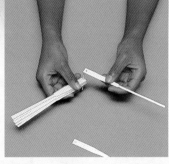

5 Stack strips. Pass a barbecue stick through holes. It must be long enough to fit through and overlap either side. Make sure strips can move freely.

6 Fold the paper backwards and forwards to form a concertina. Glue each alternate fold of the paper to the narrow ends of the strips, as shown.

7 Paint the top strip of the fan pink. Allow to dry. Cut out small card discs. Glue them over the ends of the barbecue stick to secure the strips.

Chinese Art

IN IMPERIAL CHINA, painting was believed to be the finest of all the arts. It was considered to be a mark of civilization and a suitable pastime for scholars and even emperors. Painting was based upon the same ideas of harmony and simplicity that were important in the Daoist and Buddhist faiths. Paintings appeared on scrolls of silk and paper, walls, screens and fans. Popular subjects for pictures varied over the ages. They included the misty mountains and rivers of southern China, as well as landscapes set off by lone human figures. Artists also painted birds, animals and plants, such as bamboo or lotus. Sometimes just a few brush strokes were used to capture the spirit of the subject. Chinese writing in the form of a poem often played an important part in many pictures. Chinese artists also produced woodcuts, which are prints made from a carved wooden block. Traditionally these were not valued as much as the paintings, but many beautiful woodcuts were produced during the reign of the Ming dynasty (1368–1644).

SYMBOLS OF WISDOM
To the Chinese, the dragon embodied wisdom, strength and goodness. This intricate ivory seal belonged to a Ming emperor and shows a dragon guarding the pearl of wisdom.

WINDOW ON THE PAST
A royal procession makes its way along a mountain range. This detail from a painting on silk is by the great master Li Sixun (AD651–716). Many Tang dynasty paintings show court life and royal processions, but they are far from dull. They provide a colourful glimpse of life in China at that time. This picture shows what people wore and how they travelled.

MAKE PAPER CUT-OUTS
You will need: A4 sized coloured paper, pencil, ruler, scissors.

1 Take a piece of coloured paper and lay it flat on a hard surface. Fold it exactly in half widthways. Make a firm crease along the fold, as shown above.

2 Draw a Chinese-style design on the paper. Make sure all the shapes meet up at the fold. Make a tracing of your design so you can use it again.

3 Keeping card folded, cut out shapes. Make sure you don't cut along the folded edge. Cut away areas you want to discard in between the shapes.

AT FULL GALLOP
Chinese artists greatly admired horses and loved to try to capture their strength and movement in paintings. This lively wall painting was found in a Han dynasty tomb.

PAINTING NATURE
Morning mist hangs over a mountain backdop. This detail from a masterpiece by Qiu Ying (1494–1552) is inspired by the forests and mountain landscapes of his homeland. Artists such as Qiu Ying were successful and well paid.

ART IN PORCELAIN
China's craft workers and designers were also great artists. This blue-and-white porcelain wine jar was made in the 1600s in the form of a mandarin duck and drake. Its hand-painted details would have taken many long hours of work to complete. Blue-and-white porcelain was very popular during the Ming dynasty.

SPRINGTIME ON PAPER
A watercolour painting from the 1800s shows peach blossom just as it comes into flower. It is painted in a very realistic, fresh and simple style. This approach is a common characteristic of much Chinese art.

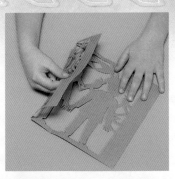

4 Now open up your design. Be careful not to tear it. To add details to the figures, fold paper again. Mark the details to be cut along the crease.

5 Using a pair of scissors, carefully cut out the detail along the crease. The cut-out detail will be matched perfectly on the other side of the figure.

Carefully open up your finished cut-out. Display the design by sticking it to a window, so that light shines through. In China, paper cut-outs are traditionally used to bring luck and good fortune.

The Written Word

THE CHINESE LANGUAGE is written with symbols called characters, which stand for sounds and words. They have changed and developed over the ages. A dictionary published in 1716 lists over 40,000 of them. Each character was written by hand with a brush, using 11 basic brush strokes. The painting of these beautiful characters is called calligraphy, and was always seen as a form of art.

The Chinese began using woodblocks for printing in about 1600BC. Before that, books had often been handwritten on bamboo strips. Ancient Chinese writers produced all sorts of practical handbooks and encyclopedias. Poetry first developed about 3,000 years ago. It was the Chinese who invented paper, nearly 2,000 years ago. Cloth or bark was shredded, pulped and dried on frames. Movable type was invented in the 1040s. During the 1500s popular folk tales such as *The Water Margin* were published, and in the 1700s the writer Cao Xuequin produced China's greatest novel, *A Dream of Red Mansions*.

MAGICAL MESSAGES
The earliest surviving Chinese script appears on animal bones. They were used for telling fortunes in about 1200BC. The script was made up of small pictures representing objects or ideas. Modern Chinese script is made up of patterns of lines.

ART OF CALLIGRAPHY
This text was handwritten during the Tang dynasty (AD618–906). Traditional Chinese writing reads down from right to left, starting in the top right-hand corner.

汉興六十餘載海
内乂安府庫充實
而四夷未賓制度
多闕上方欲用文
而不可及始
武蒲輪迎枚生見
主父蒲輪迎枚生見
式技於牛之亦已
簿於奴僕日彈牧青奮羊出
舊築飯人之於孫簿為
敬之得兒則公
漢儒雅則寬篤行
盛仲舒石建石慶推賢
董石赏卜式直
則汉黯趙禹張湯時
則韓安司馬遷方相
定令稽則東嚴助喜
文章則滑稽則數對
如皋應對則蔥
朱買臣慈
部各下品率川

MAKE PRINTING BLOCKS
You will need: plain white paper, pencil, paint, soft Chinese brush or thin paintbrush, water pot, tracing paper, board, self-drying clay (15cm x 20cm, 2.5cm thick), modelling tool, wood glue, block printing ink, damp rag.

1 Copy or trace the characters from the reversed image block (see opposite). Start off with a pencil outline, then fill in with paint. Leave to dry.

2 Copy design on to tracing paper. Turn the paper over. Place it on the clay. Scribble on the clean side of the paper to leave a mirror image in the clay.

3 Use a modelling tool to carve out characters. Cut away clay all around characters to make a relief (raised pattern). Smooth clay base with your fingertips.

THE BEST WAY TO WRITE

A calligrapher of the 1840s begins to write, surrounded by his assistants. The brush must be held upright for the writing of Chinese characters. The wrist is never rested on the table. Many years of practice and study are necessary to become a good calligrapher.

INKS AND COLOURS

Watercolours and inks were based on plant and mineral pigments in reds, browns, blues, greens and yellows. Black ink was made from carbon, obtained from soot. This was mixed with glue to form a solid block. The ink block would be wetted during use. Brushes were made from animal hair fitted into bamboo handles.

Chinese brushes

THE PRINTED PAGE

The Buddhist scripture called the Diamond Sutra *(shown right)* is probably the oldest surviving printed book in the world. It includes both text and pictures. The book was printed from a woodblock on 11 May AD868 and was intended to be distributed at no cost to the public.

reversed image   *actual image*

Block rubbings of characters were an early form of printing.

Moon Ruler

Mouth Sun

4 When the relief has dried, paint the clay block with wood glue. Leave it to dry thoroughly. When dry, the glue seals and protects the pattern.

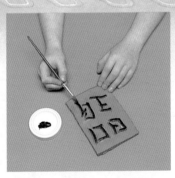

5 Now paint the design. Apply a thick layer of printing ink to the raised parts of the clay with a Chinese brush or a soft paintbrush.

6 Lay a thin piece of plain white paper over the inked block. Use a dry brush to press the paper into the ink, so that the paper takes up the design.

7 Lift up the paper to reveal your design. Look after your printing block by cleaning it with a damp rag. You can then use it again and again.

Musicians and Performers

THE EARLIEST CHINESE POETRY was sung rather than spoken. *Shijing* (the Book of Songs) dates back over 3,000 years and includes the words to hymns and folk songs. For most of China's history, musicians were employed in rich households. Orchestras played drums, gongs, pan pipes, racks of bronze bells, fiddles and other stringed instruments. Music was considered an important part of life, and models of musicians were often put in tombs to provide entertainment in the afterlife.

Musicians were frequently accompanied by acrobats, jugglers and magicians. Such acts were as popular in the markets and streets of the town as in the courtyards of nobles. Storytelling and puppet shows were equally well loved. Plays and opera became hugely popular in the AD1200s, with tales of murder, intrigue, heroism and love acted out to music. Most of the female roles would be played by men.

THE COURT DANCER
Arching her right arm upwards, an elegant dancer performs at the royal court. The model's flowing dress belongs to the fashions of the Tang dynasty (AD618–906).

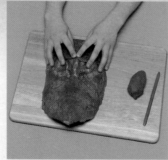

PUTTING ON A PUPPET SHOW
Children put on a show with marionettes (puppets moved by strings) in the 1600s. Drumming was used to provide musical accompaniment, just like in a professional play of the period.

MAKE A MASK

You will need: tape measure, large block of self-drying clay, board, modelling tool, petroleum jelly, newspaper, wood glue and brush, scissors, thick card, masking tape, 2 large white beads, paintbrush, paints (grey, cream, terracotta and yellow), water pot, needle, black wool, string.

1 Measure the width and length of your face with a tape measure. Make a clay mould. Carve out the eyes and attach a clay nose to the mask.

2 Paint front of mask with petroleum jelly. Apply 4–6 layers of papier-mâché. This is made by soaking torn newspaper in water and glue. Leave to dry.

3 Remove mask from the clay mould. Cut a 2.5cm wide strip of card long enough to fit around your face. Bend it into a circle, and tape to the mask.

MUSIC IN THE GARDEN

Musicians in the 1800s play *qins* (lutes) and *sheng* (flutes) in a garden setting. The music tried to reflect nature's harmony. It was intended to make the listener feel peaceful and spiritual.

CHINESE OPERA

These stars of the Chinese opera are performing in the 1700s. Well-known folk tales were acted out to the dramatic sound of crashing cymbals and high-pitched singing. Elaborate make-up and fancy costumes made it clear to the audience whether the actor was playing a hero or a villain, a princess or a demon.

SOUND THE DRUMS!

The cavalcade that followed an important government official or general might have included mounted drummers or trumpeters. These figures of musicians on horseback were found in the tomb of a high-ranking official from the Tang dynasty.

Elaborate masks like these were worn to great effect in Chinese opera. When your mask is finished, you can wear it to scare your friends!

4 Cut 2 pointed ear shapes from card. Fold card at the edge to make flaps. Cut out and glue on small, decorative pieces of card. Glue ears to the mask.

5 Glue on 2 large white beads for the eyes. Cut out more small pieces of card. Glue these on above the eyes. Add another piece of card for the lips.

6 Paint the mask with the grey base colour first. Leave to dry. Then add details using the brighter colours. When dry, varnish with wood glue.

7 Use a needle to thread black wool through for the beard. Tape wool to back of the mask. Thread string through side of mask behind ears to tie it on.

Games and Pastimes

FROM EARLY IN CHINA'S history, kings and nobles loved to go hunting for pleasure. Horses and chariots were used to hunt deer and wild boar. Dogs and even cheetahs were trained to chase the prey. Spears, bows and arrows were then used to kill it. Falconry (using birds of prey to hunt animals) was commonplace by about 2000BC.

In the Ming and Qing dynasties ancient spiritual disciplines used by Daoist monks were brought together with the battle training used by warriors. These martial arts (*wu shu*) were intended to train both mind and body. They came to include the body movements known as tai chi (*taijiquan*), sword play (*jianwu*) and the extreme combat known as kung fu (*gongfu*).

Archery was a popular sport in imperial China. The Chinese also loved gambling, and may have invented the first card games over 2,000 years ago.

PEACE THROUGH MOVEMENT
A student of tai chi practises his art. The Chinese first developed the system of exercises known as tai chi more than 2,000 years ago. The techniques of tai chi were designed to help relax the human body and concentrate the mind.

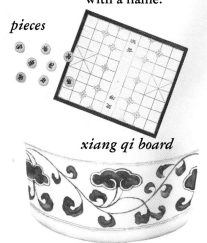

CHINESE CHESS
The traditional Chinese game of xiang qi is similar to western chess. One army battles against another, with round discs used as playing pieces. To tell the discs apart, each is marked with a name.

pieces

xiang qi board

MAKE A KITE

You will need: 30cm barbecue sticks (x12), ruler, scissors, glue and brush, plastic insulating tape, A1-size paper, pencil, paint (blue, red, yellow, black and pink), paintbrush, water pot, string, piece of wooden dowel, small metal ring.

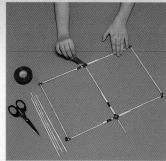

1 Make a 40cm x 30cm rectangle by joining some of the sticks. Overlap the sticks for strength, then glue and tape together. Add a centre rod.

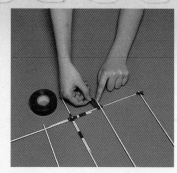

2 Make another rectangle 15cm x 40cm long. Overlay the second rectangle on top of the first one. Tape rectangles together, as shown above.

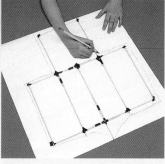

3 Place frame on to a sheet of white A1-size paper. Draw a 2.5cm border around outside of frame. Add curves around the end of the centre rod.

BAMBOO BETTING

Gamblers place bets in a game of *liu po.* Bamboo sticks were thrown like dice to decide how far the counters on the board should move. Gambling was a widespread pastime during the Han dynasty. People would bet large sums of money on the outcome of card games, horse races and cock fights.

POLO PONIES

These women from the Tang dynasty are playing a fast and furious game of polo. They are probably noblewomen from the Emperor's royal court. The sport of polo was originally played in India and central Asia. It was invented as a training game to improve the riding skills of soldiers in cavalry units.

ALL-IN WRESTLING

This bronze figure of two wrestling muscle men was made in about 300BC. Wrestling was a very popular entertainment and sport in imperial China. It continues to be an attraction at country fairs and festivals.

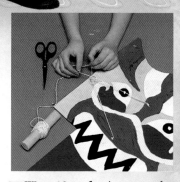

Chinese children today still play with home-made paper kites. Kites were invented in China in about 400BC.

4 Cut out the kite shape from the paper. Using a pencil, draw the details of your dragon design on the paper. Paint in your design and leave to dry.

5 Cut a triangular piece of paper to hang from the end of your kite as a tail. Fold tail over rod at bottom of kite, as shown. Tape tail into position.

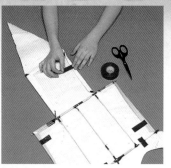

6 Carefully tape and glue your design on to the frame. Fold over border that you allowed for when cutting out the paper. Tape to back of paper, as shown.

7 Wrap 10m of string around dowel. Tie other end to ring. Pass 2 pieces of string through kite from the back. Tie to centre rod. Tie other ends to ring.

Travel by Land

THE CHINESE EMPIRE was linked by a network of roads used only by the army, officials and royal messengers. A special carriageway was reserved for the emperor himself. Ordinary people travelled along dusty or muddy routes and tracks.

China's mountainous landscape and large number of rivers meant that Chinese engineers became expert at bridge-building. Suspension bridges made of rope and bamboo were being used from about AD1 onwards. A bridge suspended from iron chains crossed the Chang Jiang (Yangzi River) as early as AD580. A stone arch bridge built in about AD615 still stands today at Zhouxian in Hebei province. Most people travelled by foot and porters often had to carry great loads on their backs. They also carried wealthy people from place to place on litters (chairs).

China's small native ponies were interbred with larger, stronger horses from central Asia sometime after 100BC. This provided fast, powerful mounts that were suitable for messengers and officials, and they were also capable of pulling chariots and carriages. Mules and camels were widely used along the trade routes of the north, while shaggy yaks carried loads in the high mountains of the Himalayas. Carts were usually hauled along by oxen.

HEADING OUT WEST
Chinese horsemen escort the camels of a caravan (trading expedition). The traders are about to set out along the Silk Road. This trading route ran all the way from Chang'an (Xian) in China right through to Europe and the lands of the Mediterranean.

RIDING ON HORSEBACK
A Chinese nobleman from about 2,000 years ago reins in his elegant horse. Breaking in the horse would have been difficult, as the rider has no stirrups and could easily be unseated. Metal stirrups were in general use in China by AD302. They provided more stability and helped to improve the rider's control of the horse.

CARRIED BY HAND

A lazy landowner of the Qing dynasty travels around his estates. He is carried along in a litter, a platform supported by the shoulders of his tired, long-suffering servants. An umbrella shades the landowner from the heat of the summer sun.

CAMEL POWER

Bactrian (two-humped) camels were originally bred in central Asia. They could endure the extremes of heat and cold of the region, and travel for long distances without water. This toughness made them ideal for transporting goods along the Silk Road.

HAN CARRIAGE

During the Han period, three-horse carriages were used by the imperial family only. This carving from a tomb brick is probably of a messenger carrying an important order from the emperor.

TRAVELLING IN STYLE

During the Han dynasty, government officials travelled in stylish horse-drawn carriages. This picture is taken from a decorative brick found in a Han tomb. After larger, stronger breeds of horses were introduced into China from central Asia, the horse became a status symbol for the rich and powerful. Such horses were considered to be celestial (heavenly).

Junks and Sampans

FROM EARLY IN CHINA'S history, its rivers, lakes and man-made canals were the country's main highways. Fishermen propelled small wooden boats across the water with a single oar or pole at the stern. These small boats were often roofed with mats, like the sampans (which means "three planks" in Chinese) still seen today. Large wooden sailing ships, which we call junks, sailed the open ocean. They were either keeled or flat-bottomed, with a high stern and square bows. Their sails were made of matting stiffened with strips of bamboo. By the AD800s, Chinese shipbuilders had built the first ships with several masts and proper rudders.

In the 1400s, admirals Zheng He and Wang Jinghong led seven sea expeditions that visited Southeast Asia, India, Arabia and East Africa. The flagship of their 300-strong naval fleet was over five times the size of the largest European ships of the time.

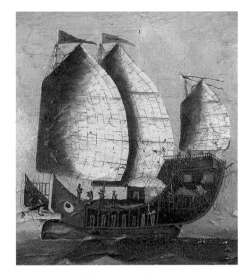

IN FULL SAIL
Junks were a type of sailing vessel used by merchants in the East and South China seas. They were also used by pirates. The China seas could be blue and peaceful, but they were often whipped into a fury by typhoons (tropical storms).

RIVER TRAFFIC
All sorts of small trading boats were sailed or rowed along China's rivers in the 1850s. River travel was often difficult and could be dangerous. Floods were common along the Huang He (Yellow River), which often changed course. The upper parts of China's longest river, the Chang Jiang (Yangzi River), were rocky and had powerful currents.

MAKE A SAMPAN

You will need: ruler, pencil, thick and thin card, scissors, glue and brush, masking tape, 6 wooden barbecue sticks, string, thin yellow paper, paint (black, dark brown), paintbrush, water pot.

39cm
1cm
Runner A (x2)

33.5cm
Side B (x2)
5cm
15cm

Base C (x2)
7cm

Base D

15cm
18cm

Floor E
7cm
10cm

4cm

Floor F (x2)
7cm

Edge G (x2)
6.5cm
1cm

Cut pieces B, C, D and G from thick card. Cut pieces A, E, and F from thin card.

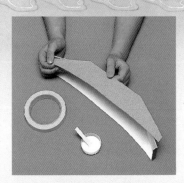

1 Glue base pieces C and D to side B, as shown. Hold the pieces with masking tape while the glue dries. When dry, remove the masking tape.

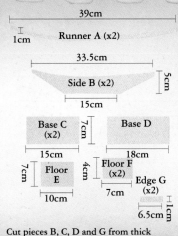

2 Glue remaining side B to the boat. Stick runner A pieces to top of the sides. Make sure the ends jut out 2.5cm at the front and back of the boat.

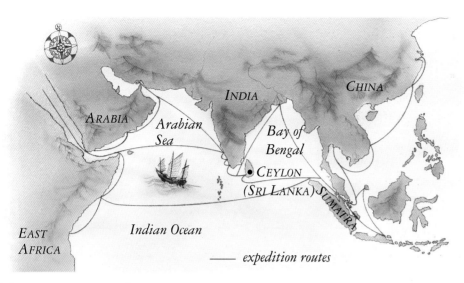

THE VOYAGES OF ZHENG HE

Chinese admirals Zheng He and Wang Jinghong carried out seven fantastic voyages of exploration between 1405 and 1433. This map shows how far and wide they travelled on these expeditions. Their impressive fleets included over 60 ships crewed by about 27,000 seamen, officers and interpreters. The biggest of their vessels was 147 metres long and 60 metres wide.

THE FISHING TRIP

A fisherman poles his boat across the river in the 1500s. The bird shown in the picture is a tamed cormorant, used for catching the fish. The cormorant was normally attached to a line, with a ring around its neck to prevent it from swallowing the fish.

FISHERMEN'S FEASTS

Seas, lakes and rivers were an important food source in imperial China. Drying fish was often the only way to preserve it in the days before refrigeration. Dried fish made strong-tasting sauces and soups. Popular seafoods included crabs, prawns and squid.

dried fish

dried squid

To add the finishing touch to your sampan, make a boatman and oar to propel the vessel through the waterways.

3 Glue floor E to centre of base. Add floor F pieces to the ends of the base, as shown. Stick edge G pieces in between the ends of the runners.

4 Bend 2 barbecue sticks into 10cm high arches. Cut 2 more sticks into five 10cm struts. Glue and tie 2 struts to sides of arches and 1 to the top.

5 Repeat step 4 to make a second roof. To make roof matting, cut thin yellow paper into 1cm x 10cm strips. Fold strips in half and stick to roofs.

6 Paint boat and roofs. Allow to dry. Glue the matting strips to the roofs, as shown. When the glue is dry, place roofs inside the boat.

Soldiers and Weapons

IN CHINA'S EARLY HISTORY, bitter warfare between local rulers devastated the countryside with an appalling cost in human lives. Battle tactics and campaigns were discussed in *The Art of War* by Master Sun, who lived in the 500s BC at around the same time as the thinker Kong Fuzi (Confucius). This was the first book of its kind and its ideas are still studied today. After the empire was united in 221BC, rulers still needed large armies to stay in power and to guard against invasion.

The first Chinese armies fought with horse-drawn chariots and bronze weapons. Later, battles were fought with iron weapons, horsemen and hundreds of thousands of footsoldiers. Armour was made of metal, lacquered leather or padded quilting. Weapons included bows and arrows, powerful crossbows, swords and halberds (long blades on poles). As the empire grew, the Han Chinese came into conflict with the many peoples whose lands now lay in China.

PRECIOUS SPEAR
This spearhead is over 3,200 years old. It was made from the precious stone jade set in bronze and turquoise. The spear was intended for ceremonial use, as it was far too precious to be used in combat.

SOLDIER ON HORSEBACK
A Tang dynasty warrior sits astride his horse, ready for battle. His horse is also ready to fight, covered by a protective jacket. The warrior's feet are supported by stirrups. These were useful in combat, as they allowed a soldier to remain steady in the saddle as he fought.

MAKE CHINESE ARMOUR

You will need: 150cm x 70cm felt fabric, scissors, large sewing needle, string, silver card, ruler, pencil, tape, split pins, silver paint, paintbrush, water pot, thick card, glue and brush.

1 Fold felt fabric in half. Cut a semicircle along fold to make a neck hole. Put garment on. Trim so it just reaches your hips and covers your shoulders.

2 Use scissors to make 2 holes either side of the waist. Pass string through holes. Secure as shown. The string will be used to tie the garment to your waist.

3 Cut 70 squares (5cm x 5cm) out of silver card. Lay a row of overlapping squares face down at the top of the fabric. Tape the rows together.

FIGHTING ON THE GREAT WALL

In 1884–1885, heavily armed French soldiers engaged in battle with the Chinese. The empire was in decline by the 1880s, and its outdated tactics were no match for the superior might of the French forces.

BATTLING HAN

This battered-looking helmet would once have protected a Han soldier's head from crossbow bolts, sword blows and arrows. Young men were conscripted into the Chinese army and had to serve as soldiers for at least two years. During this time they received no payment. However, they were supplied with food, weapons and armour.

FRONTIER GUARD

A battle-hardened soldier keeps guard with his shield and spear. A warrior like this would have kept watch over the precious Silk Road in a distant outpost of the Chinese empire. This model dates from the reign of the Tang emperor Taizong (AD626–649).

To put on your armour, pull the undergarment over your head. Ask a friend to help with the waist ties. Make holes in the shoulder pads and tie on with string.

4 Make enough rows to cover fabric. Trim card to fit at neck. Tape rows together. Take armour off fabric and turn over. Attach split pins at all corners.

5 Place armour over fabric. Push split pins through top and bottom corners of armour. Pass pins through fabric and fasten. Paint split pins silver.

6 Cut shoulder pads out of thick card. Cut out 5cm squares of silver card to cover pads. Glue to card. Push split pins through. Paint pins silver.

Festivals and Customs

THE CHINESE FESTIVAL best known around the world today is the New Year or Spring Festival. Its date varies according to the traditional Chinese calendar, which is based on the phases of the moon. The festival is marked by dancers carrying a long dragon through the streets, accompanied by loud, crackling firecrackers to scare away evil spirits. The festival has been celebrated for over 2,000 years and has always been a time for family feasts and village carnivals. The doorways of buildings are traditionally decorated with hand-written poetry on strips of red paper to bring luck and good fortune for the coming year.

Soon after New Year, sweet dumplings made of rice flour are prepared for the Lantern Festival. Paper lanterns are hung out to mirror the first full moon of the year. This festival began during the Tang dynasty (AD618–906). In the eighth month of the year, the autumn full moon is marked by the eating of special moon cakes. Chinese festivals are linked to agricultural seasons. They include celebrations of sowing and harvest, dances, horse races and the eating of specially prepared foods.

DANCING ANIMALS
Chinese New Year parades are often headed by a lion (*shown above*) or dragon. These are carried by dancers accompanied by crashing cymbals. The first month of the Chinese calendar begins on the first full moon between 21 January and 19 February.

HORSE RACING
The Mongols, who invaded China in the 1200s, brought with them their love of horses and superb riding skills. Today, children as young as three years old take part in horse-racing festivals in northern China and Mongolia. Archery and wrestling competitions are also regularly held.

MAKE A LANTERN

You will need: thick card, pencil, ruler, scissors, compasses, glue and brush, red tissue paper, blue paint, paintbrush, water pot, thin blue and yellow card, wire, tape, bamboo stick, torch, fringing fabric.

25cm
Frame (x4)
18cm
1cm
2.5cm
18cm
Side (x4)
16cm
End (x2)
18cm

Using the measurements above, draw the 10 pieces on to thick card (pieces not drawn to scale). Cut out pieces with scissors.

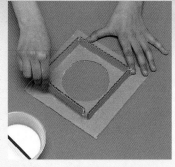

1 Using compasses, draw an 8cm diameter circle in the middle of one of the end pieces. Cut out the circle with scissors. Glue on the 4 sides, as shown.

2 Glue together the frame pieces. Then glue the end pieces on to the frame. When dry, cover frame with red tissue paper. Glue one side at a time.

DRAGON BOATS

In the fifth month of the Chinese year, races are held in the Dragon Boat festival. This is in memory of a famous statesman called Qu Yuan, who drowned himself in 278BC when his advice to his ruler was ignored. Rice dumplings are eaten at the Dragon Boat festival every year in his memory.

CHINESE LANTERNS

Elaborate paper lanterns brighten up a wedding in the 1800s during the Qing dynasty. Lanterns were also strung up or paraded on poles at other private celebrations and during Chinese festivals.

Light up your lantern by placing a small torch inside it. Decorate with a fringe. Now you can join in Chinese celebrations!

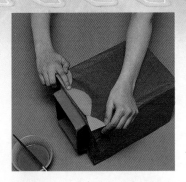

3 Paint top of lantern blue. Cut borders out of blue card. Glue to top and bottom of frame. Stick a thin strip of yellow card to bottom border.

4 Make 2 small holes opposite each other at top of lantern. Pass the ends of a loop of wire through each hole. Bend and tape ends to secure wire.

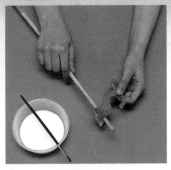

5 Make a hook from thick card. Split end opposite hook. Glue and wrap around bamboo stick. Hang lantern by wire loop from hook.

ANCIENT JAPAN

Japan is made up of almost 4,000 islands. Its people became experts at surviving in a harsh land surrounded by sea. They hunted animals and collected shellfish. Around 1,500 years ago, the rulers of Yamato in central Japan claimed the right to control all Japan and to be honoured as emperors. They were later succeeded by the military rulers known as shoguns. Samurai swordsmen helped the warlords rule their lands.

FIONA MACDONALD

CONSULTANT
HEIDI POTTER, JAPANESE FESTIVAL SOCIETY

The Land of the Rising Sun

IMAGINE YOU COULD TRAVEL BACK in time 32,000 years. That was when the first settlers reached Japan – a chain of islands between the Asian mainland and the vast Pacific Ocean. On their arrival, the early settlers would have encountered a varied and extreme landscape of rugged cliffs and spectacular volcanoes. Over the centuries, a distinctive Japanese civilization grew up, shaped by this dramatic environment. The Japanese people became experts at surviving in a harsh land. Emperors and shoguns, feuding samurai and peasant workers all played their part in the history of these islands. Many castles, temples, inventions and works of art have survived from the past to tell us what Japanese life was like in ancient times.

ANCIENT POTTERY
This decorated clay pot was made by Jomon craftworkers around 3000BC. The Jomon people were some of the earliest inhabitants of Japan. Jomon craftworkers were probably the first in the world to discover how to bake clay in fires to produce tough, long-lasting pots.

EARLY SETTLERS
The Ainu people live at the northern tip of Japan. They look unlike most other people in Japan, and speak a different language. Historians believe that they are probably descended from early settlers from Siberia.

TIMELINE 30,000BC–AD550

From around 30,000BC onwards the Japanese islands have been inhabited. For long periods during its history, Japan was isolated from the outside world. In 1854 that isolation came to an end.

*c.*30,000BC The first inhabitants of Japan arrive, probably across a bridge of dry land, from the continent of Asia.

*c.*20,000BC Sea-levels rise and the Japanese islands are cut off from the rest of the world.

early pottery

*c.*10,000BC The JOMON PERIOD begins. The Jomon people are hunter-gatherers who live mainly on the coasts. The world's first pottery is invented in Japan.

*c.*3000–2000BC People from the Jomon culture move inland. They begin to grow food crops.

*c.*2000–300BC The Jomon people move back towards the coasts and develop new sea-fishing techniques.

rice fields

*c.*300BC The YAYOI PERIOD begins. Settlers from South-east Asia and Korea arrive in Japan, bringing knowledge of paddy-field rice cultivation, metalwork and cloth-making techniques. Japanese society is transformed from wandering groups of hunters and gatherers. Communities of farmers live together in settled villages.

Yayoi bell

30,000BC	10,000BC	500BC	AD300

DAIMYO AND SAMURAI

A samurai swordsman is shown locked in mortal combat in this woodblock print. Daimyo (noble warlords) and samurai (highly trained warriors) played an important part in the history of Japan. Daimyo controlled large areas of Japan (domains), and served as regional governors. Samurai helped them to keep control of their lands, and fight rival warlords.

CHINA
RUSSIA
NORTH KOREA
SOUTH KOREA
Sea of Okhotsk
HOKKAIDO
JAPAN
Sea of Japan
HONSHU
N
SHIKOKU
KYUSHU
Pacific Ocean

MAGNIFICENT CASTLES

During the 1500s and 1600s, Japanese craftworkers built many magnificent castles. This one at Matsumoto was completed in 1594–97. Originally, castles were built for defence, but later they became proud status symbols. They were signs of their owners' great power and wealth.

THE ISLANDS OF JAPAN

The four main islands of Japan stretch across several climate zones, from the cold north-east to the semi-tropical south-west. In the past, each island had its own character. For example, northerners were said to be tough and patient, people from the central region were believed to value glory and honour more than money, while men from the south were regarded as the best fighters.

*c.*AD300 KOFUN (Old Tomb) PERIOD begins. A new culture develops. New bronze- and iron-working techniques are invented. Several small kingdoms grow up in different regions of Japan. Rulers of these kingdoms build huge mound-shaped tombs. There are wars between the kingdoms.

royal tomb

花刺蟲飛

Chinese writing

*c.*AD400 The Chinese method of writing arrives in Japan. It is brought by Buddhist scholars and monks who come from China to work for the emperors of Japan.

*c.*AD500 The YAMATO PERIOD begins. Kings from the Yamato region become powerful. They gradually take control of large areas of Japan by making alliances with local chiefs. The Yamato rulers also claim spiritual power, by descent from the Sun goddess, Amaterasu. Calling themselves emperors, they set up a powerful imperial court, appoint officials and award noble titles.

Mount Fuji

AD400

AD500

AD550

Eastern Islands

JAPAN IS MADE UP of four main islands – Kyushu, Shikoku, Honshu and Hokkaido – plus almost 4,000 smaller islands around the coast. According to legend, these islands were formed when tears shed by a goddess dropped into the sea. The first settlers arrived on the Japanese islands about 30,000BC and by 10,000BC, a hunter-gatherer civilization, called Jomon, had developed there. At first, the Jomon people lived by the sea and survived by collecting shellfish and hunting animals. Later, they moved inland, where they cultivated garden plots. After 300BC, settlers arrived from Korea, introducing new skills such as rice-growing and iron-working. People began to live in rice-growing villages around AD300 and, in time, groups of these villages came to be controlled by local lords.

Around AD500, the rulers of Yamato in central Japan became stronger than the rulers of the other regions. They claimed the right to rule all of Japan, and to be honoured as emperors. These emperors built new cities, where they lived with their courtiers. However, by 1185 rule of the country had passed to the shogun (a military ruler). There were bitter civil wars when rival warlords fought to become shogun. In 1600, the wars ended when the mighty Tokugawa Ieyasu became shogun. For over 250 years the shogun came from the Tokugawa family. This family controlled Japan until 1868, when Emperor Meiji regained the emperor's ancient ruling power.

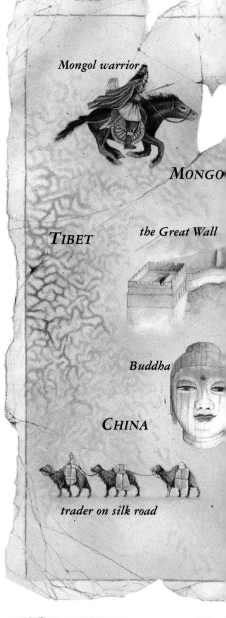

Mongol warrior

MONGO

TIBET

the Great Wall

Buddha

CHINA

trader on silk road

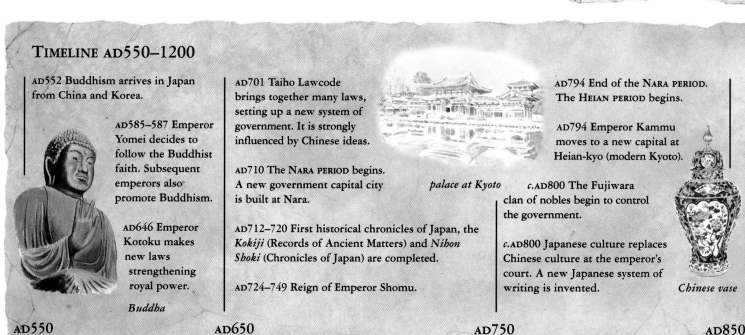

TIMELINE AD550–1200

AD552 Buddhism arrives in Japan from China and Korea.

AD585–587 Emperor Yomei decides to follow the Buddhist faith. Subsequent emperors also promote Buddhism.

AD646 Emperor Kotoku makes new laws strengthening royal power.

Buddha

AD701 Taiho Lawcode brings together many laws, setting up a new system of government. It is strongly influenced by Chinese ideas.

AD710 The NARA PERIOD begins. A new government capital city is built at Nara.

AD712–720 First historical chronicles of Japan, the *Kokiji* (Records of Ancient Matters) and *Nihon Shoki* (Chronicles of Japan) are completed.

AD724–749 Reign of Emperor Shomu.

palace at Kyoto

AD794 End of the NARA PERIOD. The HEIAN PERIOD begins.

AD794 Emperor Kammu moves to a new capital at Heian-kyo (modern Kyoto).

c.AD800 The Fujiwara clan of nobles begin to control the government.

c.AD800 Japanese culture replaces Chinese culture at the emperor's court. A new Japanese system of writing is invented.

Chinese vase

AD550   AD650   AD750   AD850

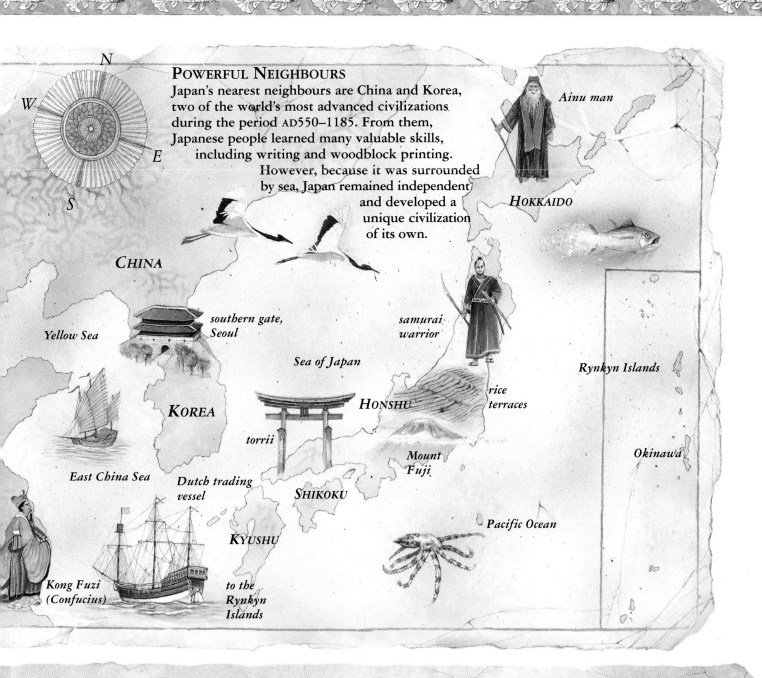

POWERFUL NEIGHBOURS

Japan's nearest neighbours are China and Korea, two of the world's most advanced civilizations during the period AD550–1185. From them, Japanese people learned many valuable skills, including writing and woodblock printing. However, because it was surrounded by sea, Japan remained independent and developed a unique civilization of its own.

Ainu man

HOKKAIDO

CHINA

southern gate, Seoul

Yellow Sea

samurai warrior

Sea of Japan

KOREA

HONSHU

Rynkyn Islands

rice terraces

torrii

East China Sea

Dutch trading vessel

SHIKOKU

Mount Fuji

Okinawa

Kong Fuzi (Confucius)

KYUSHU

to the Rynkyn Islands

Pacific Ocean

AD894 Links with China are broken.

*c.*AD900 The invention of new scripts for written Japanese leads to the growth of various kinds of literature. These works include collections of poetry, diaries, notebooks and novels. Many of the finest examples are written by rich, well-educated women at the emperor's court.

*c.*AD965 The birth of Sei Shonagon. Sei Shonagon is a courtier admired for her learning and for her witty and outspoken comments on people, places and events. She writes a famous pillow book (diary).

*c.*AD1000 *The Tale of Genji*, written by Lady Murasaki Shikibu, is completed. This was the story of love, politics and intrigue within the royal court. *The Tale of Genji* is one of the world's first novels. Lady Murasaki was the daughter of a powerful nobleman. She began to write after the death of her husband.

Lady Murasaki

AD1159 The Heiji civil war breaks out between two powerful clans, the Taira and the Minamoto. The Taira are victorious.

AD1185 Successive emperors lose control of the regions to warlike nobles. The HEIAN PERIOD ends. The Minamoto family, led by Minamoto Yoritomo, defeat the Taira. They gain control of most of Japan and set up a rival government at Kamakura, far from the imperial capital of Kyoto. Yoritomo takes the title of shogun.

Minamoto Yoritomo

AD1000   AD1100   AD1200

The Powerful and Famous

THE HISTORY OF ANCIENT JAPAN records the deeds of famous heroes, powerful emperors and bold warriors. Men and women who had won respect for their achievements in learning, religion and the arts were also held in high regard. In early Japanese society, royal traditions, honour, skill and bravery in battle were considered to be important, as was devotion to serious study. These principles mattered far more than the accumulation of wealth, or the invention of something new. Business people, no matter how successful, were in the lowest social class. However, during the Tokugawa period (1600–1868) many did gain financial power. Hard-working farmers, though in theory respected, led very difficult lives.

PRINCE YAMATO
Many stories were told about the daring adventures of this legendary hero. Prince Yamato probably never existed, but he is important because he symbolizes the power of Japan's first emperors. These emperors came from the Yamato region.

EMPRESS JINGU (ruled *c.*AD200)
According to Japanese legends, Empress (Kogo) Jingu ruled in about AD200, on behalf of her son. Many legends tell of her magic skills, such as her ability to control the waves and tides.

TIMELINE AD1200–1868

*c.*AD1200 Trade increases and a new coinage is developed. Zen Buddhism becomes popular during this period, especially with samurai warriors.

AD1274–1281 Mongols attempt to invade, but are driven back by storms.

samurai warrior

AD1331–1333 Emperor Godaigo tries to win back royal power. He fails, but his bid leads to a rebellion against the shogun.

AD1336 Ashikaga Takauji takes power and installs Emperor Komyo. He moves his court to Kyoto and encourages art and culture. Links with China are re-opened.

AD1338 Ashikaga Takauji takes the title shogun. The MUROMACHI PERIOD begins.

samurai swords

AD1467–1477 The Onin War – a civil war between rival nobles and provincial governors. The shogun's power collapses for a time. This is the first in a series of civil wars lasting until the 1590s. New daimyo (warlords) conquer vast territories in different regions.

AD1540 The first European traders and missionaries arrive in Japan. European traders hope to find spices and rich silks. European missionaries want to spread the Christian faith throughout Japan.

Portuguese sailor

AD1200   AD1300   AD1400   AD1500

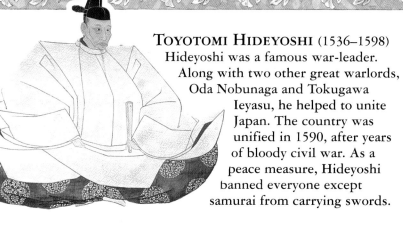

TOYOTOMI HIDEYOSHI (1536–1598)

Hideyoshi was a famous war-leader. Along with two other great warlords, Oda Nobunaga and Tokugawa Ieyasu, he helped to unite Japan. The country was unified in 1590, after years of bloody civil war. As a peace measure, Hideyoshi banned everyone except samurai from carrying swords.

LADY MURASAKI SHIKIBU (c.AD978–1014)

The writer Lady Murasaki spent much of her life at the royal court as an attendant to Empress Akiko. Her book, *The Tale of Genji*, tells the story of the life and loves of Genji, a Japanese prince, in a sensitive and poetic style.

THE MEIJI EMPEROR (1852–1912)

The Meiji imperial family are shown in this painting. The emperor began his reign in 1867. The following year the shoguns' long period in office was ended when nobles (daimyo) engineered their downfall. The nobles then installed the emperor as a figurehead ruler.

AD1500s Splendid castles are built and furnished by warlords.

AD1573 THE MOMOYAMA PERIOD begins.

AD1590 Civil wars end when warlord Hideyoshi wins control of all Japan.

Himeji castle

AD1600 MOMOYAMA PERIOD ends and the TOKUGAWA PERIOD begins.

AD1603 Tokugawa Ieyasu becomes shogun and rules all Japan. Shoguns from the TOKUGAWA DYNASTY rule Japan for the next 267 years. Edo (modern Tokyo) becomes the new capital.

Kabuki actor

AD1603 A long period of peace begins. Towns and trade expand and new popular forms of art and entertainment develop.

AD1600

AD1853 and 1854 USA sends Black Ships to demand the right to trade with Japan.

AD1868 End of the TOKUGAWA PERIOD. Tokugawa shoguns lose power. Emperor Meiji is made head of state and begins a programme of modernization.

Commander Perry's Black Ships

AD1800

God-like Emperors

THE JAPANESE PEOPLE began to live in villages in about 300BC. Over the next 600 years, the richest and most powerful of these villages became the centres of small kingdoms, controlling the surrounding lands. By about AD300, a kingdom based on the Yamato Plain in south-central Japan became bigger and stronger than the rest. It was ruled by chiefs of an *uji* (clan) who claimed to be descended from the Sun goddess. The chiefs of this Sun-clan were not only army commanders – they were priests, governors, law-makers and controllers of their people's treasure and food supply. Over the years, their powers increased. By around AD500, Sun-clan chiefs from Yamato ruled over most of Japan. They claimed power as emperors, and organized lesser chiefs to work for them, giving them noble titles as a reward. Each emperor chose his own successor from within the Sun-clan, and handed over to him the sacred symbols of imperial power – a jewel, a mirror and a sword. Sometimes, if a male successor to the throne was not old enough to rule, an empress would rule as regent in his place.

Descendants of these early emperors still rule Japan today. However, at times they had very little power. Some emperors played an active part in politics, but others spent their time shut away from the outside world. Today, the emperor has only a ceremonial role in the government of Japan.

HANIWA FIGURE
From around AD300 to AD550, hollow clay figures were placed around the edges of tombs. These figures, shaped like humans or animals, are known as Haniwa.

NARA
This shrine is in the ancient city of Nara. Originally called Heijokyo, Nara was founded by Empress Gemmei (ruled AD707–715) as a new capital for her court. The city was planned and built in Chinese style, with streets arranged in a grid pattern. The Imperial Palace was situated at the northern edge.

FANTASTIC STORIES

Prince Shotoku (AD574–622) was descended from the imperial family and from another powerful clan, the Soga. He never became emperor, but ruled as regent for 30 years on behalf of Empress Suiko. Many fantastic stories were told about him – for example, that he was able to speak as soon as he was born. It was also said that he could see into the future. More accurate reports of his achievements list his introduction of a new calendar, and his reform of government, based on Chinese ideas. He was also a supporter of the new Buddhist faith, introduced from China.

LARGEST WOODEN STRUCTURE

The Hall of the Great Buddha at Nara was founded on the orders of Emperor Shomu in AD745. The whole temple complex is said to be the largest wooden structure in the world. It houses a bronze statue of the Buddha, 16m tall and weighing 500 tonnes, and was also designed to display the emperor's wealth and power. There is a treasury close to the Hall of the Great Buddha, built in AD756. This housed the belongings of Emperor Shomu and his wife, Empress Komyo. The treasury still contains many rare and valuable items.

BURIAL MOUNDS

The Yamato emperors were buried in huge, mound-shaped tombs surrounded by lakes. The largest, built for Emperor Nintoku, is 480m long. From above, the tombs have a keyhole-shaped layout. Inside, they contain many buried treasures.

THE SUN GODDESS

The Sun goddess Amaterasu Omikami is shown emerging from the earth in this print. She was both honoured and feared by Japanese farmers. One of the emperor's tasks was to act as a link between the goddess and his people, asking for her help on their behalf. The goddess's main shrine was at Ise, in central Japan. Some of its buildings were designed to look like grain stores – a reminder of the Sun's power to cause a good or a bad harvest.

Nobles and Courtiers

IN EARLY JAPAN, everyone from the proudest chief to the poorest peasant owed loyalty to the emperor. However, many nobles ignored the emperor's orders – especially when they were safely out of reach of his court. There were plots and secret schemes as rival nobles struggled to influence the emperor and to seize power for themselves.

Successive emperors passed laws to try to keep their nobles and courtiers under control. The most important new laws were introduced by Prince Shotoku (AD574–622) and Prince Naka no Oe (AD626–671). Prince Naka considered his laws to be so important that he gave them the name Taika (Great Change). The Taika laws created a strong central government, run by a Grand Council of State, and a well-organized network of officials to oversee the 67 provinces.

BUGAKU
A Bugaku performer makes a slow, stately movement. Bugaku is an ancient form of dance that was popular at the emperor's court over 1,000 years ago. It is still performed there today.

POLITE BEHAVIOUR
A group of ladies watches an archery contest from behind a screen at the edge of a firing range. The behaviour of courtiers was governed by rigid etiquette. Noble ladies had to follow especially strict rules. It was bad-mannered for them to show their faces in public. Whenever men were present, the ladies crouched behind a low curtain or a screen, or hid their faces behind their wide sleeves or their fans. To protect their faces when travelling, they concealed themselves behind curtains or sliding panels fitted to their ox-carts. They also often left one sleeve dangling outside.

THE SHELL GAME
You will need: fresh clams, water bowl, paintbrush, gold paint, white paint, black paint, red paint, green paint, water pot.

1 Ask an adult to boil the clams. Allow them to cool and then remove the insides. Wash the shells and leave them to dry. When dry, paint the shells gold.

2 Carefully pull each pair of shells apart. Now paint an identical design on to each of a pair of clam shells. Start by painting a white, round face.

3 Add features to the face. In the past, popular pictures, such as scenes from the *Tale of Genji,* were painted on to the shell pairs.

NOBLES AT COURT

Two nobles are shown here riding a splendid horse. Noblemen at the imperial court spent much of their time on government business. They also practised their riding and fighting skills, took part in court ceremonies, and read and wrote poetry.

THE IMPERIAL COURT

Life at court was both elegant and refined. The buildings were exquisite and set in beautiful gardens. Paintings based on the writings of courtiers show some of the famous places they enjoyed visiting.

THE FUJIWARA CLAN

Fujiwara Teika (1162–1241) was a poet and a member of the Fujiwara clan. This influential family gained power at court by arranging the marriages of their daughters to young princes and emperors. Between AD724 and 1900, 54 of the 76 emperors of Japan had mothers who were related to the Fujiwara clan.

A LOOK INSIDE

This scroll-painting shows rooms inside the emperor's palace and groups of courtiers strolling in the gardens outside. Indoors, the rooms are divided up by silken blinds and the courtiers sit on mats and cushions.

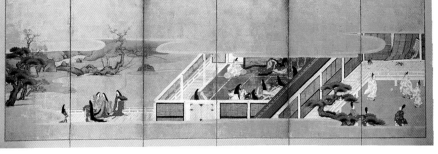

4 Paint several pairs of clam shells with various designs. Make sure that each pair of shells has an identical picture. Leave the painted shells to dry.

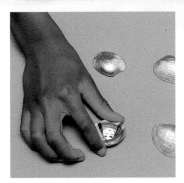

5 Turn all your shells face down and mix them up well. Turn over one shell then challenge your opponent to pick the matching shell to yours.

6 If the two shells do not match, turn them over and try again. If they do match, your opponent takes the shells. Take it in turns to challenge each other.

The person with the most shells wins! Noble ladies at the imperial court enjoyed playing the shell game. This is a simplified version of the game they used to play.

Shoguns and Civil Wars

In 1159, a bloody civil war, known as the Heiji War, broke out in Japan between two powerful clans, the Taira and the Minamoto.

The Taira were victorious in the Heiji War, and they controlled the government of the country for 26 years. However, the Minamoto rose again and regrouped to defeat the Taira in 1185.

Yoritomo, leader of the Minamoto clan, became the most powerful man in Japan and set up a new headquarters in the city of Kamakura. The emperor continued to act as head of the government in Kyoto, but he was effectively powerless.

For almost the next 700 years, until 1868, military commanders such as Yoritomo were the real rulers of Japan. They were known by the title *sei i tai shogun*, an army term meaning Great General Subduing the Barbarians.

SHOGUN FOR LIFE
Minamoto Yoritomo was the first person to take the title shogun and to hand the title on to his sons. In fact, the title did not stay in the Minamoto family for long because the family line died out in 1219. But new shogun families soon took its place.

FIRE! FIRE!
This scroll-painting illustrates the end of a siege during the Heiji War. The war was fought between two powerful clans, the Taira and the Minamoto. The rival armies set fire to buildings by shooting burning arrows and so drove the inhabitants out into the open where they could be killed.

MAKE A KITE
You will need: A1 card, ruler, pencil, dowling sticks tapered at each end (5 x 50cm, 2 x 70cm), masking tape, scissors, glue, brush, thread, paintbrush, paints, water pot, paper (52cm x 52cm), string, bamboo stick.

1 Draw a square 50cm x 50cm on card with a line down the centre. Lay the dowling sticks on the square. Glue the sticks to each other and then tape.

2 When the glue has dried, remove the masking tape. Take the frame off the card. Bind the corners of the frame with the strong thread.

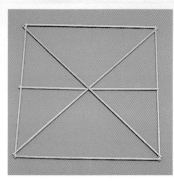

3 Now position your two longer dowling sticks so that they cross in the middle of the square. Glue and then bind the corners with the strong thread.

DYNASTY FOUNDER

Tokugawa Ieyasu (1542-1616) was a noble from eastern Japan. He was one of three powerful warlords who brought long years of civil war to an end and unified Japan. In 1603 he won the battle of Sekigahara and became shogun. His family, the Tokugawa, ruled Japan for the next 267 years.

RESTING PLACE

This mausoleum (burial chamber) was built at Nikko in north-central Japan. It was created to house the body of the mighty shogun Tokugawa Ieyasu. Three times a year, Ieyasu's descendants travelled to Nikko to pay homage to their great ancestor.

UNDER ATTACK

Life in Nijo Castle, Kyoto, is shown in great detail on this painted screen. The castle belonged to the Tokugawa family of shoguns. Like emperors, great shoguns built themselves fine castles, which they used as centres of government or as fortresses in times of war. Nijo Castle was one of the finest buildings in Japan. It had 'nightingale' floors that creaked loudly when an intruder stepped on them, raising the alarm. The noise was made to sound like a bird call.

Kites were sometimes used for signalling during times of war. The Japanese have also enjoyed playing with kites for over 1,000 years.

4 Paint a colourful kite pattern on to the paper. It is a good idea to tape the edges of the paper down so it does not move around or curl up.

5 Draw light pencil marks 1cm in from the corners of the paper on all four sides. Carefully cut out the corners of the paper, as shown.

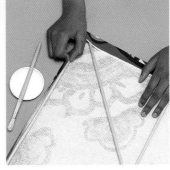

6 Glue the paper on to the kite frame. You will need to glue along the wooden frame and fold the paper over the edge of the frame. Leave to dry.

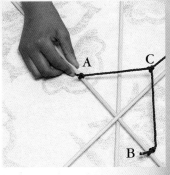

7 Tie a short length of string across the centre of the kite frame (A to B). Knot a long kite string on to it as shown (C). Wind the string on the bamboo.

Samurai

BETWEEN 1185 AND 1600 there were a great many wars as rival nobles (known as 'daimyo') fought to become shogun. Some emperors also tried, unsuccessfully, to restore imperial rule. During this troubled time in Japanese history, emperors, shoguns and daimyo all relied on armies of well-trained samurai (warriors) to fight their battles. The samurai were men from noble families, and they were skilled at fighting battles. Members of each samurai army were bound together by a solemn oath, sworn to their lord. They stayed loyal from a sense of honour – and because their lord gave them rich rewards. The civil wars ended around 1600, when the Tokugawa dynasty of shoguns came to power. From this time onwards, samurai spent less time fighting. Instead, they served their lords as officials and business managers.

RIDING OFF TO WAR
Painted in 1772, this samurai general is in full armour. A samurai's horse had to be fast, agile and strong enough to carry the full weight of the samurai, his armour and his weapons.

TACHI
Swords were a favourite weapon of the samurai. This long sword is called a *tachi*. It was made in the 1500s for ceremonial use by a samurai.

METAL HELMET
Samurai helmets like this were made from curved metal panels, carefully fitted together, and decorated with elaborate patterns. The jutting peak protected the wearer's face and the nape-guard covered the back of the neck. This helmet dates from around 1380.

SAMURAI HELMET

You will need: *thick card, pin, string, felt-tip pen, ruler, scissors, tape measure, newspaper, bowl, water, PVA glue, balloon, petroleum jelly, pencil, modelling clay, bradawl, paper, gold card, paints, brush, water pot, glue brush, masking tape, paper fasteners, 2 x 20cm lengths of cord.*

1 Draw a circle 18cm in diameter on card using the pin, string and felt-tip pen. Using the same method, draw two larger circles 20cm and 50cm.

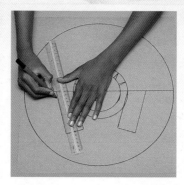

2 Draw a line across the centre of the three circles using the ruler and felt-tip pen. Draw tabs in the middle semi-circle. Add two flaps as shown.

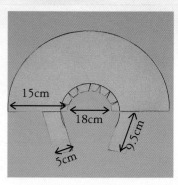

15cm · 18cm · 9.5cm · 5cm

3 Now cut out the neck protector piece completely, as shown above. Make sure that you cut around the tabs and flaps exactly.

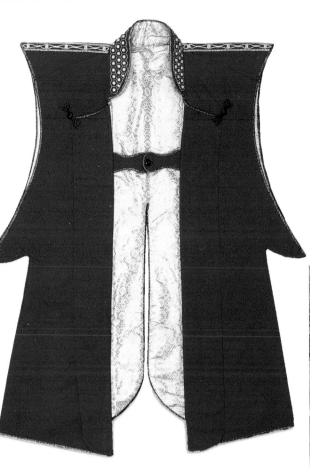

PROTECTIVE CLOTHING

This fine suit of samurai armour dates from the Tokugawa period (1600–1868). Armour gave the samurai life-saving protection in battle. High-ranking warriors wore suits of plate armour, made of iron panels, laced or riveted together and combined with panels of chain mail or rawhide. Lower-ranking soldiers, called *ashigaru*, wore thinner, lightweight armour, made of small metal plates. A full suit of samurai armour could weigh anything up to 18kg.

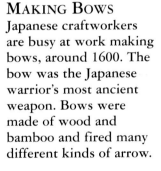

SURCOAT FINERY

For festivals, ceremonies and parades samurai wore surcoats (long, loose tunics) over their armour. Surcoats were made from fine, glossy silks, dyed in rich colours. This example was made during the Tokugawa period (1600–1868). Surcoats were often decorated with family crests. These were originally used to identify soldiers in battle, but later became badges of high rank.

MAKING BOWS

Japanese craftworkers are busy at work making bows, around 1600. The bow was the Japanese warrior's most ancient weapon. Bows were made of wood and bamboo and fired many different kinds of arrow.

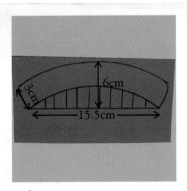

4 Draw the peak template piece on another piece of card. Follow the measurements shown in the picture. Cut out the peak template.

5 To make papier-mâché, tear the newspaper into small strips. Fill the bowl with 1 part PVA glue to 3 parts water. Add the newspaper strips.

6 Blow up the balloon to the size of your head. Cover with petroleum jelly. Build up three papier-mâché layers on the top and sides. Leave to dry between layers.

7 When dry, pop the balloon and trim. Ask a friend to make a mark on either side of your head.

Instructions for the helmet continue on the next page...

The Way of the Warrior

SAMURAI were highly-trained warriors who dedicated their lives to fighting for their lords. However, being a samurai involved more than just fighting. The ideal samurai was supposed to follow a strict code of behaviour, governing all aspects of his life. This code was called *bushido* – the way of the warrior. *Bushido* called for skill, self-discipline, bravery, loyalty, honour, honesty, obedience and, at times, self-sacrifice. It taught that it was nobler to die fighting than to run away and survive.

Many samurai warriors followed the religious teachings of Zen, a branch of the Buddhist faith. Zen was introduced into Japan by two monks, Eisai and Dogen, who went to China to study in the 1100s and 1200s and brought Zen practices back with them. Teachers of Zen encouraged their followers to meditate (to free the mind of all thoughts) in order to achieve enlightenment.

THE TAKEDA FAMILY
The famous daimyo (warlord) Takeda Shingen (1521–1573), fires an arrow using his powerful bow. The influential Takeda family owned estates in Kai province near the city of Edo and kept a large private army of samurai warriors. Takeda Shingen fought a series of wars with his near neighbour, Uesugi Kenshin. However, in 1581, the Takeda were defeated by the army of General Nobunaga.

SWORDSMEN
It took young samurai many years to master the skill of swordsmanship. They were trained by master swordsmen. The best swords, made of strong, springy steel, were even given their own names.

8 Place clay under the pencil marks. Make two holes – one above and one below each pencil mark – with a bradawl. Repeat on the other side.

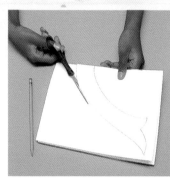

9 Fold a piece of A4 paper and draw a horn shape on to it following the design shown above. Cut out this shape so that you have an identical pair of horns.

10 Take a piece of A4 size gold card. Place your paper horns on to the gold card and draw around them. Carefully cut the horns out of the card.

11 Paint the papier-mâché helmet brown. Paint a weave design on the neck protector and a cream block on each flap. Leave to dry.

OFF TO WAR

A samurai warrior (on horseback) and foot-soldiers set off for war. Samurai had to command and inspire confidence in others, so it was especially important for them to behave in a brave and honourable way.

MARTIAL ARTS

Several sports that people enjoy playing today have developed from samurai fighting skills. In aikido, players try to throw their opponent off-balance and topple them to the ground. In kendo, players fight one another with long swords made of split bamboo. They score points by managing to touch their opponent's body, not by cutting or stabbing them!

kendo   *aikido*

SURVIVAL SKILLS

Samurai had to know how to survive in wild countryside. Each man carried emergency rations of dried rice. He also used his fighting skills to hunt wild animals for food.

ZEN

The Buddhist monk Rinzai is shown in this Japanese brush and ink scroll-painting. Rinzai was a famous teacher of Zen ideas. Many pupils, including samurai, travelled to his remote monastery in the mountains to study with him.

Samurai helmets were often decorated with crests made of lacquered wood or metal. These were mounted on the top of the helmet.

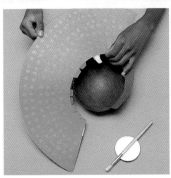

12 Bend back the tabs on the peak piece. Position it at the front of the helmet. Stick the tabs to the inside with glue. Hold in place with tape.

13 Now take the neck protector. Bend back the front flaps and the tabs. Glue the tabs to the helmet, as shown. Leave the helmet to dry.

14 Stick the horns to the front of the helmet. Use paper fasteners to secure, as shown. Decorate the ear flaps with paper fasteners.

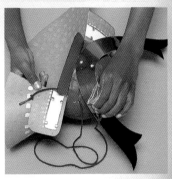

15 Thread cord through one of the holes made in step 8. Tie a knot in the end. Thread the other end of the cord through the second hole. Repeat on the other side.

Peasant Farmers

Until the 1900s, most Japanese people lived in the countryside and made a living either by fishing or by farming small plots of land. Japanese farmers grew crops for three different reasons. They grew rice to sell to the samurai or to pay taxes. Barley, millet, wheat and vegetables were used for their own food.

Traditionally, Japanese society was divided into four main classes – samurai, peasant farmers, craftworkers and merchants. Samurai were the most highly respected. Farmers and craftworkers came next because they produced useful goods. Merchants were the lowest rank because they produced nothing themselves.

During the Tokugawa period (1600–1868), society began to change. Towns and cities grew bigger, small industries developed and trade increased. Farmers began to sell their crops to people who had no land of their own. For the first time, some farmers had money to spend on better clothes, houses, and more food.

WRESTLERS
Sumo wrestling has long been a favourite sport in Japan. It developed from religious rituals and from games held at farmers' festivals in the countryside. Sumo wrestlers are usually very fat. They use their massive weight to overbalance their opponents.

RICE FARMING
Planting out tiny rice seedlings in shallow, muddy water was tiring, back-breaking work. Rice farming was introduced to Japan soon after 300BC. Most varieties of rice need to grow in flooded fields, called *tanbo* (paddy-fields). To provide extra food, farmers also reared fish in the *tanbo*.

TERRACING
It was difficult to find enough flat land for growing crops in Japan, so terraces were cut, like steps, into the steep hillsides. Farmland could be shaken by earthquakes or ruined by floods. In years when the harvests failed, there was often famine.

FAVOURITE FOODS

Soya beans and *daikon* (white radishes) were two popular Japanese foods. The Japanese developed storage methods that would allow them to last for months. The radishes were covered in earth and the beans were dried to provide essential winter food supplies. Farmers grew vegetables like these in small garden plots or in terraced fields.

daikon
radish

soya beans

A HARD LIFE

A woman farm-worker carries heavy baskets of grain on a wooden yoke. Although farmers were respected, their lives were often very hard. Until the late 1800s, they had to pay heavy taxes to the emperor or the local lord and were not free to leave their lord's land. They were also forbidden from wearing silk clothes, and drinking tea or *sake* (rice wine).

THRESHING

Japanese farmers are busy threshing wheat in this photograph taken in the late 1800s. Although this picture is relatively recent, the method of threshing has changed little over the centuries. The workers at the far right and the far left are separating the grains of wheat from the stalks by pulling them through wooden sieves. In the background, one worker carries a huge bundle of wheat stalks, while another stands ready with a rake and a winnowing fan. The fan was used to remove the chaff from the grain by tossing the grain in the air so that the wind blew the chaff away.

Treasures from the Sea

JAPAN IS A NATION OF ISLANDS, and few people live very far from the sea. From the earliest times, Japanese people relied on the sea for food. Farms, fishing villages and huts for drying fish and seaweed were all built along Japan's rugged coastline. Heaps of oyster shells and fish bones, thrown away by the Jomon people, have survived from over 10,000 years ago.

Japanese men and women took many different kinds of food from the sea. They found crabs, shrimps and limpets in shallow water by the shore, or set sail in small boats to catch deep-sea varieties such as tuna, mackerel, shark, whale and squid. Japanese people also gathered seaweed (which contains important minerals) and other sea creatures such as jellyfish and sea-slugs. Underwater, they found treasures such as pearls and coral which were both highly prized. Specially trained divers, often women, risked their lives by holding their breath for long periods underwater to harvest these precious items. The sea also provided salt, which was collected in salt-pans (hollows built next to the sea). Salt was used to preserve fish and vegetables and to make pickles of many different kinds.

INSPIRATIONAL
Strange and beautiful sea creatures inspired Japanese painters and print-makers to create many works of art. This painting shows two flat fish and a collection of shellfish. Tuna, sea bream and salmon were all popular fish caught around the coast of Japan. They were usually grilled or preserved by salting or drying.

DANGEROUS SEAS
Japanese sailors and their boat are tossed around by wind and waves in a rough sea. This scene is depicted in a woodblock print by Utagawa Kuniyoshi. The seas around Japan's rocky coasts are often wild and stormy. Being a fisherman was, and still is, a very risky job. Late summer is the most dangerous season to go fishing because monsoon winds from the Pacific Ocean cause very violent typhoon storms. These storms can easily sink a fishing boat.

SEAFOOD

Sea products have always been very important in Japan. Oysters were collected for their pearls and also for eating. Oyster stew is still a favourite dish in southern Japan. Mussels were cooked to make many tasty dishes. They flourish in the wild, but in Japan today they are also farmed. Seaweed was used to give flavour to foods. Today it is also used as the wrapping for *maki sushi* (rolls of vinegared rice with fish and vegetable fillings).

oysters

seaweed

mussel

FISHING METHODS

For many centuries, Japanese fishermen used only baited hooks and lines. This limited the number of fish they could catch on any one trip. But after 1600 they began to use nets for fishing, which allowed them to make bigger catches.

MOTHER-OF-PEARL

Made around 1500, this domed casket is decorated with mother-of-pearl, a beautiful material that forms the coating on the inside of an oyster shell. With great skill and patience, Japanese craftworkers cut out and shaped tiny pieces of mother-of-pearl. These pieces were used to decorate many valuable items.

OYSTER COLLECTING

Gangs of oyster gatherers collect shellfish from the sea bed. Both men and women are shown working together. Oysters have thick, heavy shells, so the workers have to be fit and strong to carry full buckets back to the shore.

GATHERING SHELLFISH

Painted in the 1800s, this picture makes shellfish-gathering look like a pleasant task. In fact, hands and feet soon became numb with cold and the salt water made them red and raw.

Meals and Manners

JAPANESE FOOD has always been simple but healthy. However, for many centuries famine was a constant fear, especially among the poor. The traditional Japanese diet was based on grains – rice, millet, wheat or barley – boiled, steamed or made into noodles. Many foods were flavoured with soy sauce, made from crushed, fermented soya beans. Another nutritious soya product, *tofu* (beancurd), was made from soya beans softened and pulped in water. The pulp was formed into blocks and left to set. *Tofu* has a texture somewhere between custard and cheese, and a mild taste.

What people ate depended on who they were. Only the wealthy could afford rice, meat (usually poultry) or the finest fish. Poor families lived on what they could grow or catch for themselves.

Until the 1900s, people in Japan did not eat red meat or dairy products. But Japanese farmers grew many fruits, including pears, berries and oranges. One small, sweet orange is named after the Satsuma region in the warm southern lands of Japan.

FRESH VEGETABLES

A vegetable seller is shown here taking his produce to market. He carries it in big baskets hanging from a yoke supported on his shoulders. This photograph was taken around 1900, but the tradition of going to market every day to sell vegetables started some time around 1600. At this time many more people began to live in towns. The Japanese have always liked their food to be very fresh.

ONIGIRI - RICE BALLS

You will need: 7 cups Japanese rice, saucepan, wooden spoon, sieve, bowls, 1 tbsp salt, cutting board, 1 tbsp black sesame seeds, $1/2$ sheet yaki nori seaweed (optional), knife, cucumber, serving dish.

1 Ask an adult to boil the rice. Sieve to drain, but do not rinse. The rice should remain gluey. Place the rice in one bowl and the salt into another one.

2 Wet the palms of both hands with cold water. Next, put a finger into the bowl of salt and rub a little on to your palms.

3 Place one eighth of the rice on one hand. Use both hands to shape the rice into a triangle. You should use firm but not heavy pressure.

SAKE

This *sake* bottle was made almost 600 years ago, in the Bizen pottery style. *Sake* is a sweet rice wine. It was drunk by wealthy noble families and by ordinary people on very special occasions. Traditionally, it was served warm from pottery flasks or bottles such as this one and poured into tiny cups.

CHOPSTICKS

Japanese people eat using chopsticks. Traditionally, chopsticks were made from bamboo, but today many different materials, including lacquered wood, are used. In the past, rich nobles used silver chopsticks. This was mainly to display their wealth. However, they also believed the silver would help them detect any poison that had been slipped into their food. They thought that on contact with the poison, the silver would turn black.

ornate chopsticks

ordinary chopsticks

TEA

A servant offers a bowl of tea to a seated samurai. The Japanese believed that no matter how poor or humble people were, it was important to serve food in a gracious way. Good table manners were essential.

TABLEWARE

Food was served and eaten in pottery bowls and on plates. In contrast to the round and flat dishes found in many other countries, Japanese craftworkers often created tableware in elegant shapes, such as this six-sided dish.

4 Make more rice balls in the same way. Place each rice ball in one hand and sprinkle sesame seeds over the rice ball with the other.

5 If available, cut a strip of yaki nori seaweed into four and wrap some of your rice balls in it. To serve your *onigiri*, garnish them with sliced cucumber.

Rice was introduced to Japan in AD100. It has remained the staple food of the islands ever since. Serve your Japanese meal on a pretty dish and eat it with chopsticks.

Family Life

FAMILIES IN ANCIENT JAPAN survived by working together in the family business or on the family land. Japanese people believed that the family group was more important than any one individual. Family members were supposed to consider the well-being of the whole family first, before thinking about their own needs and plans. Sometimes, this led to quarrels or disappointments. For example, younger brothers in poor families were often not allowed to marry so that the family land could be handed on, undivided, to the eldest son. Daughters would leave home to marry if a suitable husband could be found. If not, they also remained single, in their parents' house.

Family responsibility passed down the generations, from father to eldest son. Japanese families respected age and experience because they believed it brought wisdom.

LOOKING AFTER BABY
It was women's work to care for young children. This painting shows an elegant young mother from a rich family dressing her son in a *kimono* (a robe with wide sleeves). The family maid holds the belt for the boy's *kimono*, while a pet cat watches nearby.

WORK
A little boy uses a simple machine to help winnow rice. (Winnowing separates the edible grains of rice from the outer husks.) Boys and girls from farming families were expected to help with work around the house and farmyard, and in the fields.

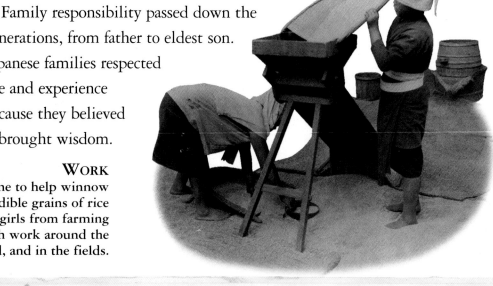

CARP STREAMER

You will need: pencil, 2 sheets of A1 paper, felt-tip pen, scissors, paints, paintbrush, water pot, glue, wire, masking tape, string, cane.

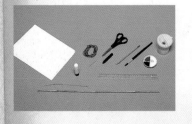

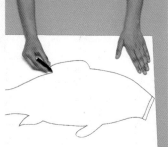

1 Take the pencil and one piece of paper. Draw a large carp fish shape on to the paper. When you are happy with the shape, go over it in felt-tip pen.

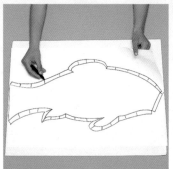

2 Put the second piece of paper over the first. Draw around the fish shape. Next, draw a border around the second fish and add tabs, as shown.

3 Add scales, eyes, fins and other details to both of the fishes, as shown above. Cut them both out, remembering to snip into the tabs. Paint both fishes.

PLAYTIME

These young boys have started two tops spinning close to one another. They are waiting to see what will happen when the tops touch. Japanese children had many different toys with which to play. As well as the spinning top, another great favourite was the kite.

TRADITIONAL MEDICINE

Kuzu and ginger are ingredients that have been used for centuries as treatments in traditional Japanese medicine. Most traditional drugs are made from vegetables. The *kuzu* and ginger are mixed together in different ways depending on the symptoms of the patient. For example, there are 20 different mixtures for treating colds. Ginger is generally used when there is no fever.

kuzu   *ginger*

HONOURING ANCESTORS

A mother, father and child make offerings and say their prayers at a small family altar in their house. The lighted candle and paper lantern help guide the spirits to their home. Families honoured their dead ancestors at special festivals. At the festival of Obon, in summer, they greeted family spirits who had returned to earth.

4 Put the two fish shapes together, with the painted sides out. Turn the tabs in and glue the edges of the fish together, except for the tail and the mouth.

5 Use picture or garden wire to make a ring the size of the mouth. Twist the ends together, as shown Then bend them back. Bind the ends with masking tape.

6 Place the ring in the fish's mouth. Glue the ends of the mouth over the ring. Tie one end of some string on to the mouth ring and the other end to a garden cane.

Families fly carp streamers on Boy's Day (the fifth day of the fifth month) every year. One carp is flown for each son. Carp are symbols of perseverence and strength.

Houses and Homes

JAPANESE BUILDERS faced many challenges when they designed homes for Japan's harsh environment. They built lightweight, single-storey houses made of straw, paper and wood. These materials would bend and sway in an earthquake. If they did collapse, or were swept away by floods, they would be less likely than a stone building to injure the people inside.

Japanese buildings were designed as a series of box-like rooms. One room was sufficient for the hut of a farming family, but a whole series of rooms could be linked together to form a royal palace. The space within was divided by screens which could be moved around to suit people's needs. Most houses had raised timber floors that were about $^1/_2$m off the ground.

LAMPS

This pottery lantern has a delicate, cut-out design and was probably for use outdoors. Inside, Japanese homes were lit by candles. A candle was placed on a stand which had four paper sides. The paper protected the candle from draughts. One side could be lifted to insert and remove the candle. There were many different styles and designs. House-fires, caused by cooking and candles, were a major hazard. They were a particular problem because so many homes were made of wood.

SILK HOUSE

For many people in Japan, home was also a place of work. Tucked under the thatched roof of this house in Eiyama, central Japan, was an attic where silk producers bred silk-worms.

MAKE A SCREEN

You will need: gold paper (44cm x 48cm), scissors, thick card (22cm x 48cm), craft knife, metal ruler, cutting board, glue stick, ruler, pencil, paints, paintbrush, water pots, fabric tape.

1 Cut two pieces of gold paper (22cm x 48cm). Use a craft knife to cut out a piece of card the same size. Stick the gold paper to both sides of the card.

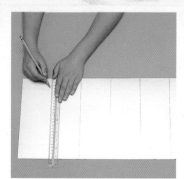

2 Use a ruler and pencil to carefully mark out six equal panels, on one side of the card. Each panel should measure 22cm x 8cm.

3 Now turn your card over. Paint a traditional picture of Japanese irises, as shown above. When you have finished, leave the paint to dry.

RICH FURNISHINGS

The interior of a richly furnished building is shown in this print from 1857. Japanese furnishings were often very plain and simple. However, this house has a patterned mat and a carpet on the floor, a tall lampstand, a black and gold side table, and a brightly coloured screen dividing the room. There is also a musical instrument called a *koto* with 13 silk strings.

SCREENS

Wood and paper screens were used to make both outer and inner walls. These could be pushed back to provide peaceful garden views and welcome cool breezes during Japan's hot summers.

ON THE VERANDA

Japanese buildings often had verandas (open platforms) underneath their wide, overhanging eaves. These could be used for taking fresh air, keeping lookout or enjoying a beautiful view. The people at this inn are relaxing after taking a bath in the natural hot springs.

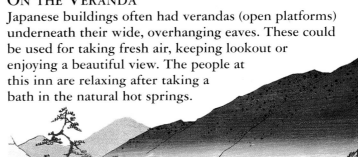

4 Turn the screen over, so the plain side is facing you. Using scissors or a craft knife, cut out each panel completely along the lines you have drawn.

5 Now use fabric tape to join each of your panels, leaving a small gap between every other panel. The tape will work as hinges for the screen.

Japanese people liked to decorate their homes with pictures of iris flowers. Traditionally, irises reminded them of absent friends.

The City in the Clouds

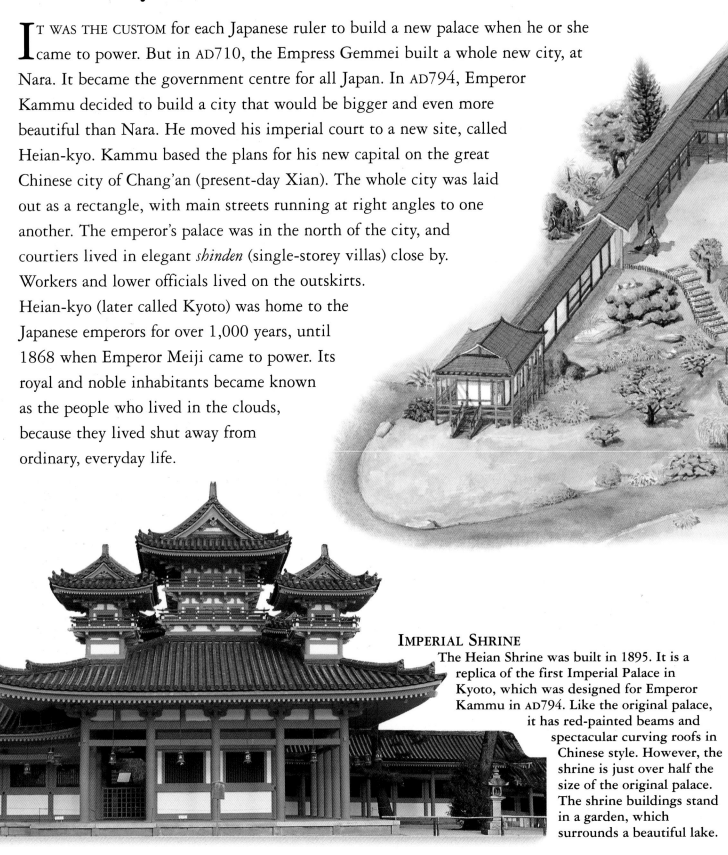

IT WAS THE CUSTOM for each Japanese ruler to build a new palace when he or she came to power. But in AD710, the Empress Gemmei built a whole new city, at Nara. It became the government centre for all Japan. In AD794, Emperor Kammu decided to build a city that would be bigger and even more beautiful than Nara. He moved his imperial court to a new site, called Heian-kyo. Kammu based the plans for his new capital on the great Chinese city of Chang'an (present-day Xian). The whole city was laid out as a rectangle, with main streets running at right angles to one another. The emperor's palace was in the north of the city, and courtiers lived in elegant *shinden* (single-storey villas) close by. Workers and lower officials lived on the outskirts. Heian-kyo (later called Kyoto) was home to the Japanese emperors for over 1,000 years, until 1868 when Emperor Meiji came to power. Its royal and noble inhabitants became known as the people who lived in the clouds, because they lived shut away from ordinary, everyday life.

IMPERIAL SHRINE

The Heian Shrine was built in 1895. It is a replica of the first Imperial Palace in Kyoto, which was designed for Emperor Kammu in AD794. Like the original palace, it has red-painted beams and spectacular curving roofs in Chinese style. However, the shrine is just over half the size of the original palace. The shrine buildings stand in a garden, which surrounds a beautiful lake.

LIFE IN A *SHINDEN*

In Heian-kyo, nobles and courtiers lived in splendid *shinden* houses like this one. Each *shinden* was designed as a number of separate buildings, linked by covered walkways. It was usually set in a landscaped garden, with artificial hills, ornamental trees, bridges, pavilions and ponds. Sometimes a stream flowed through the garden – and through parts of the house, as well. The various members of the noble family, and their servants, lived in different parts of the *shinden*.

GOLDEN PAVILION

This is a replica of the famous Kinkakuji (Temple of the Golden Pavilion). The original was completed in 1397 and survived until 1950. But, like many of Kyoto's old wooden buildings, it was destroyed by fire. The walls of the pavilion are covered in gold leaf, giving out a golden glow that is reflected in the calm waters of a shallow lake.

SILVER TEMPLE

The Ginkakuji (Temple of the Silver Pavilion) in Kyoto was completed in 1483. Despite its name, it was never painted silver, but left as natural wood.

THRONE ROOM

The Shishinden Enthronement Hall is within the palace compound in Kyoto. The emperor would have sat on the raised platform *(left)* while his courtiers bowed low before him. This palace was the main residence for all emperors from 1331 to 1868.

The Castle Builders

FOR MANY CENTURIES, powerful nobles lived in the city of Heian-kyo (later called Kyoto). But after about AD1000, some noble families began to build up large *shoen* (private estates in the countryside). These families often went to war against each other. They built castles on their lands to protect themselves, their *shoen* and the soldiers in their private armies.

Unlike all other traditional Japanese buildings (except temples), castles were several storeys high. Most were built on naturally well-defended sites such as rocky cliffs. The earliest had a *tenshu* (tall central tower) surrounded by strong wooden fences or stone walls. Later castles were more elaborate buildings, with ramparts, moats and inner and outer courtyards surrounding the central *tenshu*. The period 1570–1690 is often called the Golden Age of castle design when many magnificent castles were built by daimyo (noble warlord) families. These castles were so strong that they challenged the power of the shogun. In 1615, shogun Tokugawa Ieyasu banned noble families from building more than one castle on their estates.

CASTLE OF THE WHITE HERON
The largest surviving Japanese castle is Himeji Castle, in southern Japan. Some people say it is also the most beautiful. It is often called the Castle of the White Heron because of its graceful roofs, curved like a bird's wings. The castle was built by the Akamatsu family in the 1500s. It was taken over by warlord Toyotomi Hideyoshi in 1580.

CASTLE OF WOOD
Himeji Castle is made mostly of wood. The building work required 387 tonnes of timber and 75,000 roof tiles. Outside, strong wooden beams are covered with special fireproof plaster. Inside, there are floors and staircases of polished wood.

CASTLE UNDER SIEGE

The usual way to attack a castle was by siege. Enemy soldiers surrounded it, then waited for the inhabitants to run out of food. Meanwhile, they did all they could to break down the castle's defences by storming the gates and killing the guards.

RUN FOR IT!

This painted screen shows a siege at Osaka Castle in 1615. The inhabitants of the castle are running for their lives, chased by enemy soldiers. The castle moat and walls are visible in the background.

IN THE HEART OF THE CAPITAL

Nijo Castle, Kyoto, was begun by warrior Oda Nobunaga in 1569, and finished by Tokugawa Ieyasu. It was designed to give its owner total control over the emperor's capital city – and all Japan.

BUILDING MATERIALS

Castles were built of wood such as pine and stone. For the lower walls, huge boulders were cut roughly from the quarries or collected from mountainsides. They were fitted together by hand without mortar so that in an earthquake the boulders could move slightly without the whole building collapsing. Castle stonework was usually left rough, but it was occasionally chiselled to a fine, smooth finish. Upper walls were made of wooden planks and spars, covered with plaster made from crushed stone mixed with water.

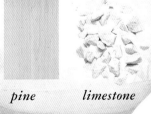

pine   *limestone*

SURROUNDED BY WATER

Castles were surrounded by wide, deep moats to keep out invaders. A typical moat might be 20m wide and 6m deep. The only way into the castle was across a wooden drawbridge guarded by soldiers at both ends. The castle was also defended by strong stone ramparts, often 5m thick. They sloped into the moat so that any attacker could easily be seen from above.

Towns and Trade

Until modern times (after around 1900) most Japanese people lived in the countryside. But after 1600, when Japan was at peace, castle-towns in particular grew rapidly. Towns and cities were great centres of craftwork and trade. As one visitor to Kyoto commented in 1691, 'There is hardly a household... where there is not something made or sold.' Trade also increased in small towns and villages, linking even the most remote districts into a countrywide network of buying and selling.

Castle-towns were carefully planned. Roads, gates, walls and water supplies were laid out in an orderly design. Areas of the town were set aside for different groups of people to live and work – nobles, daimyo and high-ranking samurai families, ordinary samurai, craftworkers, merchants and traders. Many towns became centres of entertainment with theatres, puppet plays, dancers, musicians and artists. Big cities also had pleasure districts where the inhabitants could escape from the pressures of everyday life.

TOWN WOODWORKERS
Netsuke were toggles used to attach small items to a *kimono* belt. Three carpenters are carved on this ivory example. Woodworkers were kept busy in towns, building and repairing houses.

A TRADITIONAL TOWN
This picture was drawn by a visiting European artist in 1882. It shows a narrow, busy street in a Japanese city. Although it is a relatively recent picture, it shows styles of clothes, shops and houses that had existed for several hundred years. The buildings are made of wood and the shops open directly on to the streets. The cloth hangings above the doorways represent the type of shop, for example, knife shop or fan shop. They are printed or woven with *kanji* characters or special designs. The European artist obviously could not read Japanese because the writing on the shop boards and banners is meaningless squiggles.

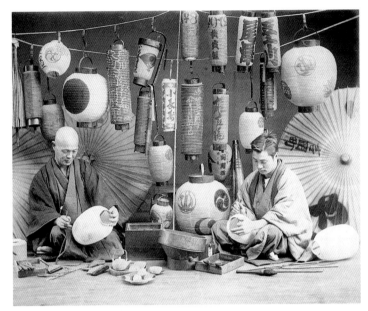

SKILLED AT WEAVING SILK

Silk was woven on a loom like the one shown here. This woodblock print dates from about 1770. Towns were great centres of cloth production. Kyoto, in particular, was famous for its silk fabrics patterned with gold and silver flowers.

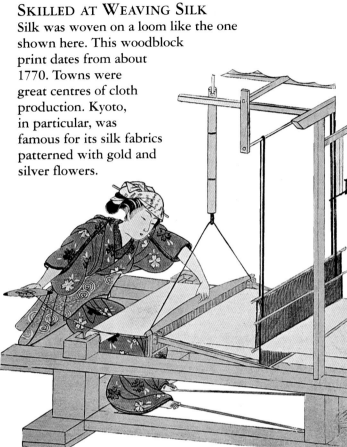

MANY DIFFERENT CRAFTS

These two men are busy making paper lanterns. From the earliest times craftworkers with many different skills worked in Japanese towns. One list of craft guilds, drawn up in Osaka in 1784, included 24 trades. They ranged from makers of porcelain, parasols and face-powder, to basket-weavers, printers, paper-sellers, paint-mixers, cotton-spinners, ivory carvers, and makers of socks.

PLEASURE PURSUIT

Actors, musicians and entertainers, like this well-dressed young woman, lived and worked in the pleasure districts of many towns. The most famous was the Yoshiwara district of Edo. In big cities, they were full of inns and restaurants. Young female entertainers were called *geisha*.

Merchants and sometimes samurai would enjoy a meal and a drink while the *geisha* danced and sang for their pleasure.

FIRE HAZARD

Fire was a constant danger in Japanese cities. This was because most buildings were made of wood and packed close together. In an effort to prevent fires from spreading, city rulers gave orders that wooden roof-coverings should be replaced by fireproof clay tiles. They also decreed that tubs of water should be placed in city streets, and watch-towers built to give advance warning of fire.

Palace Fashions

IN ANCIENT JAPAN, rich noble men and women at the emperor's court wore very different clothes from ordinary peasant farmers. From around AD600 to 1500, Japanese court fashions were based on traditional Chinese styles. Both men and women wore long, flowing robes made of many layers of fine, glossy silk, held in place by a sash and cords. Men also wore wide trousers underneath. Women kept their hair loose and long, whilst men tied their hair into a topknot and wore a tall black hat. Elegance and refinement were the aims of this style.

After about 1500, wealthy samurai families began to choose new styles. Men and women wore *kimono* – long, loose robes. *Kimono* also became popular among wealthy artists, actors and craftworkers. The shoguns passed laws to try to stop ordinary people from wearing elaborate *kimono*, but they proved impossible to enforce.

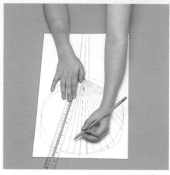

PARASOL
Women protected their delicate complexions with sunshades made of oiled paper. The fashion was for pale skin, often heavily powdered, with dark, soft eyebrows.

GOOD TASTE OR GAUDY?
This woman's outfit dates from the 1700s. Though striking, it would probably have been considered too bold to be in the most refined taste. Men and women took great care in choosing garments that blended well together.

MAKE A FAN
You will need: thick card (38cm x 26cm), pencil, ruler, compasses, protractor, felt tip pen (blue), paper (red), scissors, paints, paintbrush, water pot, glue stick.

1 Draw a line down the centre of the piece of card. Place your compasses two-thirds of the way up the line. Draw a circle 23cm in diameter.

2 Add squared-off edges at the top of the circle, as shown. Now draw your handle (15cm long). The handle should be directly over the vertical line.

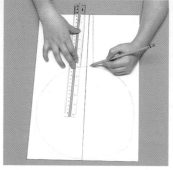

3 Place a protractor at the top of the handle and draw a semicircle around it. Now mark lines every 2.5 degrees. Draw pencil lines through these marks.

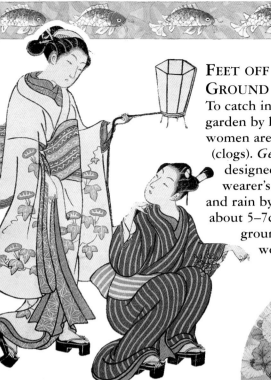

FEET OFF THE GROUND

To catch insects in a garden by lamplight these women are wearing *geta* (clogs). *Geta* were designed to protect the wearer's feet from mud and rain by raising them about 5–7cm above the ground. They were worn outdoors.

SILK *KIMONO*

This beautiful silk *kimono* was made in about 1600. Women wore a wide silk sash called an *obi* on top of their *kimono*. Men fastened their *kimono* with a narrow sash.

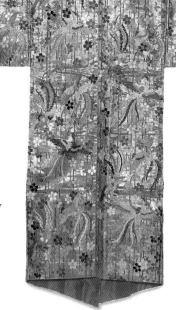

PAPER FAN

Folding fans, made of pleated paper, were a Japanese invention. They were carried by both men and women. This one is painted with gold leaf and chrysanthemum flowers.

It was the custom for Japanese noblewomen to hide their faces in court. They used decorated fans such as this one as a screen. Fans were also used to help people keep cool on hot, humid summer days.

BEAUTIFUL HAIR

Traditional palace fashions for men and women are shown in this scene from the imperial palace. The women have long, flowing hair that reaches to their waists – a sign of great beauty in early Japan.

4 Draw a blue line 1cm to the left of each line you have drawn. Then draw a blue line 2mm to the right of this line. Add a squiggle between sections.

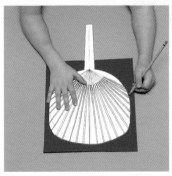

5 Cut out your card fan. Now use this as a template. Draw around the fan top (not handle) on to your red paper. Cut out the red paper.

6 Now cut out the in-between sections on your card fan (those marked with a squiggle). Paint the card fan brown on both sides. Leave to dry.

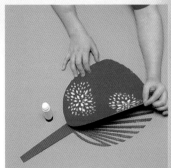

7 Paint the red paper with white flowers and leave to dry. Paste glue on to one side of the card fan. Stick the undecorated side of the red paper to the fan.

Working Clothes

ORDINARY PEOPLE IN JAPAN could not afford the rich, silk robes worn by emperors, nobles and samurai families. Instead, they wore plain, simple clothes that gave them freedom to move easily as they went about their daily tasks. Men wore baggy jackets and loose trousers, whilst women wore simple, long wrap-over robes.

Ordinary clothes were made from rough, inexpensive fibres, woven at home or purchased in towns. Cotton, hemp and ramie (a plant rather like flax) were all popular. Many other plants were also used to make cloth, including plantain (banana) and the bark of the mulberry tree. From around 1600, clothes were dyed with indigo (a blue dye) and were sometimes woven in complicated *ikat* patterns.

Japan's climate varies from cold and snowy in winter to hot and steamy in summer, so working peoples' clothes had to be adaptable. Usually people added or removed layers of clothing depending on the season. To cope with the rainy summers, they made waterproof clothes from straw. In winter, they wore padded or quilted jackets.

PROTECTIVE APRONS
These women are making salt from sea water. They are wearing aprons made out of leather or heavy canvas cloth to protect their clothes. The woman on the right has tied back her long hair with a scarf.

LOOSE AND COMFY
Farmworkers are shown hard at work planting rice seedlings in a flooded paddy-field. They are wearing loose, comfortable clothes – short jackets, baggy trousers tied at the knee and ankle, and shady hats. For working in water, in rice-fields or by the seashore, ordinary men and women often went barefoot.

MAKE DO AND MEND

Working clothes often got frayed or torn and it was a woman's job to mend them with needle and thread. Women in poor, ordinary families usually made rough, simple clothes for their own families. Sometimes they also bought clothes from travelling pedlars or small shops.

ARMOURERS AT WORK

Loose, flowing *kimono* were originally worn only by high-ranking families. Before long other wealthy and prestigious people, such as these skilled armour makers, copied them. *Kimono* were elegant and comfortable. However, they were certainly not suitable for active outdoor work.

FITTING FOOTWEAR

Out of doors, ordinary people wore clogs or simple sandals. The sandals were woven from straw and held on by twisted straw strings. Before entering a house, people always took off their outdoor footwear so as not to bring mud, grass and dirt inside.

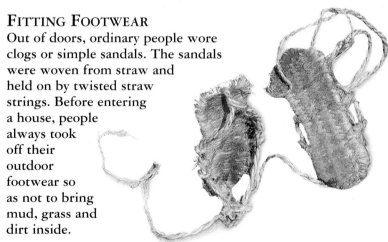

KEEPING THE RAIN OUT

Cone-shaped hats made of woven straw or bamboo protected people's heads from rain. The sloping shape of these hats helped the rainwater to run off before it had time to soak in. Farmworkers also made rain-capes out of straw matting. In this picture you can see one man bent almost double under his rain-cape (*right*). To protect themselves from the rain, rich people used umbrellas made of oiled cloth.

The Decorative Arts

THERE IS A LONG TRADITION among Japanese craftworkers of making everyday things as beautiful as possible. Craftworkers also created exquisite items for the wealthiest and most knowledgeable collectors. They used a wide variety of materials – pottery, metal, lacquer, cloth, paper and bamboo. Pottery ranged from plain, simple earthenware to delicate porcelain, painted with brilliantly coloured glazes. Japanese metalworkers produced alloys (mixtures of metals) that were unknown elsewhere in the ancient world. Cloth was woven from many fibres in elaborate designs. Bamboo and other plants from the grass family were woven into elegant *tatami* mats (floor mats) and containers of all different shapes and sizes. Japanese craftworkers also made beautifully decorated *inro* (little boxes, used like purses) which dangled from men's *kimono* sashes.

SHINY LACQUER
This samurai helmet was made for ceremonial use. It is covered in lacquer (varnish) and decorated with a diving dolphin. Producing shiny lacquerware was a slow process. An object was covered with many thin layers of lacquer. Each layer was allowed to dry, then polished, before more lacquer was applied. The lacquer could then be carved.

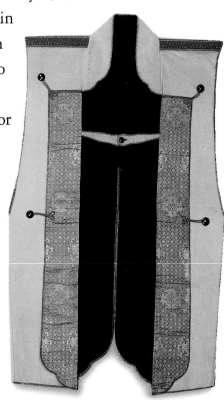

SAMURAI SURCOAT
Even the simplest garments were beautifully crafted. This surcoat (loose, sleeveless tunic) was made for a member of the noble Mori family, probably around 1800. Surcoats were worn by samurai on top of their armour.

MAKE A *NETSUKE* FOX

You will need: paper, pencil, ruler, self-drying clay, balsa wood, modelling tool, fine sandpaper, acrylic paint, paintbrush, water pot, darning needle, cord, small box (for an inro*), scissors, toggle, wide belt.*

1 Draw a square 5cm by 5cm on a piece of paper. Roll out a ball of clay to the size of the square. Shape the clay so that it comes to a point at one end.

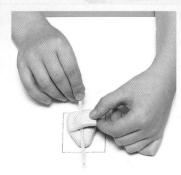

2 Turn your clay over. Lay a stick of balsa approximately 6cm long, along the back. Stick a thin sausage of clay over the stick. Press to secure.

3 Turn the clay over. Cut out two triangles of clay. Join them to the head using the tool. Make indentations to shape them into a fox's ears.

METALWORK
Craftworkers polish the sharp swords and knives they have made. It took many years of training to become a metalworker. Japanese craftsmen were famous for their fine skills at smelting and handling metals.

BOXES FOR BELTS
Inro were originally designed for storing medicines. The first *inro* were plain and simple, but after about 1700 they were often decorated with exquisite designs. These *inro* have been lacquered (coated with a shiny substance made from the sap of the lacquer tree). Inside, they contain several compartments stacked on top of each other.

MASTERWORK
This beautiful jar is decorated with a design of white flowers, painted over a shiny red and black glaze. It was painted by the master-craftsman Ogata Kenzan, who lived from 1663 to 1743.

Wear your inro *dangling from your belt. In ancient Japan,* inro *were usually worn by men. They were held in place with carved toggles called* netsuke.

4 Use the handle of your modelling tool to make your fox's mouth. Carve eyes, nostrils, teeth and a frown line. Use the top of a pencil to make eye holes.

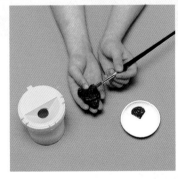

5 Leave to dry. Gently sand the *netsuke* and remove the balsa wood stick. Paint it with several layers of acrylic paint. Leave in a warm place to dry.

6 Thread cord through the four corners of a small box with a darning needle. Then thread the cord through a toggle and the *netsuke,* as shown.

7 Put a wide belt round your waist. Thread the *netsuke* under the belt. It should rest on the top of it. The *inro* (box) should hang down, as shown.

Wood and Paper

Ⓘ N ANCIENT JAPAN, woodworking was an art as well as a craft. Most large Japanese buildings, such as temples and palaces, were decorated with elaborately carved, painted and gilded wooden roofs. Doorways and pillars were also painted or carved. Inside, ceiling-beams and supporting pillars were made from strong tree trunks, floors were laid with polished wooden strips, and sliding screens had finely made wooden frames. A display of woodworking skill in a building demonstrated the owner's wealth and power. However, some smaller wooden buildings were left deliberately plain, allowing the quality of the materials and craftsmanship, and the elegance of the design, to speak for themselves.

Paper was another very important Japanese craft. It was used to make many fine objects – from wall-screens to lanterns, sunshades and even clothes. The choice of the best paper for writing a poem or painting a picture was part of an artist's task. Fine paper also showed off a letter-writer's elegance and good taste.

WOODEN STATUES
This statue portrays a Buddhist god. It was carved between AD800 and 900. Many Japanese temples contain carvings and statues made from wood.

SCREENS WITH SCENES
Screens were moveable works of art. This example, made in the 1700s, portrays a scene from Japanese history. It shows Portuguese merchants and missionaries listening to Japanese musicians.

ORIGAMI BOX
You will need: a square of origami paper (15cm x 15cm), clean and even folding surface.

1 Place your paper on a flat surface. Fold it horizontally across the centre. Next fold it vertically across the centre and unfold.

2 Carefully fold each corner to the centre point as shown. Unfold each corner crease before starting to make the next one.

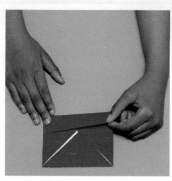

3 Using the creases, fold all the corners back into the centre. Now fold each side 2cm from the edge to make a crease and then unfold.

GRAND PILLARS

This row of red wooden pillars supports a heavy, ornate roof. It is part of the Meiji Shrine in Tokyo. Red (or cinnabar) was the traditional Japanese colour for shrines and royal palaces.

HOLY LIGHTS

Lamps made of pleated paper were often hung outside Shinto shrines. They were painted with the names of people who had donated money to the shrines.

PAPER ART

Paper-making and calligraphy (beautiful writing) were two very important art forms in Japan. This woodcut shows a group of people with everything they need to decorate scrolls and fans– paper, ink, palette, calligraphy brushes and pots of paint.

USEFUL AND BEAUTIFUL

Trees were admired for their beauty as well as their usefulness. These spring trees were portrayed by the famous Japanese woodblock printer, Hiroshige.

Japanese people used boxes of all shapes and sizes to store their possessions. What will you keep in your box?

4 Carefully unfold two opposite side panels. Your origami box should now look like the structure shown in the picture above.

5 Following the crease marks you have already made, turn in the side panels to make walls, as shown in the picture. Turn the origami round 90°.

6 Use your fingers to push the corners of the third side in, as shown. Use the existing crease lines as a guide. Raise the box slightly and fold the wall over.

7 Next, carefully repeat step 6 to construct the final wall. You could try making another origami box to perfect your technique.

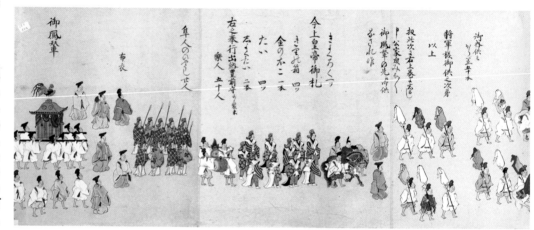

printed kanji → katakana	printed kanji → handwritten kanji → hiragana
阿 → ア	以 → ⿰ → い
伊 → イ	呂 → ろ → ろ
宇 → ウ	波 → は → は
江 → エ	仁 → に → に
於 → オ	保 → 保 → ほ

JAPANESE WRITING

Around AD800 two new writing systems, *hiragana* and *katakana,* were invented. For the first time, people could write Japanese exactly as they spoke it. The left-hand side of the chart above shows how a selection of *katakana* symbols developed from the original *kanji*. The right-hand side of the chart shows how *hiragana* symbols evolved, via the handwritten form of *kanji*.

OFFICIAL RECORDS

This illustrated scroll records the visit of Emperor Go-Mizunoo (ruled 1611–1629) to Shogun Tokugawa Iemitsu. The writing tells us that the palanquin (litter) in the picture carries the empress and gives a list of presents for the shogun.

Writing and Drawing

THE JAPANESE LANGUAGE belongs to a family of languages that includes Finnish, Turkish and Korean. It is totally different from its neighbouring language, Chinese. Yet, for many centuries, Chinese characters were used for reading and writing Japanese. This was because people such as monks, courtiers and the emperor – the only people who could read and write – valued Chinese civilization and ideas.

As the Japanese kingdom grew stronger, and Japanese culture developed, it became clear that a new way of writing Japanese was required. Around AD800, two new *kana* (ways of writing) were invented. Both used picture-symbols developed from *kanji* (Chinese characters) that expressed sounds and were written using a brush and ink on scrolls of paper. One type, called *hiragana*, was used for purely Japanese words; the other, called *katakana*, was used for words from elsewhere.

CALLIGRAPHY

You will need: paper, ink, a calligraphy brush. (Please note that you can use an ordinary paint brush and black paint if you cannot find a calligraphy brush or any ink.)

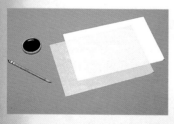

The numbers show the order of the strokes required for this character. Strokes 2, 3 & 4, and 5 & 6, are written in one movement, without lifting the brush.

1 The first stroke is called *soku*. Begin near the top of the paper, going from left to right. Move the brush sharply towards the bottom left, then lift it off the paper.

2 Strokes 2, 3 and 4 are called *roku*, *do* and *yaku*. Write them together in one movement. Apply pressure as you begin each stroke and then release again.

STORIES ON SCROLLS

Scrolls such as this one were designed to be hand-held, like a book. Words and pictures are side-by-side. Japanese artists often painted buildings with the roofs off, so that readers could see inside.

PAINTING PICTURES

A young boy is shown here mixing ink for his female companion. The ink is made from compressed charcoal that is dissolved in water to give the ink the required consistency. The artist herself has selected a broad brush to begin her painting.

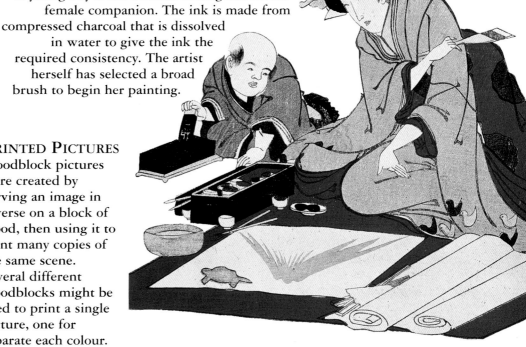

PRINTED PICTURES

Woodblock pictures were created by carving an image in reverse on a block of wood, then using it to print many copies of the same scene. Several different woodblocks might be used to print a single picture, one for separate each colour.

3 For stroke 5 (*saku*) apply an even amount of pressure as you draw your brush left to right. For 6 (*ryo*), apply pressure at the beginning and release it.

4 Stroke 7 is called *taku*. Apply even pressure overall to make this short stroke. Make sure that you also make the stroke quite quickly.

5 Stroke 8 is also called *taku*. Apply an increasing amount of pressure as the brush travels down. Turn the brush back to the right at the last moment, as shown.

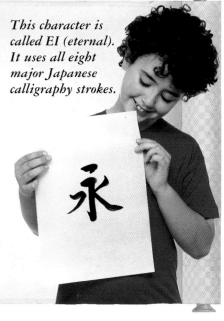

This character is called EI (eternal). It uses all eight major Japanese calligraphy strokes.

Poems, Letters and Novels

NEW WAYS OF WRITING the Japanese language were invented around AD800. This led to the growth of forms of literature such as diaries, travel writing and poems. Elegant, refined poetry (called *waka*) was very popular at the emperor's court. From about 1600, *haiku* (short poems with 17 syllables) became the favourite form. *Haiku* were written by people from the samurai class, as well as by courtiers.

Women prose writers were especially important in early Japan. The courtier, Sei Shonagon (born around AD965) won praise for her *Pillow Book* – a kind of diary. Women writers were so famous that at least one man pretended to be a woman. The male poet Ki no Tsurayuki wrote *The Tosa Diary* under a woman's name.

LITERARY LADY
Lady Chiyo was a courtier and poet in the 1700s. Nobles read and wrote a lot of poetry. It was considered a sign of good breeding to quote from literary works. Letters to and from nobles often contained lines from poems.

THE WORLD'S FIRST NOVEL
This scroll shows a scene from the *Tale of Genji*, written in about AD1000 by Lady Murasaki Shikibu. The scroll was painted in the 1700s, but the artist has used a painting style from the period in which the story was written.

MAKE PAPER

You will need: 8 pieces of wood (4 x 33cm and 4 x 28cm), nails, hammer, muslin (35cm x 30cm), staple gun, electrical tape, scissors, torn-up paper, water bowl, masher, washing-up bowl, flower petals, spoon, soft cloths.

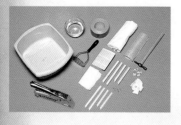

1 Ask an adult to make two frames. Staple stretched muslin on to one frame. Cover this frame with electrical tape to make the screen, as shown.

2 Put the frame and screen to one side. Soak paper scraps overnight in water. Mash into a pulp with the potato masher. It should look like porridge.

3 Half-fill the washing-up bowl with the pulp and cold water. You could add a few flower petals for decoration. Mix well with a spoon.

POET AND TRAVELLER

The poet Matsuo Basho (1644-1694) is portrayed in this print dating from the 1800s. Basho was famous as a writer of short *haiku* poems. He was also a great traveller, and in this picture he is shown (*right*) talking to two farmers he has met on his travels. Here is a typical example of a *haiku* by Basho:

The summer grasses –
All that has survived from
Brave warriors' dreams.

CRANES ON A CARD

This poem-card contains a traditional *waka* (palace-style) poem, in 31 syllables. It is written in silver and black and decorated with cranes.

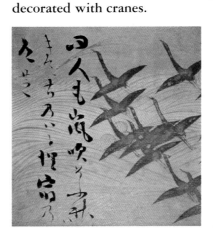

JAPANESE PAPER

Japanese craftworkers made many different kinds of beautiful paper. They used tree bark (especially the bark of the mulberry tree) or other plant fibres, which they blended carefully to create different thicknesses and textures of paper. They sometimes sprinkled the paper mixture with mica or gold leaf to produce rich, sparkling effects.

Japanese paper

mulberry bark

The personality of a Japanese writer was judged by the type of paper they used, as well as by the content of the letter.

4 Place the screen with the frame on top into the washing up bowl. As the frame and screen enter the water, scoop under the pulpy mixture.

5 Pull the screen out of the pulp, keeping it level. Gently move it from side to side over the bowl to allow a layer of pulp to form. Shake the water off.

6 Take the frame off the screen. Carefully lay the screen face down on a cloth. Mop the back of the screen with a cloth to get rid of the excess water.

7 Peel away the screen. Leave the paper to dry for at least 6 hours. When dry, turn over and gently peel away the cloth to reveal your paper.

At the Theatre

GOING TO THE THEATRE and listening to music were popular pastimes in ancient Japan. There were several kinds of Japanese drama. They developed from religious dances at temples and shrines, or from slow, stately dances performed at the emperor's court.

Noh is the oldest form of Japanese drama. It developed in the 1300s from rituals and dances that had been performed for centuries before. Noh plays were serious and dignified. The actors performed on a bare stage, with only a backdrop. They chanted or sang their words, accompanied by drums and a flute. Noh performances were traditionally held in the open air, often at a shrine.

Kabuki plays were first seen around 1600. In 1629, the shoguns banned women performers and so male actors took their places. Kabuki plays became very popular in the new, fast-growing towns.

GRACEFUL PLAYER

This woman entertainer is holding a *shamisen* – a three-stringed instrument, played by plucking the strings. The *shamisen* often formed part of a group, together with a *koto* (zither) and flute.

POPULAR PUPPETS

Bunraku (puppet plays) originated about 400 years ago, when *shamisen* music, dramatic chanting and hand-held puppets were combined. The puppets were so large and complex that it took three men to move them about on stage.

NOH THEATRE MASK

You will need: tape measure, balloon, newspaper, bowl, glue, petroleum jelly, pin, scissors, felt-tip pen, modelling clay, bradawl, paints (red, yellow, black, and white), paintbrush, water pot, cord.

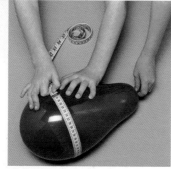

1 Ask a friend to measure around your head above the ears. Blow up a balloon to fit this measurement. This will be the base for the papier-mâché.

2 Rip up strips of newspaper. Soak in a water and glue mixture (1 part glue to 2 parts water). Cover the balloon with a layer of petroleum jelly.

3 Cover the front and sides of your balloon with a layer of papier-mâché. Leave to dry. Repeat 2 or 3 times. When dry, pop the balloon.

TRAGIC THEATRE

An audience watches a scene from an outdoor performance of a Noh play. Noh drama was always about important and serious topics. Favourite subjects were death and the afterlife, and the plays were often very tragic.

LOUD AND FAST

Kabuki plays were a complete contrast to Noh. They were fast-moving, loud, flashy and very dramatic. Audiences admired the skills of the actors as much as the cleverness or thoughtfulness of the plots.

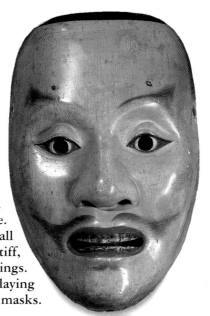

BEHIND THE MASK

This Noh mask represents a warrior's face. Noh drama did not try to be lifelike. The actors all wore masks and moved very slowly using stiff, stylized gestures to express their feelings. Noh plays were all performed by men. Actors playing women's parts wore female clothes and masks.

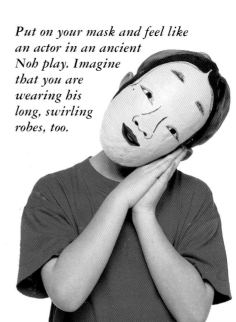

Put on your mask and feel like an actor in an ancient Noh play. Imagine that you are wearing his long, swirling robes, too.

4 Trim the papier-mâché so that it forms a mask shape. Ask a friend to mark where your eyes, nose and mouth are when you hold it to your face.

5 Cut out the face holes with scissors. Put clay beneath the side of the mask at eye level. Use a bradawl to make two holes on each side.

6 Paint the face of a calm young lady from Noh theatre on your mask. Use this picture as your guide. The mask would have been worn by a man.

7 Fit the cord through the holes at each side. Tie one end. Once you have adjusted the mask so that it fits, tie the other end.

Travel and Transport

JAPAN IS A RUGGED and mountainous country. Until the 20th century, the only way to travel through its wild countryside was along narrow, zig-zag paths. These mountain paths and fragile wooden bridges across deep gullies and rushing streams were often swept away by landslides or floods.

During the Heian period, wealthy warriors rode fine horses, while important officials, wealthy women, children and priests travelled in lightweight wood and bamboo carts. These carts were fitted with screens and curtains for privacy and were pulled by oxen. In places where the route was unsuitable for ox-carts, wealthy people were carried shoulder-high on palanquins (lightweight portable boxes or litters). Ordinary people mostly travelled on foot.

During the Tokugawa period (1600–1868) the shoguns encouraged new road building as a way of increasing trade and control. The longest road was the Eastern Sea Road, which ran for 480km between Kyoto and the shogun's capital, Edo. Some people said it was the busiest road in the world.

BEASTS OF BURDEN
A weary mother rests with her child and ox during their journey. You can see that the ox is loaded up with heavy bundles. Ordinary people could not afford horses, so they used oxen to carry heavy loads or to pull carts.

SHOULDER HIGH
Noblewomen on palanquins (litters) are shown being taken by porters across a deep river. Some of the women have decided to disembark so that they can be carried across the river. Palanquins were used in Japan right up to the Tokugawa period (1600–1868). When making journeys to or from the city of Edo, daimyo and wives were sometimes carried the whole route in palanquins.

HUGGING THE COASTLINE

Ships sail into harbour at Tempozan, Osaka. Cargo between Edo and Osaka was mostly carried by ships that hugged the coastline. The marks on the sails show the company that owned the ships.

CARRYING CARGO

Little cargo-boats, such as these at Edobashi in Edo, carried goods along rivers or around the coast. They were driven through the water by men rowing with oars or pushing against the river bed with a long pole.

STEEP MOUNTAIN PATHS

Travellers on mountain paths hoped to find shelter for the night in villages, temples or monasteries. It could take all day to walk 16km along rough mountain tracks.

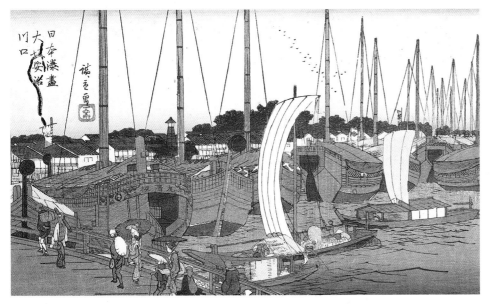

IN THE HARBOUR

Sea-going sailing ships, laden with cargo, are shown here at anchor in the harbour of Osaka (an important port in south-central Japan). In front of them you can see smaller river-boats with tall sails. Some families both lived and worked on river-boats.

Gods and Spirits

Almost all of the Japanese people followed a very ancient religious faith called Shinto. Shinto means the way of the gods. It developed from a central idea that all natural things had a spiritual side. These natural spirits – called *kami* in Japanese – were often kindly, but could be powerful or even dangerous. They needed to be respected and worshipped. Shinto also encouraged ancestor-worship – ancestor spirits could guide, help and warn. Special priests, called shamans, made contact with all these spirits by chanting, fasting, or by falling into a trance.

Shinto spirits were honoured at shrines that were often built close to sites of beauty or power, such as waterfalls or volcanoes. Priests guarded the purity of each shrine, and held rituals to make offerings to the spirits. Each Shinto shrine was entered through a *torii* (large gateway) which marked the start of the sacred space. *Torii* always had the same design – they were based on the ancient perches of birds waiting to be sacrificed.

AT THE SHRINE
A priest worships by striking a drum at the Grand Shrine at Izu, one of the oldest Shinto shrines in Japan. A festival is held there every August, with processions, offerings and prayers. An *omikoshi* (portable shrine) is carried through the streets, so that the spirits can bring blessings to everyone.

OFFERINGS TO THE SPIRITS
Worshippers at Shinto shrines leave offerings for the *kami* (spirits) that live there. These offerings are neatly-wrapped barrels of *sake* (rice wine). Today, worshippers also leave little wooden plaques with prayers on them.

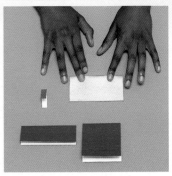

VOTIVE DOLLS
You will need: self-drying clay, 2 balsa wood sticks (12cm long), ruler, paints, paintbrush, water pot, modelling clay, silver foil, red paper, gold paper, scissors, pencil, glue stick, optional basket and dowling stick.

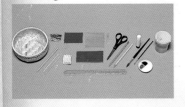

1 Place a ball of clay on the end of each of the balsa sticks. On one of the sticks, push the clay down so that it is 5mm from the end. This will be the man.

2 Paint hair and features on the man. Stand it up in modelling clay to dry. Repeat with the woman. Cover the 5mm excess stick on the man's head in foil.

3 Take two pieces of red paper, 6.5cm x 14cm and 6cm x 10cm. Fold them in half. Take two pieces of gold paper, 10.5cm x 10cm and 1cm x 7cm. Fold in half.

LUCKY GOD
Daikoku is one of seven lucky gods from India, China and Japan that are associated with good fortune. In Japan, he is the special god of farmers, wealth, and of the kitchen. Daikoku is recognized by both Shinto and Buddhist religions.

HOLY VOLCANO
Fuji-San (Mount Fuji) has been honoured as a holy place since the first people arrived in Japan. Until 1867, women were not allowed to set foot on Fuji's holy ground.

FLOATING GATE
This *torii* at Miyajima (Island of Shrines), in southern Japan, is built on the seashore. It appears to float on the water as the tide flows in. Miyajima was sacred to the three daughters of the Sun.

In some regions of Japan, dolls like these are put on display in baskets every year at Hinamatsuri (Girls' Day), on 3 March.

4 Take the folded red paper (6.5cm x 14cm). This is the man's *kimono*. Cut a triangular shape out of the bottom. Cut a neck hole out at the folded end.

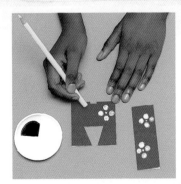

5 Dip the blunt end of the pencil in white paint. Stipple a pattern on to the red paper. Add the central dots using the pencil tip dipped in paint.

6 Slip the man's head and body into the red paper *kimono*. Then take the larger piece of gold paper and fold around the stick, as shown. Glue in place.

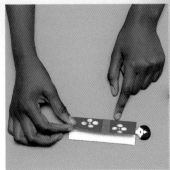

7 Now stick the gold paper (1cm x 7cm) on to the woman's *kimono*, in the middle. Slip the woman's head and body into the *kimono*. Glue in place.

Monks and Priests

MONK AND PUPIL
A Buddhist sage is pictured with one of his pupils. Thanks to such teachers, Buddhist ideas spread beyond the imperial court to reach ordinary people, and many Buddhist temples and monasteries were built.

AS WELL AS FOLLOWING SHINTO, many Japanese people also practised the Buddhist faith. Prince Siddhartha Gautama, the founder of Buddhism, was born in Nepal around 500BC. He left his home to teach a new religion based on the search for truth and harmony and the ending of all selfish desires. His followers called him the Buddha (the enlightened one). The most devoted Buddhists spent at least part of their life as scholars, priests, monks or nuns.

Buddhist teachings first reached Japan in AD552, brought by monks and scribes from China and Korea. Buddhism encouraged learning and scholarship, and, over the centuries, many different interpretations of the Buddha's teachings developed. Each was taught by dedicated monks or priests and attracted many followers. The Buddhist monk Shinran (1173–1262) urged his followers to place their faith in Amida Buddha (a calm, kindly form of the Buddha). He taught them that Amida Buddha would lead them after death to the Western Paradise. Shinran's rival, Nichiren (1222–1282) claimed that he had been divinely chosen to spread the True Word. This was Nichiren's own interpretation of Buddhism, based on an ancient Buddhist text called the *Lotus Sutra*.

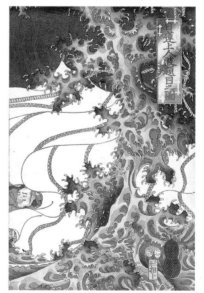

FAMOUS MONK
This woodcut of 1857 shows an episode from a story about the Buddhist monk, Nichiren. He was said to have calmed a storm by the power of his prayers. The influence of Nichiren continued long after his death, and many other stories were told about him.

SCHOLAR MONKS
A group of monks (*left*) study Buddhist scrolls. Monks were among the most important scholars in early Japan. They studied ancient Chinese knowledge and developed new Japanese ideas.

GREAT BUDDHA
This huge bronze statue of Daibutsu (the Great Buddha) is 11.3m high and weighs 93 tonnes. It was made at Kamakura in 1252 – a time when the city was rich and powerful. The statue shows the Buddha in Amida form – inviting worshippers to the Western Paradise.

GOD OF MERCY
Standing over 5m high, this statue of Kannon was made around AD700. Kannon is also known as the god of mercy. Orginally Kannon was a man – in fact, one form of the Buddha himself. However, over the years it became the custom to portray him in female shape.

HOLY FLOWERS
The lotus flower often grows in dirty water and was believed to symbolize the purity of a holy life. It has many associations in literature with Buddhism. Chrysanthemums are often placed on graves or on Buddhist altars in the home. White and yellow flowers are most popular because these colours are associated with death.

white chrysanthemum

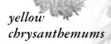

yellow chrysanthemums

lotus

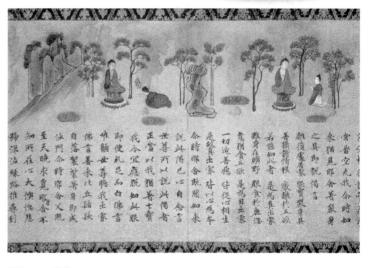

HOLY WORDS
For many years after Buddhism reached Japan, it was practised mainly by educated, wealthy people. Only they could read the beautiful Buddhist *sutras* (religious texts) like this one, created between AD645 and 794. This sutra was written by hand, but some of the world's first printed documents are Buddhist *sutras* made in Japan.

Temples and Gardens

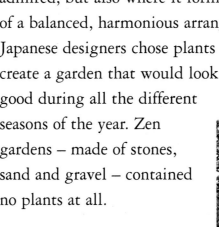

Land suitable for growing plants was very precious in Japan, so the people made the best use of it – both for growing food and for giving pleasure. All Japanese people who could afford it liked to surround their homes with beautiful gardens where they could take gentle exercise, read or entertain.

Japanese gardens were often small, but they were carefully planned to create a landscape in miniature. Each rock, pool, temple or gateway was positioned where it could best be admired, but also where it formed part of a balanced, harmonious arrangement. Japanese designers chose plants to create a garden that would look good during all the different seasons of the year. Zen gardens – made of stones, sand and gravel – contained no plants at all.

PLANTS TO ADMIRE
Artists created and recorded delicate arrangements of blooms and leaves. This scroll-painting of branches, blossom and flowers dates from the 1500s.

ZEN GARDEN
This is part of a Zen Buddhist garden, made of lumps of rock and carefully-raked gravel. Gardens like this were designed to help people pray and meditate in peaceful surroundings.

HARMONY IN DESIGN
The Eastern Pagoda at the Yakushiji Temple in Nara is one of the oldest temples in Japan. It was founded in AD680 and the pagoda was built in 730. Pagodas are tall towers, housing statues of Buddha or other religious works of art. Often, they form part of a group of buildings standing in a garden.

MAKING AN *IKEBANA* ARRANGEMENT
You will need: vase filled with water, scissors, twig, raffia or string, 2 flowers (with different length stems), a branch of foliage, 2 stems of waxy leaves.

1 Cut the twig so that it can be wedged into the neck of the vase. This will provide a structure to build on and to control the position of the flowers.

2 Remove the twig from the vase. Next, using raffia or string, tie the twig tightly on to the longest flower about halfway down the stem.

3 Place the flower stem in the vase. As you do this, gently slide the twig back into the neck of the vase and wedge it into position as before.

TREES IN MINIATURE

Bonsai is the Japanese art of producing miniature but fully-formed trees. This is achieved by clipping roots and carefully regulating the water supply. Bonsai originated in China, but became popular in Japan around 1500. A tree that might naturally grow to about 6m could end up just 30cm tall after bonsai treatment. Some bonsai trees are grown to achieve a dramatic slanting or twisted shape.

bonsai maple   *bonsai pine*

CHINESE STYLE

The Tenryuji Temple, Kyoto, stands in one of the oldest Buddhist gardens still surviving in Japan. The garden was created before 1300. It is designed in the Chinese style and made of rocks, gravel, water and evergreen plants.

GARDENERS AT WORK

A gardener, his wife and son prepare to plant cedar tree saplings. In the foreground, you can see a wooden bucket for watering plants, and a wooden hoe for digging up weeds. At the back, there are nursery beds where seedlings are carefully tended. Cedar trees were, and still are, popular in Japan. The wood is used in the building of houses and the beautiful trees themselves are used to decorate many gardens.

Ikebana *means "living flowers". The three main branches of an arrangement represent heaven, earth and human beings.*

4 Add the shorter-stemmed flower to the longer stem. Position it so that it slants forwards. Carefully lean it against the twig and the longer stem.

5 Slip the branch of foliage between the two stems. It should lean out and forward. The foliage should look as though it is a branch growing naturally.

6 Position some waxy leaves at the neck of the vase. *Ikebana* is the arrangement of anything that grows. Foliage is as important as the flowers.

7 Add a longer stem of waxy leaves at the back of the vase. This simple arrangement is typical of those Japanese people have in their homes.

Festivals and Ceremonies

THE JAPANESE PEOPLE CELEBRATED FESTIVALS (*matsuri*) all year round, but especially during the warm months of spring and summer. Many of these festivals had ancient origins and were connected with farming or to the seasons. Others were linked to Shinto beliefs or to imported Buddhist ideas. There were two main kinds of festival. National holidays, such as New Year, were celebrated throughout Japan. Smaller local festivals were often linked to a Buddhist statue or temple, or to an ancient Shinto shrine.

One of the most important ceremonies was the tea ceremony, first held by Buddhist monks between 1300 and 1500. During the ceremony, the host served tea to his or her guests with great delicacy, politeness and precision.

BOWLS FOR TEA
At a tea ceremony, two types of green tea are served in bowls like these. The bowls are often plainly shaped and simply decorated. According to Zen beliefs, beauty can be found in pure, calm, simple things. Toyotomi Hideyoshi fell out with the tea master Sen no Rikyu over this. Hideyoshi liked tea bowls to be ornate rather than plain.

LOCAL FESTIVAL
A crowd of people enjoy a festival day. Local festivals usually included processions of portable Shinto shrines through the streets. These were followed by lots of noisy and cheerful people.

TEA BOWL
You will need: self-drying clay, cutting board, ruler, modelling tool, cut-out bottom of a plastic bottle (about 10cm in diameter), fine sandpaper, paints, paintbrush, water pot, soft cloth, varnish and brush.

1 Roll out a snake of clay 25cm long and 1cm thick. Starting from the centre, curl the clay tightly into a circle with a diameter of 10cm.

2 Now you have made the base of the bowl, start to build up the sides. Roll out more snakes of clay, 25cm long. Join the pieces by pressing them together.

3 Sculpt the ridges of the coil bowl together using your fingers and modelling tool. Use the bottom of a plastic bottle for support (see step 4).

CHERRY BLOSSOM

This woodblock print shows two women dressed in their best *kimonos* strolling along an avenue of flowering cherry trees. The cherry-blossom festival, called Hanami, was a time to meet friends and enjoy an open-air meal in the spring sunshine. Blossoms appeared in late February in the far south, but not until early May in the colder northern lands of Japan.

BLOSSOM

The Japanese looked forward to the sight of plum blossom emerging, usually in mid February. The plum tree was the first to blossom. In March and April, cherry trees followed suit by producing clouds of delicate pink and white blossom. People hurried to admire the cherry blossom before its fragile beauty faded away. This joyful festival was also tinged with sadness. Spring is the rainy season in Japan and one storm could cause the blossom to fail. The cherry blossom was a reminder that human lives could soon disappear.

plum blossom

cherry blossom

TEA CEREMONY

Hostess and guests sit politely on *tatami* (straw mats) for a Zen tea ceremony. This ritual often lasted for up to four hours. Many people in Japan still hold tea ceremonies, as a way of getting away from hectic modern life.

Design your bowl in a pure, elegant style, like the Zen potters. If you want to add any decoration, make sure that is very simple, too.

4 Roll out another coil of clay 19cm long and 1cm wide. Make it into a circle 8cm in diameter. Join the ends. This will form a stand for the bowl.

5 Turn the bowl over – still using your drinks bottle for support. Join the circular stand to the bottom of the bowl. Mould it on using your fingers.

6 Leave the bowl to dry. Once dry, remove the plastic bottle and sand the bowl gently. Paint the base colour over it. Leave until it is dry.

7 Apply your second colour using a cloth. Lightly dapple paint over the bowl to make it appear like a glaze. Varnish the bowl inside and out.

Glossary

A

abacus A wooden frame with beads on rods, used for calculating.

acupuncture The treatment of the body with fine needles to relieve pain or cure illness.

agriculture Growing crops and breeding animals; farming.

aikido A Japanese martial art in which players try to overbalance their opponents.

Ainu The original inhabitants of northern Japan.

alloy A substance made by mixing two or more different metals.

ancestor An individual from whom one is descended, such as a great, great-grandfather.

Anno Domini (AD) A system used to calculate dates after the supposed year of Christ's birth. Anno Domini dates in this book are prefixed AD up to the year 1000 (e.g. AD521).

After 1000, no prefixes are used (e.g. 1912).

anonymous Without the name of the writer.

archaeologist Someone who studies ancient ruins, tools, coins, seeds, etc., to learn about the past.

archaeology The study of ancient remains and ruins.

Aryans A group of people who migrated into India around 1500BC.

ascetics Monks or religious wanderers who rejected home life to pursue enlightenment.

ashigaru A Japanese samurai (warrior) with a low rank.

astrology The study of the position and movement of the stars and planets in order to foretell the future.

astronomy The scientific study of stars, planets and other heavenly bodies. In ancient times it was often not separate from astrology, the belief that such heavenly bodies shape our lives.

B

banquet A rich, elaborate feast served with great ceremony to celebrate an important event.

barter To trade by exchanging goods rather than by paying money.

Before Christ (BC) A system used to calculate dates before the supposed year of Christ's birth. Dates are calculated in reverse (e.g. 200 BC is longer ago than 1 BC). Before Christ dates are followed by the letters BC (e.g. 455 BC).

bellows A mechanism for pumping air into a fire or furnace.

bodhi tree Symbol of the Buddha. The tree he sat under when he achieved enlightenment.

booty Valuable things and goods taken away by a victorious army.

brahmi Oldest script in India.

brahmins The priests, members of the highest caste in India.

Buddha The name (meaning "the enlightened one") given to Siddhartha Gautama, an Indian prince who lived around 500BC. He taught a new philosophy, based on seeking peace (nirvana).

Buddhism The religious teachings of the Buddha, which first came to China from India.

bugaku An ancient dance form that was popular at the court of the Japanese emperor.

bultu A doctor's prescription in Mesopotamia.

bunraku Japanese plays performed by puppets.

bushido A strict code of brave, honourable behaviour, meant to be followed by Japanese samurai (warriors).

C

campaign A series of battles fought by a ruler to bring an area under his control.

caste One of four social classes into which Hindus were divided in India.

character One of the many symbols used in Chinese script.

chauri A whisk, usually made of yak tail, for fanning away flies.

citadel Fortress near to or inside a city.

city-state A city, its surrounding villages and countryside with its own god and ruler.

civil servant Someone who works for the Government.

civilization A human society that is well governed and has made advances in the law, technology and the arts.

clan A group of people related to each other by ancestry or marriage.

collyrium A black paste used as eyeliner in India.

conch A type of large, colourful sea shell.

Confucianism The Western name for the teachings of the Chinese philosopher Kong Fuzi (Confucius), which call for social order and respect for one's family and ancestors.

cormorant A coastal and river bird that can be trained to catch fish.

courtier Person attending at royal court.

cowrie A seashell used as the lowest form of currency near the coastal regions of ancient India.

crossbow A mechanical bow that fires small arrows called bolts.

cuneiform The wedge-shaped writing invented by the Sumerians and also used by the Babylonians and Assyrians.

D

daimyo A Japanese nobleman or warlord.

Daoism A Chinese philosophy based on contemplation of the natural world. It later became a religion with a belief in magic.

dargah Shrine to a Sufi saint in India.

decipher To work out the meaning of signs and symbols in ancient writing.

deity A god or goddess.

derrick The tower-like frame that supports drilling equipment.

dhoti Traditional Indian dress worn by Hindu men.

discus A heavy disc, symbol of the Hindu god Vishnu.

diviner Someone who foretells the future by examining an animal's insides or other things, such as the pattern oil makes on water.

dynasty A period of rule by emperors of the same royal family.

E

edict Order issued by a king.

Eid A celebration at the end of the month of fasting in Islam.

empire A large number of different lands ruled over by a single person or government.

enlightenment Freedom from ignorance through meditation. Buddhist monks try to achieve enlightenment.

epic Long poem telling a story.

escapement A type of ratchet used in clockwork timing mechanisms.

excavate To dig in the ground to discover ancient remains.

exploits Great deeds or achievements of kings and heroes.

F

festival A special day set aside to honour a god or goddess. Sometimes it went on for several days like the New Year festival at Babylon.

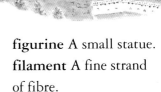

figurine A small statue.

filament A fine strand of fibre.

Forbidden City The royal palace in Beijing, China, made up of hundreds of buildings set inside high walls.

foundation deposit A group of objects placed in the foundations of a temple by the king who built it.

frieze Decorated strip along a wall or ceiling.

G

Ganesha Elephant-headed Hindu god. He is lord of Shiva's armies.

garrison A fort or similar place that is guarded by a troop of soldiers. The word garrison can also refer to the troop of soldiers.

genie A friendly spirit who drives away evil. Statues of genies appear on palace walls blessing the king.

geometric pattern A pattern made of lines, circles and triangles.

geta Wooden Japanese clogs, designed to keep feet dry in wet weather.

glazed bricks Baked bricks, which have been given a colourful, glassy coating and are often used to decorate the walls of palaces and temples.

gopuram Gate tower of a south Indian temple.

guilds Groups of skilled workers who checked quality standards, trained young people and looked after old and sick members.

gurdwara Sikh place of worship.

H

haiku A short Japanese poem, containing 17 syllables. Haiku were popular after about AD1600.

haj Pilgrimage to Mecca that every Muslim should make at least once.

Haniwa Clay figures that were buried in ancient Japanese tombs. They are a very important source of evidence about early Japan.

Hanuman Leader of the monkey army that helps Rama rescue Sita in the Indian epic Ramayana.

harmony A pleasing sense of order, based on peace and balance.

hemp A fibrous plant, which is often used to make coarse textiles and clothes.

high priest or priestess The chief priest or priestess in a temple who had a special relationship with the deity.

hilt The handle of a sword or dagger.

Hinduism Religion that includes worship of several gods and belief in reincarnation or rebirth after death in a new body.

Holi A festival celebrating the onset of spring in India.

hookah Indian water pipe used to smoke tobacco.

I

ikat A weaving technique. The threads are dyed in many different colours

then woven together to create complicated and beautiful patterns.

ikebana The art of flower-arranging that is practised in Japan.

imperial Relating to the rule of an emperor or empress.

impression The shape and pattern left on a clay tablet when a seal is pressed on to it.

incarnation Human form of a god or goddess.

inro A small, decorated box, worn hanging from the belt in Japan. Originally, inro were designed for storing medicines.

inscribed Something that is carved on stone or another similar hard material.

inscription Writing done with a reed pen on a clay tablet or with a chisel on stone.

irrigation Bringing water to the fields by means of canals and ditches.

Islam The Muslim faith, which proclaims that there is only one God and that his messenger is the prophet Muhammad.

ivory The tusks of elephants used to make furniture, boxes and handles for mirrors and fans.

J

jade Either of two hard, precious minerals called jadeite and nephrite. Jade is white or green in colour.

jama Side-fastening coat worn with trousers in Mughal times.

Jataka A story telling of a previous birth of the Buddha.

joinery Skilled woodworking needed for making fine furniture.

Jomon An early hunter-gatherer civilization in Japan. It originated in about 10,000 BC.

junk A traditional Chinese sailing ship with square sails.

K

kabuki Popular plays, performed in Japan from about AD 1600. They were fast-moving and loud.

Kali A fierce form of Shiva's wife.

kami The Japanese holy spirits.

kana The name for the Japanese method of writing.

kanji The picture symbols that were used for writing Japanese before about AD 800.

kaolin A fine white clay used in porcelain and paper making.

Kaurava One of the two feuding families of the Indian epic the Mahabharata.

kendo A martial art in which players fight one another with bamboo swords.

khanda A comb, one of the five objects carried by Sikh brotherhoods.

kimono A loose robe with wide sleeves, worn by both men and women.

kitchen god A god whose picture was kept in Chinese kitchens.

knucklebones The small round bones in the feet of animals.

Krishna Vaishnava god who is the main character in the Indian story the Mahabharata.

ksatriya A warrior, a member of the second caste in India.

kuzu A plant with a fleshy root that is dried and used in traditional Japanese medicine.

L

lacquer A thick, coloured varnish, made from the sap of trees, used to coat wood, metal or leather.

lamassu A huge stone statue of a human-headed bull or lion used to guard the entrance to a palace in Mesopotamia.

lapis lazuli A dark blue, semi-precious stone used for jewellery and seals.

libation A sacrifice of wine or oil poured out in honour of a god or goddess.

litter A portable bed.

lodestone A type of magnetic iron ore, also called magnetite.

loom A frame or machine used for weaving cloth.

lotus A type of water lily.

lychee A soft Chinese fruit.

lyre A stringed instrument similar to a harp.

M

mace Spiked club used by Hindu warriors.

magistrate An imperial officer of justice, similar to a local judge.

Mahabharata An Indian story of the contest for succession between the families of the Kauravas and Pandavas.

makara A mythical crocodile-like animal in India.

martial arts Physical exercises that are often based upon combat, such as swordplay and kung fu. Many martial arts bring together spiritual and physical disciplines.

mausoleum A burial chamber.

merchant A person who buys and sells goods for a profit.

mica A flaky, shiny metal.

millennium A period of 1,000 years.

millet A type of grain crop.

minar A tower next to a mosque in India.

minting The process by which new coins are produced.

monsoon Winds that blow at particular seasons of the year in south Asia, bringing heavy rain.

mortar Mixture that is used to stick bricks or stones together.

mosaics Tiny pieces of colourful stone, shell or glass that are used to make pictures or to decorate objects.

mosque A Muslim place of worship.

mother-of-pearl A beautiful, shiny substance found in shells, also known as nacre. It was often used by skilled craft workers in jewellery inlays or as inlays for furniture and the frames of musical instruments.

moxibustion In Chinese medicine, healing the body with burning herbs.

Muharram First month of the Muslim calendar.

mung beans The seeds of the Asian mung plant. Often used as a source of bean sprouts.

mushushshu A dragon-like creature who is the special animal of Marduk, the god of Babylon.

Muslim A follower of the prophet Muhammad.

myth Any ancient tale or legend, often describing gods, spirits or fantastic creatures.

N

Nagari The modern alphabet used for north Indian languages.

nape The back of the neck.

netsuke Small toggles, carved from ivory and used to attach items to belts in Japan.

nirvana Freedom from suffering.

noh A serious, dignified drama that originated in Japan in around 1300.

nomadic people Those who constantly move from place to place.

O

obelisk A tall, thin, four-sided monument with (in Mesopotamia) a stepped top. It was used by kings to record their victories.

obi A wide sash, worn in Japan only by women.

omen A sign of good or bad fortune in the future.

omikashi A portable shrine in Japan.

overlord The ruler of a large state who demands loyalty from a smaller one.

P

pagoda A high, multi-storey tower found in eastern and southern Asia. Pagodas were often used as libraries or places of religious worship.

paijama Tight-fitting trousers worn during Mughal times.

palanquin A seat or carriage borne on the shoulders of men.

Pandava One of the two feuding families of the Indian epic the Mahabharata.

paratha A fried wheat bread eaten in northern India.

patron Person who gives money and encouragement to the arts.

peasant A poor country dweller, who is often a farm worker.

peninsula An area of land surrounded by water on three sides, making it almost like an island.

Persian Language spoken in Persia. It came to be used by the Muslim kings who ruled India.

pigment Any material used to provide colour for paint or ink.

pilgrim Person who makes a journey to a holy place.

pillow book A collection of short notes and writings in Japan, rather like a diary or journal.

pinyin The official romanized spelling of the Chinese language, used for terms and place names in the Chinese section of this book. In pinyin, the letter q is pronounced as ch.

plate-armour Protective clothing, which is made from overlapping plates of metal.

polo A game, similar to hockey, but played on horseback.

porcelain The finest quality of pottery. It was made with kaolin and baked at a high temperature.

province Part of an empire marked off for administrative purposes and sometimes ruled by a governor on behalf of a king.

puja The act of honouring an icon of a god in India.

purification The means by which the king or priest made himself clean so as to be fit to offer sacrifices to his god.

Q

quarry A place where building stone can be hacked out of the ground.

R

Radha The favourite of lord Krishna as a youth.

raja Indian king or prince.

Rama Hero-king of the Indian epic the Ramayana.

Ramayana The story of Rama's rescue of his wife Sita from the demon Ravana.

ramie A plant rather like flax, which is used to make clothing in Japan.

Ravana Demon who is the villain of the Indian epic the Ramayana.

regent Someone who rules a country on behalf of another person.

relief A carved stone slab decorating the walls of a palace or temple.

ritual A religious ceremony carried out by a priest or priestess.

S

sake Rice wine.

sampan A small wooden Chinese boat with a cabin made of matting.

samurai Well-trained warriors in Japan.

sanctuary The most holy place in a temple.

Sanskrit Language of the Aryans. The language of the ruling classes in ancient India.

sari Traditional female Indian dress.

sceptre Ceremonial staff carried by a king.

scroll-painting A painting on a long roll of paper.

sculpture Carved figures of stone, wood or metal, either free-standing or fixed to the wall of a palace or temple.

seal Official mark made on a document.

seismoscope An instrument that reacts to earthquakes and tremors.

semi-legendary Someone who once really lived but about whom fantastic stories are told.

Semitic A family of languages, which includes Akkadian, Aramaic and modern Hebrew and Arabic.

sericulture The production of silk.

Shaivism Belief in Shiva as the lord of the Universe.

shamisen A Japanese three-stringed musical instrument.

shelwar kamiz Long tunic and trousers worn in northern India.

Shia A branch of Islam.

shikar An Indian expedition for hunting animals.

shinden A large, single-storey house in Japan.

Shinto An ancient Japanese religion, known as the "way of the gods", based on honouring holy spirits.

Shiva A chief Hindu god.

shoen A private estate in the Japanese countryside.

shogun A Japanese army commander. From 1185 to 1868, shoguns ruled Japan.

shrine Sacred place of worship.

Silk Road The overland trading route that, in ancient times, stretched from northern China through Asia to Europe.

silken Made of silk.

silkworm The larva (caterpillar) of a silkmoth. It produces silken threads that it spins into a cocoon.

sitar An Indian guitar-like instrument.

smelt To extract a metal from its ore by heating it in a furnace.

soapstone A soft, easily carved stone.

stela A large, round-topped piece of stone with the figure of a king and a written account of major events in his reign.

stupa Buddhist place of worship containing a relic of the Buddha.

sudra Servant or peasant, member of the lowest caste in India.

Sufism A mystical form of Islam.

sultan A Muslim ruler

sumo A type of wrestling popular in Japan.

surcoat A long, loose tunic worn over armour.

suspension bridge A bridge in which the roadway is suspended (hung) from towers.

T

tablet A flat piece of clay of varying shape and size that is used for cuneiform writing.

tachi The long sword that was carried by a Japanese samurai.

tanbo Flooded fields in Japan where rice was grown.

tatami A mat that covers the floor in Japan and is woven from reeds.

temple A special building where a god or goddess is worshipped.

tenshu The tall central tower of a Japanese castle.

terracotta A composition of baked clay and sand used to make statues, figurines and pottery. Reddish-brown unglazed earthenware.

textile Cloth produced by weaving threads together.

threshing Separating grains of wheat or rice from their stalks.

tofu Bean-curd – a nourishing food made from the pulp of crushed soya beans.

tomb A vault in which dead bodies are placed. In imperial China, the tombs of emperors and noblemen were often filled with beautiful jewellery and other objects of great value.

torii The traditional gateway to a Shinto shrine.

treaty An agreement between two cities or

countries or between kings and their vassals.

tribute Payment by a vassal state to the ruler of a larger one who is his overlord.

tublah A drum played in north Indian classical music.

turban Headdress worn by Muslim and Sikh men.

U

uji A clan in Japan.

Underworld The Land of the Dead. The people of Mesopotamia thought it was a very gloomy place.

V

Vaishnavism Hindu belief in Vishnu as the lord of the Universe.

vaishya Merchant or farmer, a member of the third caste in India.

vassal The ruler of a small state who acknowledges a greater king as his overlord. He promises to be loyal and pay his tribute while his overlord promises to protect him.

Veda Ancient Aryan texts.

Vishnu One of the chief Hindu gods.

vulture A bird of prey that feeds on dead flesh.

W

waka Elegant poetry, popular at the Japanese emperor's court.

ward A walled district found in the cities of imperial China.

warlord In China a man who keeps a private army and controls a large region of the country by force.

warrior A man who fights in wars.

weir A low dam built across a river or canal to control the flow of water.

winged disc A symbol of the sun god Shamash or of Ashur, the chief god of Assyria.

winnowing Separating grains of wheat and rice from their papery outer layer, called chaff.

wisteria A Chinese climbing shrub with blue flowers.

world power A country that becomes one of the most important states in the world for a time.

X

xianq qi A traditional Chinese board game, similar to the Western game of chess.

Y

yak A long-haired ox, used in Tibet as a beast of burden.

yaksi A tree spirit in India.

yin and yang The Daoist belief in two life forces that must be balanced to achieve harmony. Yin is negative, feminine and dark, while yang is positive, masculine and light.

yoke A long piece of wood or bamboo, used to help carry heavy loads. The yoke was placed across the shoulders and a load was hung from each end to balance it.

Z

zakat Alms that must be given to the poor in Islam.

Zen A branch of the Buddhist faith that was popular among the samurai in Japan.

ziggurat A solid, stepped pyramid in Mesopotamia built of mud-brick with a small temple on top, which is approached by great staircases.

Index

Acknowledgements

Anness Publishing would like to thank Scallywags and the following children for modelling this book: Mikey Ammah, Sarah Bone, Lucilla Braune, Earaneqa Carter, Stephanie Da Cova, Samara Edwards-Amos, Emma Franklin, Aileen Greiner, Otis Harrington, Gem Harrison, Rachel Herbert, Francesca Hill, Lorenzo Heron, Louis Jade, Eka Karumidze, Adam Keevash, Alex Lindblom-Smith, Sophie Lindblom-Smith, Louis Loucaides, Christina Malcolm-Hansen, Alex Martin-Simons, Ernests Milevics, Ivelin Nedkova, Daniel Ofori, Vanessa Ofori, Kayleigh Ollman, Edward Parker, Joshua Parris-Eugene, Gigi Playfair, Thaddius Rivett, Dimitry Rozamae, Levinia de Silva, Claudia Martins Silva, Victoria Sintun, Clleon Smith, Luke Spencer, Nicky Stafford, Luke Stanton, Saif Uddowlla, Kirsty Wells, Tyrene Williams and Nino Zaalishvili. Gratitude also to their parents, and to Hampden Gurney and Walnut Tree Walk Schools.

PICTURE CREDITS

b=bottom, t=top, c=centre, m=middle, l=left, r=right

MESOPOTAMIA: AKG: 12tl, 16tl, 17mr, 18tl, 22t, 24t, 26t, 27tl, 30bc, 32tl, 32mc, 34b, 35tl, 36ml, 36mr, 37tl, 38tr, 42tl, 44t, 45tr, 48t, 49ml, 51bl, 52t, 53tl, 55m, 57tr, 61tl, 66b, 67tr, 67br, 69tr; Ancient Art and Architecture Collection: 62t, 62br, 68t; Bildarchiv Preussischer Kulturbesitz: 17tr, 19bl, 22bl, 22br, 23ml, 25t, 25bl, 27tr, 34t, 35br, 37m, 41ml, 49tl, 50t, 50ml, 56b, 60tl, 62bl, 68b; Bulloz: 19br, 20tl, 34m, 37tr, 50mr; Mary Evans Picture Library: 21m; E.T. archive, 53b, 69b; Werner Forman: 28t; Robert Harding Picture Library: 13t, 27ml, 28mr, 29ml, 29mc, 35tr, 39tr, 39t, 41tr, 44b, 52br, 58, 60mr, 61ml, 63br, 65tl, 67tl; David Hawkins: 19t, 46b; Michael Holford: 13mr,16tr, 17tl, 24bl, 28ml, 30t, 30ml, 39tl, 39bl, 42ml, 51t, 58mr, 64t, 66t; Hutchison Library: 30br, 38br; Ident: 18m; Erich Lessing: 47tl; John Oakes: 31bl, 45bl; Muriel and Giovanni Dagli Orti: 20mr, 38ml, 54t; Science and Society Picture Library: 64ml.

ANCIENT INDIA: AKG: 77tr, 84tr, 84cl, 99tl, 101br, 102bl, 108tl, 112cr, 113cr, 113tr, 113cr, 117br, 120tl, 122c, 123tl, 127br; The Ancient Art and Architecture Collection Ltd: 73ct, 82t, 82b, 83tr, 88bl, 102br, 102tl, 116br; The Bridgeman Art Library : 72tr, 73tl, 79c, 79tl, 83bl, 85tl, 85tr, 85c, 86cl, 87c, 87tr, 87tl, 88tr, 89tl, 90tr, 95c, 96cl, 97tr, 99c, 100tl, 101tl, 101tr, 101bl, 103tl, 103cr, 104tl, 105tl, 108cr, 109tr, 111tl, 111tr, 111cl, 112tl, 112cl, 114tl, 115tl, 117tr, 117cl, 119c, 120b, 121bl, 124cr, 125tl, 125c, 126cr, 126cl, 127tr; Corbis: 72cl, 83br, 89br, 96tl, 106tr, 121tr, 122tl, 123cl, 124tl, 126tl; C M Dixon: 76tl, 78c; E.T. Archive: 77c, 78tr, 94tl, 97tl, 111bl, 113cl, 118tl, 118cr, 119tr, 121cr; Mary Evans Picture Library; 93bl, 94c; FLPA: 105c; Robert Harding: 92b, 93tr, 103br, 106b, 107bl, 110tl, 121bl; Hutchison Library: 83tl, 91tr, 93tl, 110bl, 114cr, 125tr; Images of India: 88br, 89tr, 90b, 90b, 109tl, 109cl, 109c; Philadelphia Museum of Art: 86tl; Ann and Bury Peerless: 77tl; Link Picture Library: 73c, 91br; V & A Picture Library: 80t, 91bl, 92t, 97c, 98tl, 98cl, 105tr, 115cl; Oxford Scientific Films: 103bl; Royal Asiatic Society: 115c; Tony Stone Images: 83c, 91tl, 95t.

THE CHINESE EMPIRE: Ancient Art and Architecture Collection Ltd: 141br, 180tl, 182cl; Bridgeman Art Library: 141tl, 142cl, 147tr, 149br, 151bl, 157tl, 157cl, 159bl, 165bl, 169tl, 170cl, 171cl, 171cr; Bruce Coleman: 151br, 163tl; James Davis Worldwide Photographic Travel Library: 131tr, 143cl; C M Dixon: 138tl, 140bl, 150tl, 156tr, 167tl, 168tr; E T Archive: 134l, 135tl, 135tr, 135bl, 137t, 137bl, 138bl, 141tr, 141bl, 143tr, 146br, 147br, 148tr, 148bl, 149bl, 150br, 151tr, 152tr, 153tr, 158bl, 164br, 167tr, 171tl, 173cl, 174cr, 178bl, 181cl, 185t; Mary Evans Picture Library: 137br, 138br, 148br, 155tl, 166br, 183tl; FLPA: 167cr, 167br; Werner Forman Archive: 136bl, 139br, 152cr, 155tr, 155cl, 162tr, 163bl, 163br, 164bl, 168cl, 172c, 174tl, 175cl, 179tr, 183tr; Michael Holford: 130tl, 161bl, 166tl, 182tr; The Hutchinson Library: 176cl, 184c, 185cl; MacQuitty Collection: 131c, 146tr, 147bl, 151tl, 153cl, 158tr, 165br, 167bl, 169tr, 170tl, 172tr, 177tl, 177tr, 177cl, 178tl, 179cl, 179br, 183cl; Papilio Photographic: 156cl; TRIP: 136br, 184tr; Visual Arts Library: 134r, 135br, 140tl, 140c, 146bl, 149tr, 154cl, 160tl, 161cl, 164tl, 165tl, 165tr, 168cr, 173tl, 175tl, 175tr, 179tl, 180cl; ZEFA: 130c, 136tr, 139tl, 139b, 142tl, 144tr, 159tl, 159br, 162tl, 163tr, 171tr.

ANCIENT JAPAN: Ancient Art and Architecture Collection: 201b, 203tl, 207br, 225tl, 226tl; E. Beintema/AAA Collection: 206tl; Ronald Sheridan/ AAA Collection: 207bl, 219tl; AKG London: 188br, 193br, 198tl, 219tl, 233tl, 234br; Heather Angel: 243br; BBC Hulton: 213c; Bridgeman Art Library, London: The Life and Pastimes of the Japanese Court 197tl;

Sumo Wrestler Abumatsu Rokunosuki by Kunisada 204tl, Fuji on a Fine Day by Kuniyoshi 207tl, Osen of the Kagiya Serving Tea by Harunobu 209bl, The Moon by Kunisada 212, Woman by Kikumaru 219bl, Standing Courtesan by Kaigetsudo 220br, Collecting Insects by Harunobu 221tl, Salt Maidens by Harunobu 222tl, Threading a Needle by Chinnen 223tr, Tales of Bunsho by Tosa 229tl, Tale of Genji by Tokugawa II 230br, Courtesan with Musical Instrument by Kuniyoshi 232tl, Urban Life 233tr, Ships Returning to Harbour by Gakutei 235tr, The Stone Bridge by Hiroshige III 235bl, Retreat in the Mountains by Tomioka 235br, Fuji in Fine Weather by Hokusai 237tl, Nicheren Calming the Storm by Yoshimoro 238bl, Juroku Rakan 238tl, Cherry Blossoms at Asakura by Hiroshige II 243tl; The following Bridgeman Art Library images are reproduced by kind permission of the Fitzwilliam Museum, Cambridge: Mother Dressing Son by Harunobu 210tl, Celebrated Beauties by Utamaro 220tl, Sudden Shower by Hiroshige 223br, Painting Party by Kunisada 227cr, Fuji from Koshigaya 227cl, Mother and Baby Resting by Kunimaru 234bl; Christies Images: 197bl, 200bl, 200br, 201tl, 203bl, 207cl, 209br, 213bl, 219br, 221tr, 224br, 225tr, 228br, 239cr, 239tl, 242tl, 242br;Bruce Coleman: 237bl; Asian Art and Architecture Inc/ Corbis: 230tl, 231tl, Corbis-Bettman: 195tl, Carmen Redondo/ Corbis: 240br, Hulton-Deutsch/ Corbis: 205tr, Sakamoto Photo Research Laboratory/ Corbis: 212tl, 221bl, 231br, 239br, Seattle Art Museum/ Corbis: 205bl, Michael S Yamashita/ Corbis: 216bl; CM Dixon: 194tl, 218tl, 229bl; Edimedia: 208bl, 210br, 222br; ET Archive: 188tl, 193tl, 195br, 196bl, 204br, 211tl, 226br, 235tr, Mary Evans: 211bl, 218bl; Werner Forman: 194bl, 197ct, 199bl, 217cl, 223tl, 224tl, 233bc; Garden Picture Library: 239bl, 239bc; Michael Holford: 192br, 200tl, 202br, 206bl, 229br, 240tl, 243bl; Hutchison/Jon Burbank: 227tl, 236tl, 239cl; Hutchison/ JG Fuller: 236bc; Hutchison/ Patricio Goycoolea: 223bl; Hutchison/ Chiran Kyushu: 213cr, 223bl, Hutchison/ Michael Macintyre: 196tl, 215bl, 215br; The Idemitsu Museum of Arts: 203cl, 221cl, 225cl; Images Colour Library: 217tr, 239bl; Japan Archive: 189tl, 189bl, 192tl, 193tc, 195tr, 195cr, 197tr, 198br, 199tl, 199tr, 201tr, 202tl, 204tl, 214bl, 215tr, 216tl, 217tl, 217bl, 227tl, 232br, 237tr, 241tr; NHPA: 243c, Tony Stone: 240bl; Superstock: 240bl.

This edition is published by Southwater

Southwater is an imprint of Anness Publishing Limited
Hermes House, 88–89 Blackfriars Road, London SE1 8HA
tel. 020 7401 2077; fax 020 7633 9499

Distributed in the UK by The Manning Partnership
251–253 London Road East, Batheaston, Bath BA1 7RL
tel. 01225 852 727; fax 01225 852 852

Published in the USA by Anness Publishing Inc.
27 West 20th Street, Suite 504, New York NY 10011
fax 212 807 6813

Distributed in Australia by Sandstone Publishing
Unit 1, 360 Norton Street, Leichhardt, New South Wales 2040
tel. 02 9560 7888; fax 02 9560 7488

Publisher: Joanna Lorenz
Managing Editor, Children's Books: Gilly Cameron Cooper
Editor: Joy Wotton
Senior Editors: Neil Kelly, Nicole Pearson
Project Editors: Edel Brosnan, Joanne Hanks, Louisa Somerville, Sophie Warne, Joy Wotton
Copy Editors: Nicola Barber, Gill Harvey, Charlotte Hurdman
Editorial Readers: Felicity Forster, Penelope Goodare, Richard McGinlay, Jonathan Marshall, Joy Wotton
Designers: Juliet Brown, Matthew Cook, Caroline Reeves, Margaret Sadler, Alison Walker
Illustrations: Rob Ashby, Vanessa Card, Stuart Carter, Chris Forsey, Shane Marsh, Rob Sheffield, Clive Spong
Photography: John Freeman
Stylists: Konica Shankar, Thomasina Smith, Melanie Williams
Production Controller: Wendy Lawson

Previously published in four separate volumes, *Step Into Mesopotamia*, *Step Into Ancient India*, *Step Into the Chinese Empire* and *Step Into Ancient Japan*.